D0705761

The Frantic Assembly

Book of Devising Theatre

'This is a close companion to Frantic Assembly's practice and one that is written with an open and engaging, even disarming, tone … A rich, rewarding and compelling text.'

Stuart Andrews, *University of Surrey*

As Frantic Assembly move into their twentieth year of producing innovative and adventurous theatre, this new edition of their well-loved book demystifies the process of devising theatre in an unusually candid way. Scott Graham and Steven Hoggett offer an intimate and invaluable insight into their evolution and success, in the hope that sharing their experiences of devising theatre will encourage and inspire students and fellow practitioners.

The Frantic Assembly Book of Devising Theatre is a uniquely personal account of the history and practice of this remarkable company, and includes:

- practical exercises;
- essays on devising, writing and choreography;
- suggestions for scene development;
- a 16-page colour section, and illustrations throughout; and
- a companion website featuring clips of rehearsals and performances at www.routledge.com/cw/graham.

This is an accessible, educational and indispensable introduction to the working processes of Frantic Assembly, whose playful, intelligent and dynamic productions continue to be acclaimed by audiences and critics alike.

Scott Graham and Steven Hoggett are the co-founders of Frantic Assembly.

The Frantic Assembly

Book of Devising Theatre

SECOND EDITION

SCOTT GRAHAM AND STEVEN HOGGETT

LONDON AND NEW YORK

First edition published 2009, this edition published 2014
by Routledge
2 Park Square, Milton Park, Abingdon, Oxon OX14 4RN

and by Routledge
711 Third Avenue, New York, NY 10017

Routledge is an imprint of the Taylor & Francis Group, an informa business

Text © 2009, 2014 Scott Graham and Steven Hoggett

All photographs © Scott Graham, unless otherwise credited

The right of Scott Graham and Steven Hoggett to be identified as authors of this work has been asserted by them in accordance with sections 77 and 78 of the Copyright, Designs and Patents Act 1988.

All rights reserved. No part of this book may be reprinted or reproduced or utilised in any form or by any electronic, mechanical, or other means, now known or hereafter invented, including photocopying and recording, or in any information storage or retrieval system, without permission in writing from the publishers.

Trademark notice: Product or corporate names may be trademarks or registered trademarks, and are used only for identification and explanation without intent to infringe.

British Library Cataloguing in Publication Data
A catalogue record for this book is available from the British Library

Library of Congress Cataloging in Publication Data
Graham, Scott, 1971-
The Frantic Assembly book of devising theatre / by Scott Graham and Steven Hoggett.
pages cm
Includes bibliographical references.
1. Frantic Assembly (Group) 2. Experimental theater–Great Britain. 3. Theatrical companies–Great Britain. 4. Improvisation (Acting) I. Hoggett, Steven, 1971- II. Title.
PN2595.13E97G73 2014
792.02'2–dc23
2014000797

ISBN: 978-1-138-77700-2 (hbk)
ISBN: 978-1-138-77701-9 (pbk)
ISBN: 978-1-315-76871-7 (ebk)

Typeset in Univers
by Saxon Graphics Ltd, Derby

Printed and bound by CPI Group (UK) Ltd, Croydon, CR0 4YY

This book is dedicated to the following:

Liz Heywood for seeing something at the very start – thank you
Sally Harris for *teaching us everything you knew!*
Sian, Marcia and Carys Graham
In memory of Nigel Charnock and Marcia Pook

Contents

Acknowledgements

In our experience, Frantic Assembly has been exactly that – a frantic blast through some astounding experiences surrounded by an assembly of wonderful people. Together we inspire and support each other.

We have been lucky enough to work with and learn from some incredibly talented and generous collaborators and advisers. Big thanks are due to Lisa Maguire, Laura Mallows, Inga Hurst, Tom Morris, Ben and Claire Chamberlain, Vicky Featherstone, John Tiffany, Georgina Lamb, Natasha Chivers, Liam Steel, Simon Mellor, Dan O'Neill, Simon Stokes, David Sibley, Spencer Hazel, Korina Biggs, Cait Davis, Laura Hopkins, Merle Hensell, Abi Morgan, Eddie Kay, Despina Tsatsas ... the list goes on!

Special mention to Vicki Middleton (née Coles), the vital element in our unholy founding trinity. The three of us formed the company and stumbled through the first ten years before she was whisked off to Australia with a promise of sunshine, surf and snags on the barbie.

All of the above allowed and encouraged us to be what we are and for that we truly love and thank you.

And thanks to Talia Rodgers ... for the suggestion, the encouragement, and the patience.

An introduction

The book – an introduction by Scott Graham

Knowledge is surprising. It sneaks up on you. You can wait for it, look out for it and even, if you are confident enough, expect it. When it arrives it does so unannounced. This book represents what we know after 18 years of making work together.

It also marks a significant change in the relationship at the heart of Frantic Assembly as Steven Hoggett leaves to pursue a freelance career. Within these pages we shall talk about the discoveries we have made together, the work we struggled to make, the revelations that rewarded many hours of hard sweat. And the many hours we made it up as we went along.

Throughout this book you will read how 'we' worked or what 'we' tried. Despite being sole artistic director of Frantic Assembly I don't think I will quickly get out of the habit of using 'we'. This is not an aspiration to royalty. It is just that 'we' feels right for a company built on collaboration, a company that has prided itself on its openness and accessibility. As I take Frantic Assembly forward I look forward to the new collaborators and the new discoveries 'we' will find. Over time I will not rule out the rise of 'I' but for now I do take pleasure, solace and pride in 'we'.

Writing this book remains a fascinating exercise. Like I said, it is the process of writing that reveals the knowledge. It bubbles up. You start with a vague notion you have something you want to say, something that might be relevant to someone, somewhere struggling to make work. You want to tell them that it is going to be ok. You want to tell them that there is a way through the maze. You want to tell them that things can be much simpler than they initially seem. This is what drives this book. So much of theatre seems to perpetuate the myth that the process is torturous. This does not have to be the case. Yes, it can be very hard work. Yes, there can be days where the task seems insurmountable but if you can look at the situation in another way then opportunities can present themselves. If this book provides the reader with anything, I hope it is at least the ability to look at the problem differently.

What you will find here is a determined effort to demystify the devising process. To this end, the book falls into two parts. The first includes a selection of scenes that cover the creative output of the company from early shows such as *Klub* (1995) through to *Little Dogs* (2012). Each of these scenes are taken and examined in terms of the initial idea followed by the methods used in transferring that idea from a scrap of conversation or grotty notebook into the production and onto the stage. We then look at possible ways in which this existing scene might be developed or how the creative process could be harnessed to create something different. The last section expresses our belief that the reader should not think about the ideas here being an end point. When running workshops, we are always at pains to point out to participants that the most important part to take away from the workshop is not the creative end point we might have reached but the means by which we got there. It is the understanding of the process that is valuable. We are certainly not unique in being a company who continue to work on the production throughout its tour. The development of ideas is essential once the production begins to seek validity in front of an audience.

Part One also includes a number of essays that cover some of the elements and ideas that have become central to the Frantic method of thinking about and creating theatre. As well as revealing the places where we find ideas and inspiration, it is hoped that this section might encourage the practitioner to reconsider their own inspirational locations and, in doing so, free up the frequently self-imposed restrictions on where to be looking for creative motivation.

Part Two is a comprehensive guide through the creation of our work and how it might help your work, starting with warm-up advice and games through to advanced choreographic exercises before looking at specific uses of music and text in our theatre practise. Each exercise has been tried and tested by the company over a number of years working with a wide variety of practitioners ranging in age and ability.

We hope that the reader of this book will find enough points of interest to instigate their own search for good practice. In our own experience, it has been important to establish both starting points and departure points for us. This book should work in the same way – a healthy balance of agreeable and disagreeable pointers, thoughts, exercises and suggestions. It is an attempt to provoke the reader into looking for new means of creating theatre performance. Our own non-theatre background meant that we had no choice but to forge our own understanding of how to create work. This in itself might have been a blessing, as we have never felt beholden to any particular school of thought or theatrical tradition. It led to a freedom in picking and choosing what appeared interesting or relevant no matter where that inspiration lay. We were open enough to take advice, ignorant enough to look for inspiration anywhere and brave enough to ask for help. Over time we found what we liked mostly through finding out what we didn't like. But this never led to definitions and rules. We always retained the right to change our minds as we became aware that inspiration could come from the most unexpected places and take the most unexpected forms. A rigid sense of what theatre *should* be will always be the enemy of devised theatre. The 'what might be' is essential.

An introduction will usually go to great lengths to define the terms central to the book. Having spent years wrestling with the term 'physical theatre', we have found ourselves less and less sure of its definition and even its relevance. It is a phrase we never utter in the rehearsal room. It exists outside and as such it proves that other people are much better placed to comment on definitions. It can be argued that all theatre is physical and that all theatre is, to some extent, devised. That argument is not one we care about enough to dedicate space to here. It is a waste of precious time. Let's just get on with it! We also encourage practitioners to get into the rehearsal room, make the work and let others be the ones to speculate on the definition of what it is they just experienced.

Ok, ok, we will talk about physical theatre. Later.

Actually, before we get on with it, a quick word on the book itself.

Having written this book remains a great source of pride for us. To hear that it has a value within rehearsal rooms or in the 'manbags' of aspiring theatre makers is a tremendous thrill. Returning to update it is a brutal reminder of our initial fear when asked to write it. What if we change our minds about these thoughts? Committing them to print seemed reckless and rash. Surely they will come back to bite us as we develop and they date?

It is true that passing time does make the voice a little unfamiliar but it has mostly been a pleasant and fairly informative return to the book. Yes there may be things that we might have done differently and things we might never do again (we are not going to point them out!) but on the whole, who cares? Things we believed then that we might not be so sure about now still retain a certain validity. We have come to realise that this book is less about capturing pronouncements that define the universe and more about sharing processes that might lead to something significant for your work. Not that we ever tried to define the universe! The revelation just means that it is easier to write knowing that one day we might not hold these 'truths' so dear. That is ok, for in the meantime they hopefully mean something to the reader and help open up theatrical possibilities for them.

It fills us with immense pride when people remark how the book has helped them make work. It is almost surreal. There was a moment at a book signing a few years back (now that WAS surreal) when a young woman apologised for the tattered and bent state of the book she was asking us to sign. She did not realise that this was the moment that possibly thrilled us the most, when the significance of having written a book actually hit home. It was not the signing itself. It was the fact that the book was being used. It had suffered from being stood on in a sweaty rehearsal room. How wonderful is that? It was never meant to gather dust on a shelf. The ambition was always for it to be a partner to your creativity and how fitting for it to wear the bruises and scars of the rehearsal room with pride!

Right, now we *can* get on with it.

A brief history of Frantic Assembly

This book is not about the history of our company but a little background information might explain a lot about our company ethos.

The nature of how we came to be has been a massive influence on our drive to make our work accessible. It has informed all our efforts in education and training.

We were both English Literature students at Swansea University. We met as an unused understudy and a bored prompt on a student drama society production of *Educating Rita*.

Swansea University does not have a drama department but it does have a fantastic theatre that hosts the drama society three or four times a year presenting the usual talcum headed Chekhov and vanity projects. That is what we thought theatre was.

As students we individually took part in and watched a student production directed by Volcano Theatre Company (*Savages* by Christopher Hampton). This was the life-changing moment. We did not know that theatre could be like this. We had experienced this production from both sides of the fourth wall and it had blown our preconceptions apart. It was also clear that this was what we both wanted to do with our lives.

Volcano were a massive inspiration to us. They were alternative and sexy, intelligent and fierce. They were the perfect role models for us, being Politics and Psychology graduates from Swansea who had been inspired by another director to set their company up and create their own work. They recognised the inspiration and expertise they could give us and actively encouraged, advised and nurtured us during the early days. This is why our education and training programmes are so important to us.

With Volcano's encouragement we presented *Savages* at the Edinburgh Fringe Festival. For 'we' you should read 'Swansea University Drama Society'. Before signing up for the festival we were to be found around a thesaurus trying to agree on a company name. For some reason we felt that Swansea University Drama Society was not going to bring the punters in. We all agreed on Chaos then found out there was a Kaos Theatre Company. Then someone proposed Frantic and Frantic it was.

The next year we directed *As Is* by William M. Hoffman and took it to Edinburgh, again as Frantic Theatre Company. We managed to sell out both runs and garner good national reviews. It was felt that if we could fool the public so far maybe we should give it a go full time. That is when Vicki Middleton (née Coles), Scott Graham and Steven Hoggett decided to hatch a plan and turn a hobby into a job.

We got other (proper) jobs for the year while we waited for each other to finish our studies before returning to Swansea to start the company properly. The reason for starting out in Swansea had everything to do with Volcano, the goodwill and encouragement of those at the Taliesin Theatre, the lower cost of living and the prospect of immediately being a small fish in a small pond. We felt that in being anywhere else, even Cardiff, we would get swamped in the clamour for new companies to get noticed.

We formed the company proper under the name Frantic Theatre Company Limited in 1994 on a government scheme called Enterprise Allowance. In real terms this meant being unemployed for at least six weeks and taking a £10 pay cut from your Job Seekers' Allowance and attending seminars and meetings on finance and business. Being on the scheme meant that we did not have to sign on for the year as we built the business up. Enterprise Allowance contributed £30 a week to each of our wages and the company added another £10.

We had decided that our approach to building the company would be all or nothing. We would not get part-time jobs so that we could concentrate fully on Frantic. This mostly meant tapping out letters to artistic directors on an old typewriter, stuffing envelopes and waiting for the phone to ring.

Our first tour saw us take a radical reworking of *Look Back In Anger* to mystified audiences in arts centres throughout Wales and a few dates in England.

With each production came an intense learning curve gained from working with a talented freelance choreographer. Their input was our training. We had little more to offer than boundless energy and enthusiasm (which of course should never be underestimated). We were also brave and driven both in our desire to try new things and make an impact on the theatrical world. *Look Back In Anger* was our way in. From then on we felt that we could do what we wanted.

That has meant the odd distraction and the odd blind alley but we have always been lucky enough to make our own mistakes and honest enough to learn from them.

Throughout this book we will refer to past productions and specific scenes from past shows. An anthology of our work can be found on this book's companion website: www.routledge.com/cw/graham. Futher information for all productions can be found on the Frantic Assembly website: www.franticassembly.co.uk.

Artistic aims of the company

Frantic Assembly is one of the UK's leading contemporary theatre companies, producing thrilling, energetic and uncompromising theatre, constantly attracting new audiences. In collaboration with a wide variety of artists, Frantic Assembly continues to create new work that places equal emphasis on movement, design, music and text. Since its formation in 1994 Frantic Assembly has toured extensively throughout the UK and abroad, establishing a reputation for excellence with work which combines striking physicality and the best new writing. In addition to its productions Frantic Assembly is deeply committed to its extensive Learn and Train programme which has run since the company's inception and now serves over 6,000 participants each year reaching every county of England and throughout the UK and across the world. In addition, Frantic Assembly also run the highly succesful Ignition programme aimed at bringing raw male talent into the sector, much in the same way its founding artistic directors were drawn into and encouraged to develop within theatre. This is a nationwide initiative focusing on unearthing untapped talent in sports, youth groups and those not in education or employment.

How can this book help you?

Sometimes we have had suggestions to structure the exercises in this book into a kind of beginners/intermediate/advanced format. There is a little resistance to this on our part as we don't believe that it is necessarily the exercise that is 'advanced' but how you apply it and who you apply it to. Some of the more apperantly simple exercises can be used by professionals of great experience to access new movement and see things in new ways. Similarly we believe that each exercise aims for a simplicity of building blocks that should offer something to the more inexperienced practitioner/student/teacher. We urge you not to see any of the exercises as off limits because you might define yourself as beginner/intermediate/advanced. The process for Scribble (see Chapter 2) remains the same when used by young students as it does when used by experienced dancers. That the results will be different (possibly in style and quality) does not matter. The process is not about replicating our version that appeared in *Beautiful Burnout*. The process is there to open up different possibilities for you and those involved. The scene was *our* result from the process. What will *yours* be?

That said, it would be churlish not to offer some guidance to using this book. Not that there is a secret blueprint to getting the best out of this book. Any guidance we offer is merely us guessing what might work for you! And what about you? Are you a teacher, a curious student, an actor, a dancer, a director? Experienced? Are you looking to get sweaty? Do you want to get your group lifting? Are you working with a large group? Are you trying to work with text? Are you making work from scratch?

OK, let's try this. From this point you might want to jump past Chapter 1, 'Frantic essays' (we need to think of a better word than essays!) and get stuck in. Fine. If that works for you. We are not suggesting you do, just trying to guess where you are coming from.

Can we recommend you have a look at 'Why warm up?' (page 91) before you get started? Setting the initial tone can be so important. As they say, you never get a second chance to make a first impression.

Even if you are gagging to get stuck in, don't overlook the rest of the 'Suggestions for constructive warm-ups' section (page 100). Those simple, calm exercises go a long way in influencing the quality of the more dynamic and 'advanced' exercises.

You can see there are a few warm-up games to pick from. Clear The Space is your bog standard but is so important for breaking down any inhibitions about touching and physical contact. Even experienced performers appreciate the opportunity to play a silly game and get a lot of hugs coming their way first thing in the morning.

If you have a boisterous group that are a little afraid or prejudiced against what they think drama or theatre might be then go for the recognisable simplicity of Relays. Like Clear The Space it subtly works its magic on the group.

Quad can be used with all levels of ability and can be returned to every day as it is a useful tool to show how a group are progressing. It introduces participants to the task of moving and counting within music too.

To be fair (and contradicting ourselves slightly) you might get the best results from Marcia Take Down with a slightly more experienced group. That does not mean it is not worth trying though!

Chapter 4, 'Choreography' should be accessible and relevant to all levels. Passives (in 'New physical vocabulary/restrictions and freedom') is fairly simple exercise that might actually be more relevant to the experienced performer who has got stuck in their movement palette. That said it should still take the body to new positions. When looking at these exercises, do not think about the end product as defined by our productions. Look for the building blocks that support the process. These are the most important parts and what make the processes accessible.

'Advanced exercise – pushing the potential' suggests just that. Ok, you have got us there. Maybe these are more advanced but maybe they are also a way of returning to a simple process and rethinking its end point. Ideally, this is how you look at any of the processes. Ask yourself, 'How can I take the building blocks and create something new and relevant to my theatrical aspirations?'

If you are working on a production, then Chapter 5, 'Devising and words', could be a rich source but, again, please do not presume that any aspect of this book is irrelevant just because it refers to an existing or dead show. Everything in this book is here to suggest a way of moving forward. Chapter 2, 'Scenes and their Creation', is not a history lesson. It is about offering up the processes to the work you want to make today.

Which brings us back to Chapter 1, 'Frantic essays' (still working on a better title). They are not musings from a comfy leather armchair. They are here because they are discoveries that have opened up our understanding of how we can make work. They are often Eureka moments. We offer them here as a response to the comments we hear from students/teachers/practitioners as they struggle to make their own work. They might offer a new way of looking at the problem, or a new way of getting over it. So have a look and see if they answer the question even if you haven't asked it yet.

A glossary of terms

It struck us that, at times, you might not know what we are talking about. We hope this helps.

A String of material	Through our devising processes, participants are usually set tasks to come up with several moves to be retained and performed in a specific order. This is often referred to as a string of material.
Contact work	The more lifty side of choreography. When actors bump up against each other.
Beats per minute	The, er, beats per minute contained within a music track. Has a profound effect on the listener.
Gestural	Gestural can be considered movement based on gesture. Or more simply, movement based on arm

	and hand movements. It can be incredibly detailed choreography.
Unison	Identical movement. An absolute minefield!
Canon	More complex group work. Or what happens when unison goes wrong.
Core strength	Referring to the internal muscles that offer control and stability
Building Block	At the heart of how we disseminate our creative devising processes (see Building blocks).
Transitions	Often when performing newly created choreography you can see where sections and moves have been joined and learned. You have to work on these transitions to create a smooth, flowing piece of movement.
Calippo	An iced lolly. Also, the perfect inspiration for a group lift that appears and feels fairly effortless.

part one
documentation

chapter one

Frantic essays

Here are some thoughts that might give you an insight into our creative process. We also attempt to answer some of the more frequently asked questions about our company, our work and our working relationship.

What is the Frantic Assembly devising process?

This is a question that we have found fairly difficult to answer. This book goes some way to answering it but what it will only ever do is give some indication to what it has been so far. It is not Frantic Assembly nailing its colours to the mast and saying this is the way it will be forever. This is not the only way Frantic Assembly will ever seek to make work.

It is always about finding new ways. Standing still is dangerous. You have to look for new ways to see the world and new ways of telling the world what you think of it.

The term 'devising' or 'devised' inspires different connotations in different people. The companies that might legitimately lay claim to devising as their creative process might make vastly different work.

One of the most common presumptions is that it excludes the presence of a writer or script. This has certainly not been the case in our work. The biggest difference from the more traditional model is that the initial idea comes from Frantic Assembly and then we match that with a writer. That idea might be a fragment (*Hymns*, *Sell Out*) or it could be an idea much more detailed and fully formed (*Stockholm*). It might take years for that idea to evolve from spark to rehearsal draft. These sparks have originated in a wide variety of ways in a number of different forms. *Flesh* was inspired by a comment made in the early 80s by Norman Tebbit, a Conservative MP. *Sell Out* was a response to a fraught year of touring in the back of a very cramped Frantic van. *Hymns* started as a response to a couple of untimely funerals we attended. *Peepshow* was inspired by a music video. *Pool (no water)* by a book of photography. *Stockholm* came after overhearing a domestic argument. *Lovesong* was partly inspired by a question and answer session after a Frantic performance. Some of these are obvious enough and some are not. They were all, ultimately, rich in what they provided. But more importantly, there was and is no pattern here. Just keeping eyes and ears open and truly trusting that the spark might appear at anytime *from any source*.

We initially take the kernel of the idea and test this to see if it is interesting enough to us and if 'it has got legs' – whether it will stand up to scrutiny and be interesting to anyone else. This 'testing' is pretty much talking about the idea, letting it sit for a while and then returning to it with a wiser head to see if it still excites us. If we still have the conviction then we take the idea to our favoured writer. The idea has to ignite that writer. They are not writing to order. They are engaging in an idea that is multifaceted and our devising process intends to give the writer many tools and collaborators to work with.

This leads to a period of research and development. Often this has meant entering a rehearsal room with actors and/or dancers (usually a mix of the two) and working solidly for two weeks without the writer writing a single word. They observe and absorb the many situations and stories explored through physicality. Sometimes these physical moments are a launch pad to a written scene. Sometimes they become the scene themselves as the writer brilliantly laces them through the script.

We have found it desirable to have as many of our creative team as possible at these development sessions. They see ideas as they are formed but more importantly it invites them to make sure their roles are not passive or reactive. They are not lighting or designing 'our' world. We should be making this world together. Their vision, experience and expertise are invaluable. They should be commenting on the physical and influencing the text. This should be a mutual flow of energy and ideas.

Ultimately the writer could be working with the brilliance of the designer in mind, with the potential of sound to gently manipulate, with action and potentially silence speaking louder than words. This does not suit every writer and it is important to consider the best possible working relationship for all collaborators. Feel free to make demands but make sure they all work towards bringing the best out of everyone on board.

Some writers can be very open in their process. Others might appear to be up to point and then require space and freedom to write. We have to respect and be sensitive to this. The collaborative devising is often done in the initial set-up, the development sessions. This is what gives the writer all the practical tools to create the show we need. There is never a scenario where a writer is tapping away at their laptop with a director and designer hovering over their shoulders. From the development sessions onwards the process for a writer working on a show for Frantic Assembly might be very similar to that experienced elsewhere.

Working with writers like Bryony Lavery and Abi Morgan has been the most exhilarating and empowering experience. It was Bryony who really gave us the confidence to 'write' in movement. She understood image and aspired to write in it as much she wrote in text.

The development sessions might look much more like the preconception of devising but it is without the reductive pressure of existing within a dwindling rehearsal time. It is not rehearsals. It is focused and disciplined but it is definitely the time to be playing with 'what if?' It can be physically led, or it could be about developing story and text. We might explore character work either textually or physically but all work will be within a clearly defined subject. We would have talked about our aims and created techniques to explore them, partly wanting to be proved successful and partly wanting to be surprised by the outcome.

All of this leads towards a draft of the full script for day one of rehearsals.

Building blocks

When working with performers (and students), all of our devising is broken down into tasks. These remain as simple as they can be. They are bite sized and self-contained. We call them *building blocks*. Like building blocks they are simple and robust. They are not the house. They come together to make the house. They never set out to encapsulate the whole production idea or solve the entire demands of the text. They are merely building blocks, created to support more blocks.

By setting tasks you allow your performers to offer much creative input into the devising of choreography without burdening them with the responsibility of creating the whole show. Such burdening may not bring out the best of your performer. The shaping of theatre and choreography requires an outside eye and it is this objective influence that can liberate the performer to be brave, take risks and try things new. We, as the director/choreographers, are liberated too as the performer is now providing a palette so much larger and richer than our own imaginations could provide. We feel this relationship and process sets both performers and directors free to use their full imaginations as well as working with ideas we would never have thought about.

We are firm believers that limitations create freedoms and breed creativity. Asking performers to improvise in a void can be really counterproductive. It is the pain of personal experience that has shaped this approach as well as the influence and approaches of the very talented choreographers we have worked with. They recognised the need to simplify things for us, to see what we could do and then use this. We responded to their use of rules and parameters and have taken this process and developed it as our own. This is probably why we never teach choreography from the front of the room. In rehearsals we never teach 'steps'. The moves come from what the performers find they are capable of through the specific tasks set. We believe this is the most productive, honest and accessible method for us.

Our favourite devising processes are the ones where the lines of creativity start to blur. A successful production for us will be one where it is hard to distinguish which came first between, say, words and movement or movement and music. This is achieved in a rehearsal room where the creative team act as one unit, sitting in front of the same scene or image or moment and all feeding into the process not just as, say, lighting designer but as a potential audience member and a Frantic theatre maker.

During a development period for *Stockholm*, we invited Martin Holbraad, an anthropologist at University College London, to spend the week in the room with us. To begin with there was no agenda as there was no notion as to what might be of interest for anthropological study. As a company, we were simply inquisitive as to how our creative process was seen to operate from the outside and how we might look to adapt or improve it. One interesting observation Martin made was our constant use of anecdotes and breakouts into storytelling. One director has recently written about the rehearsal room being, for them, an environment where the anecdote is not welcome. This could not be further from the truth for us. These early stages of development are littered with the entire creative team hurling anecdotes around the room. This interface between the central idea or theme and the personal experiences of the collective people in the room is where we start to understand the actual validity of the idea as a point of interest.

It was noted by Martin that these alternative templates were all about creating an environment of anti-pretentiousness. Following this observation through in a conversation, we talked about how it feels counterproductive for us to allow the individual to go solo within the rehearsal room for too long. The practice of sharing was critical to the working dynamic. This led Martin to conclude that 'membership of the group (was) openness'. In considering what are the ideal conditions for devising theatre, this sentiment is one that we believe sits at the heart of *our* understanding and practice of devising theatre.

Pre-show

From the very start there was the notion of the pre-show. For us, these were those unique minutes between entering the performance space and the start of the performance proper. These minutes are there for the taking – a time when the level of expectation is palpable and yet malleable, a time that naturally fuels slightly animated conversation; and yet even this very personal factor can be manipulated.

The drive behind the pre-show had a lot to do with being a company about to set out on a multi-venue tour for the first time. In creating a pre-show we felt we achieved two vital factors. One was the claiming of the space. From the moment each audience member entered the auditorium, they were instantly made aware that the space was ours, had been claimed by Frantic. No matter that they were long-serving season ticket holders, used to swinging through those same doors twice a month. Our aim was not necessarily to wrong-foot them – in most cases this was never going to be possible with a couple of bits of Tri-Lite and a swathe of MDF (i.e. our set). The ambition was to stake out our territorial claim, that in some way tonight might be different from what they might usually expect, that things were in our control for tonight. During those early tours, venues changed dramatically from town to town and night to night. Wings suddenly disappeared or were only found on one side. The audience were on top of us one night and then were somewhere out there in the darkness the next. The speaker systems were right behind us, kicking out decibels that created involuntary movement among us, or consisted of a tiny speaker somewhere up in the lighting rig and in front of us so that we were effectively performing in silence on stage. Such oscillations in stage experiences were par for the course once the show began so it was always a relief to feel that those starting minutes would be something we could set off with, collectively. A few precious moments of control before the technical capacity of the venue and the responses of the audience that night started to have their own effect.

The pre-shows varied from piece to piece but the underlying principle was (and still is) to create the idea that something *has already started*. That the price of your ticket wasn't enough to contain the start of the work, that this was a place where you would be asked to keep up, a place where the stuffy conventions of polite chatter were not an option.

For our very first pre-show (*Look Back in Anger*) we gauged a moment when we figured approximately 50 per cent of the audience had taken their seats. At this point, there was a 30-second blast from a Nine Inch Nails track (famed American Industrial/Techno/Grunge artist Trent Reznor) during which we emerged from both wings (when available) and executed a furious blast of movement upon each other, at the end of which we disappeared until the start of the show when the entire audience were in. A sort of 'blink and you miss it' sequence or 'miss it completely 'cos you were still getting your ticket ripped' sequence. Whichever, it got the seated audience wired and created a great 'we saw this weird beginning thing/what are you talking about?' divide in the bar afterwards.

From there, pre-shows have ranged from blasting the audience with pounding techno music as they enter (*Klub*), the entire cast being concealed within a toilet cubicle on stage while a soundtrack relays the recorded events of an alcohol-fuelled evening together (*Sell Out*) and the performers casually chatting while suspended as high as the venue would allow from four separate golden ladders (*Hymns*). Our personal favourite was the pre-show for *Flesh* which we based on an account given to us in interview by a male prostitute during our research for the show. He described how he would pick up clients on street corners by 'jigging around a bit'. From this we created a start to the show where the four performers would prowl the stage as the audience entered, eyeing them up and staring at various people, intermittently dropping into various 'jigs' as a means of flirtation. The collective task was to 'find your person'. At the same time, we considered ourselves as something definitely not sexy but something closer to 'butcher's cuts'. The biggest crowd pleaser seemed to be the run-up to the opening of *Zero*. Five performers squeezed into an impossibly small children's Wendy house for sometimes up to 25 minutes as an unsuspecting (and as it sometimes felt, uncaring) audience sauntered in. Once the show properly began, the house began to pulse as the performers pressed into the little plastic walls before all bursting from the doors and windows, trying desperately not to show the extent of chronic cramp and pins and needles.

Some pre-shows did cause confusion for some audiences. A second pre-show for *Look Back in Anger* involved the performers on stage rehearsing the show for themselves quietly as the audience began to arrive, with a music track playing in the foreground. A rather elderly audience in Croydon, unable to hear what we were saying, began to yell at us furiously, telling us that they couldn't hear us, that we would have to speak up, that we had to have the music turned down.

Even at its most basic, the pre-show was a carefully selected music track played at a volume level that forced the incoming audience to shout slightly if they wished to talk to one another once they were seated. An attempt to raise the adrenalin and create an underlying level of *event*.

As with all things, there were exceptions and mistakes. The pre-show for *Tiny Dynamite* was a bare stage with the gentle sound of crickets, easily drowned out by audience chatter. The piece was a break from many practices for both Frantic and Paines Plough and to experiment in this way felt totally in keeping with the project as a whole. An initial pre-show for *Klub* involved the use of mid-level classical music which we felt was a trick that the audience could see through immediately. The first night that we swapped Schubert for The Aloof at top levels, the audience cheered as the lights went down before a single thing had happened on stage.

For us, the pre-show is a precious device, not in the sense of being delicate or even necessarily well crafted (though we did spend weeks working on the pre-show for *Flesh*), but precious as in valuable, an essential part of what we perceive to be the theatrical experience of coming to see a Frantic show. Laying claim to a theatre space like this demonstrates that we are taking full responsibility for what is about to happen and in fact, it is already happening. It creates a sense of event by asking the audience to commit to the experience just that little bit earlier than they might usually expect, to give just that little bit more. It is this kind of contact that Frantic wishes to engage in and to provide.

Othello further blurred the line between pre-show and actual show. The audience came into the auditorium to a typically inviting Hybrid track but on clearance from the front-of-house staff the track would shift to Hybrid's 'Just For Today'. The volume would rise imperceptably until the tipping point at which, on a good night, the audience realised they were being dealt with an increasing volume level at the very same moment that the lights snapped to a blackout, leaving the pinball machine flickering away in the dark. This would catch the audience out. It would be a shock to be suddenly plunged into darkness and find the show somehow alive before you. Most shows ease their audience in. *Othello* made a huge statement with its pre-show. 'Do not expect this to be a polite experience! Maybe your rules don't apply here!' This affirmed our context for the show. It had to be edgy and unexpected.

The pre-show consistently created a charge in the auditorium as the lights went down. Often the darkness would illicit screams and cheers. This felt like a thrilling achievement. We had already transformed what many young people or first time theatre goers could have feared would have been a stuffy and incomprehensible experience into a potentially exciting and dangerous experience.

We could still make mistakes though. Initially we tried to resist the temptation to go for a banging pre-show track for *Beautiful Burnout*. We aimed for something much more ethereal until it dawned on us it just was not working. If ever a show deserved an energetic pre-show it was *Beautiful Burnout*! We made a sudden decision to go for the biggest, beefiest Underworld track but omitted to tell one of our actors that we had changed anything. As the soundsystem strained and the seating jumped with the bass, one of our more seasoned actors, on her first Frantic Assembly show, got so caught up in the energy of it she thought she was having a heart attack! Not ideal but it does at least confirm the power of the pre-show!

Accidents and creativity

The Frantic rehearsal room is a well-considered space but not always the most organised. There will always be a source of sugar somewhere in the room and a good-sized pair of speakers to contend with, but the actual plan for the day falls well short of a military-type strategy with hours mapped out and scenes to be ticked off. One of the occasional pitfalls of sharing the directorial responsibility is believing that you can ignore a scene or section that feels tricky to initiate or start, hoping that the other will pick it up and run. The problem in our case is that we always have the same reluctance about the exact same scenes. The physical element in our work means that there is quite a methodical approach to the physical side of rehearsals but we are long-term advocates of a slightly looser approach to theatre making when it comes to creating and developing scenes. This is partly because of the many fortuitous moments that have occurred in rehearsals by way of keeping an eye on everything that is happening in the room. This means allowing even the most random event to shape and alter an exercise, to leave the path or idea prescribed maybe only moments earlier and to free up the room in order to make the most of a newfound impulse, influence or inclination. We have always maintained that on day one of rehearsals, the notebooks we carry into the rehearsal room will be of the highest quality (we spend weeks on the search for working notebooks that satisfy all the requisite standards) but will not contain all the answers. They are there for us to map out the gradual process of how each show comes into being, not ticking off pre-decided scenes and sequences already mapped out.

An early example of this was on our first day of rehearsals for *Zero*, which was a devised performance working around the idea of pre-millennial tension coming to a climax during a house party on New Year's Eve 1999. We had strong reservations about a set that represented the inside of a house. All pre-rehearsal conversations regarding the look and feel of the house and its room or rooms proved fruitless. This was at a time when there was no designer employed on our productions, and in this instance we strongly felt the lack of that individual who provides expert input on aesthetic issues, practicality and possibility. On entering the sports hall of the Welsh girls' school that was to be our home for the next five weeks, we were met by a slightly embarrassed looking children's Wendy house into which we all promptly disappeared for the next hour (the five of us all being under the national average height was, in this instance, a blessing, meaning we could just fit in en masse). Our whole problem of the interior of the space, all the choices that would have to go into the presentation of our playing environment, was erased as we realised the answer lay in this tatty plastic house that stood approximately four feet high. Our capacity to present a party going on inside this tiny house was priceless – allowing us to flip between riotous action by the house itself and then scenes of personal, private introspection practically anywhere else on stage by virtue of it being outside the house. Our entire playing space freed itself up to many possibilities, and the capacity for the house party to be the best of all possible parties was unquestioned, it only being glimpsed every now and again through the tiny windows and door. The fact that so many people wanted to be in such a small space went some way to representing the desirability for all the characters to be at the party, even though in real terms it often meant much discomfort for the performers and some very intimate physical encounters in there – some expected, some not.

Another example occurred during rehearsals for *Hymns* and an early improvisation for a scene we finally called Lullaby. At the time, we were improvising a scene around a table between the four characters using the simple practice of physically 'listening' to one another and attempting to construct a sequence using physical impulses taken from each other. As a character objective, we didn't want to be seen communicating anything too committed but at the same time yearned for just the simplest form of connection that remained elusive. We ran a number of sessions attempting to set this sequence, each time working with a track by the band lamb that was the final track on their album *Fear of Fours*. It was felt that the rhythm contained in the track drove the urgency of the exercise in a way that was useful in conveying a sense of insistence, of wanting to connect. During a late run of the exercise, as the track finished, nobody pressed stop on the CD player. Unusually for us, the exercise continued in silence after the track had completed. What we didn't realise was that lamb had a tendency to include 'hidden' tracks on their CDs – a track that plays some time after the ending of the last listed track. In this case it was some time before the track 'Lullaby' quietly drifted out of the speakers. At first, no-one really knew what was happening but what became apparent was that this was a whole new mood and tempo being offered. The exercise switched, becoming something far more delicate. The rhythms slowed and the painful misses in trying to connect with one another came to the fore. Playing to the music, we totally rediscovered the scene for ourselves and less than three minutes later we had what was very close to the completed version of our scene. This was one of the first rehearsal periods where we had use of a video camera and it is this 'Lullaby' episode that we often cite as the turning point for us in the way that we record and create work in the rehearsal room.

A second 'happy accident' occurred during the making of Lullaby a few weeks later when we moved to a rehearsal studio at Battersea Arts Centre, which had a huge window at one side. As we were running and recording the sequence, a sudden dramatic flurry of clouds scudded across the sky outside, breaking up the sun's rays and sending long shadows shifting across the table at which we were all sat. The sudden speed of the light moving around the room looked like time-lapse photography. Luckily, the video recording was as dramatic looking as the actual event and we were able to hand the tape over to Natasha Chivers, our lighting designer, who replicated the sequence of light for the actual show.

While dance companies gravitate to light and airy rooms with polished mirrors we have found that the slightly more down-market rooms have actually had more impact on the rehearsals. When rehearsing *Hymns* we spent the first three weeks in an extremely plush dance studio in a new purpose-built venue. And we found it less than perfect. The beautiful, clean lines may have been conducive to pure dance and to be fair we did work very hard creating a large proportion of the more dancy elements of the show, but we struggled to get any theatrical inspiration. A case of all perspiration and no inspiration. We were in danger of leaving that space still unsure about ideas surrounding set and design. We knew we wanted ladders but how could we tour with them? How could we slide down them like we imagined without shredding our hands? What was the overall aesthetic of the piece? It was when we were looking through a maintenance cupboard for a mop to clean up a spill on the immaculate sprung floor that we found a ladder. The sides were smooth and it broke down into 90 centimetre sections which meant we could potentially create the 5 metre ladders we hoped for and still be able to tour with it. We contacted the manufacturer and they sent us our ladder pieces. This accidental discovery was probably the most important moment of our three weeks rehearsing at a premiere dance studio.

Accidents that have befallen our actors have made it into final productions. During a late rehearsal for *Rabbit*, one section involved the actress Sue Kyd suddenly turning on her daughter and marching across the room towards her. On this occasion, as Sue rounded the set and set off on her trajectory, her heel collapsed and rather than stopping, she carried on her path, but in this instance her march had turned into a lurch as Sue tried to navigate the constantly shifting balance of her walking pattern, rising and falling like a careering, stunned animal about to crash to the ground. The effect was startling and encapsulated the moment so precisely that, in the final production, we not only had her repeat the event, but also armed her with a bottle of vodka in each hand just to add to the swagger of the moment.

Examples such as these are less about pre-thought ideas proving to be wrong and more about the essential practice of being truly receptive to ideas and influences that occur around the rehearsal period. It is not unknown for us to work on an image that one of us might have spotted on an advertising billboard on the way into work that morning. The set for *Tiny Dynamite* was a direct reference to the series of *Big Brother* that we were all watching on TV that summer. The show's title was a pure mistake, taken from a song by

Cocteau Twins that is actually called 'Tiny Dynamine'. It is important to remember that happy accidents can never be relied on. Nothing is more terrifying for us than the notion of turning up in a room and just 'seeing what happens', but what we have also discovered is that if the rehearsal process is structured and ordered to the point of being sanitised, then you don't allow the space for these happy accidents to happen.

What is physical theatre? (and why we hate answering that question)

We get asked this a lot. We always try to answer to the best of our abilities but therein lies the problem. Each time we answer we feel that the person asking the question actually knows more about the subject than we do.

This is not a question that occupies much of our time, despite the number of times we get asked it. 'Physical theatre' is actually quite a frustrating phrase as it barely manages to describe what we do never mind the wide range of styles and influences that are clustered under its banner.

When we have tried to avoid the question it is only partly through boredom and mostly through ignorance. We will do our best now to explain what it means to us but that won't be easy. We do not come from a formal theatre background and have not been instructed in the history of performance. We are not particularly familiar with terms and definitions that are often contained within the questions addressed to us. Once, in front of a class of theatre undergraduates, when asked to talk about how Artaud had influenced us, we started to rattle off venue names, how each audience was different and the joys of sleeping in a Transit van. We thought they wanted to know about our tour. This was not just a case of mishearing. The students were horrified to find that we had never heard of Artaud. In fact there was honesty and relevance in our accidental answer. The Transit van we used to tour actually did have much more influence over our work than any practitioner in a textbook.

It appears 'physical theatre' is used as an umbrella term for aspects of performance including dance theatre, mime, clowning and traditional pictorial or visual theatre. (We are already way out of our comfort zone!) Within this is an enormous range of 'physicality' from the limb-threateningly expressive to the delicate and demonstrative. It can be said that our brand of theatre sits somewhere within this realm and could rightly be termed physical theatre.

When we started our company we were proud and excited to be labelled under the physical theatre banner. We were fit and fearless and just wanted to bang the drum for the physical theatre cause.

As we developed and the questions about physical theatre mounted up we started to realise that it was not particularly applicable to our creative process. The question 'What is physical theatre?' only crossed our mind replying to e-mails from students. We were not interested in definitions as, to us, they felt like limitations. Our unorthodox route into theatre had actually presented us with a world of possible styles and approaches. We realised quickly that this was our strength. We were not developed through a house style as can happen at some establishments. We were not dedicated to exploring theatre through Brechtian terms. The world was our oyster.

It is true to say that we set out to be Volcano Theatre Company clones, such was their immediate influence on us, but that soon faded. We were not as politicised or as angry as Volcano. We had a lighter touch. Watching a Volcano show that we did not enjoy was possibly one of the most liberating experiences as it helped us find what we did like. This is a pattern that continued for many years, acting instinctively and finding out what we did like by noticing what we didn't. This experience did not dull our appreciation of Volcano. It just told us that we were not Volcano.

We became influenced by the dance films of DV8. Through attending workshops we encountered influential practitioners from dance companies such as V-TOL and the Featherstonehaughs. Even at this early stage we did not see distinctions between movement and theatre. It was all there to be harnessed. This was not, however, through a desire to be genre breaking. It was because we were not aware of definitions.

As we have developed we have become more aware of the dangers of existing under a banner. People expect you to deliver work along those lines. Being aware meant that we have openly reserved the right to make the kind of theatre we like. That was our reason for starting off and that must not change. When we made *Tiny Dynamite* we were desperate to remain true to its need for a gentle and tender physicality. It was still a physical show in our minds. It just had none of the bombast and spectacle of what one might expect from 'physical theatre'.

It is this expectation that frightens us. We do not want to simply deliver the expected.

Video camera in rehearsal

Our rehearsal rooms are now full of sound systems and people tapping away at laptops. It is a long way from the empty rooms and the vacant looks that accompanied our initial rehearsals. The technological revolution in the way we work has mostly crept up on us, but there was a moment when we took a great lurch forward. It was a time when the video camera became a necessity in the rehearsal room.

We started making *Heavenly* in January 2002. We were working with a close friend as fellow writers, directors, choreographers and performers. For most rehearsal sessions it was just the three of us trying to make work that

From rehearsal to production – Richard Winsor and Ifan Meredith as Monster and Victor Frankenstein in *Frankenstein* (2008). Image by Scott Graham

was poignant and funny. For three people who could make each other laugh effortlessly we found the whole process of turning material into a show torturous. We were lost and alone and losing all confidence. We struck upon the idea of bringing in a video camera and setting up improvisations we could all take part in. We set the camera up and ran the exercise. When we had finished we rushed to the camera and rewound it knowing there were some good moments in there. Watching it back gave us a bit of a shock. All of the good bits were accidental; all of the bits we thought were good were anything but. This might have been a deflating experience had the camera not given us all of these moments we had missed. It was up to us now to gather them up and consciously put them into our work.

The video camera had saved us on that project. We made sure that we took it into subsequent productions, thinking that it is one thing for us to stand out front and tell performers where their improvisations were and were not working, and another to sit down with them and analyse what they were doing and the possibilities that emerge accidentally and get captured by the camera. The performers can then recreate those moments and claim them for their own.

The video camera is not just for capturing and documenting what you know is there. It is also for capturing all the possibilities that emerge by accident. It is there to show you what you don't yet know. It is also a great shorthand way of explaining to a performer what you liked and what you want them to do. Watching a recording of an improvisation enables you to specify moments by the minute and second they occurred. This means that performers can recreate the moments and move towards a final version that is an amalgamation of killer moves from longer improvisations. This process was invaluable on productions like *Frankenstein* (adapted by Lisa Evans), where the improvisations were so physically and mentally draining that the performers had no sense of what worked and what did not. This process allowed them to go straight to those moments, saving them from the exhaustion of repeating the improvisations.

Frantic music and the notion of soundtracking

Throughout the development of Frantic Assembly, one of the most invigorating and exciting artistic discoveries has been that afforded by the exploration of music in our work. As a form, it has been the most essential of influences, not just in terms of creating the soundtracks for our shows but as a tool for setting up the right rehearsal environment, inspiring theatrical scenarios, offering inspiration through lyrical and compositional content, providing structure for improvisation sessions right through to the tracks used to accompany promotional material created by the company.

When facing the challenge of our first purely devised performance, *Klub*, we were liberated from all the constricts of a well-structured play, but with so much freedom at our disposal we were floundering in the vast sea of possibilities. Around this time we were starting to work with Andy Cleeton, a DJ also based in Swansea, which enjoyed a thriving club scene at the time. After hearing a particularly blistering set from Andy one weekend, we asked him how, when faced with so much vinyl to choose from, did he make choices in structuring his set. The answer we anticipated was something along the lines of just feeling it in the moment, but Andy revealed a method that was to be instrumental in the way that we structured theatre.

Over a three-hour set, Andy would begin with tracks with a tempo around 120 bpm (beats per minute). This was more than just a desire to start with a relatively pedestrian tempo – this was DJ etiquette. The DJ prior to Andy's set would, towards the end, slow the tempo down to something around 120 bpm in order to allow the incoming DJ to warm themselves up over a number of tracks as they became accustomed to the crowd. (120 bpm is the tempo for most pop and dance tracks and some theorists have gone to great lengths studying the effects this tempo has on the human body, pointing out that it is no coincidence that all the most popular pop and dance songs over the past 30 years sit within a range of 2 bpm difference.) Over the next 45 minutes, Andy would increase the bpm rate to around 140, drop it back to 120 over the next 15 minutes then build it up to a high of perhaps 145 over the next 30 minutes. This pattern would then repeat, forming a clear set of peaks and troughs before settling down and signing off when the DJing baton would be passed on to the incoming DJ at a sedate rate of 120 bpm. This was like a newfound science to us, instantly understandable as one that centred around the focus and capacity of a crowd/audience to be moved. For us, the mapping out of tempo like this was exactly the same as the rhythm we felt we needed to create for our own work – a rhythm that carried the audience along confidently, pushing them to points of intensity but also carrying them confidently out of that intensity, allowing breathing space and something like recovery or at least respite from events but all the while preparing the way for a further high or peak. On a good night, Andy's capacity to create an environment where he appeared totally in control was masterful and we wanted to achieve the same thing.

Taking the structure of a DJ set as laid out by Andy, we started to examine the existing scenes we had for *Klub*. One immediate realisation was that, unlike an incoming DJ, nobody was providing us with a handover. This had huge implications on our practice of creating a pre-show environment. We inverted Andy's model in order to fulfil what we needed at the start of our own work. Rather than building from a trough, *Klub* (and the following two shows *Flesh* and *Zero*) started with a peak, a physical sequence that was our equivalent of the 140 bpm track – full, hard, loud, exhilarating. From this point we allowed the rhythm of the show to settle for a while, allowing the audience to get the measure of the piece but with a steady sense of increasing pace leading up to a second physical sequence. It does not always follow that physical sequences and text scenes represented the peaks and troughs respectively. The intensity of a particular textual scene would be considered a peak and placed within the overall structure accordingly. Over the space of those first few shows (each one lasting approximately 75 minutes) there would be three peak scenes, one at the beginning, one somewhere near the middle and one as the penultimate scene. These would be the most intense points in the show and the rest of the piece would rise and fall between these points.

Another way in which music influenced the structure of our work was the running time of the scenes. For the Generation Trilogy, each scene lasted, on average, three and a half minutes, which is the running time of the average pop song. In this way, we aimed for the performances to be similar to watching MTV for an hour or so, a response to the prevailing theories in abundance at that time about the average attention span sitting within this time frame. This structural policy meant that each scene had to get to the point and conclude with precision and economy – no bad objective when devising material, be it textual, physical or a combination of the two.

As a creative device, we have used music to create soundtracks for every Frantic show. We use the term 'soundtrack' in an admitted nod towards its filmic implications. One reason for this is a term we use to describe the kind of music that we find particularly inspiring. That term is 'bedroom cinematic' and it is hard to describe exactly what this means but we know it when we hear it. It is often found in music that has a sense of the personal and yet involves the most lush, vast orchestration. A good starting point for discovering this type of music would be practically anything by the band Hybrid. It is in the throb of a punishing techno track that still has within it the sense of a heart breaking. Within these points there is an implicit sense of drama, which also might be a way of defining the essential element in music that we look for. Soundtracking also seems like an accurate term as many of the tracks we use are from existing film soundtracks. Film soundtracks are a very useful rehearsal tool. Many of them consist of short tracks and can often swing wildly from track to track in terms of mood. When improvising, we often use soundtracks like this as the aural wallpaper, an element for the performers to work alongside. The brevity of the tracks prevents the improvising performers getting lost in themselves and the irregular structural nature of the music means that people are not able to improvise in a way that they might do if using songs or music that follows the traditional verse/chorus/verse/chorus/middle eight/chorus model. Performers are not always aware of using such structures, but this does not mean that they are not falling into the same rhythmic patterns on a subconscious level. Avoiding this makes for a purer improvisation that truly has to respond to the unexpected.

As with film scores, several Frantic shows have attempted to create a consistent sound and in this way create an arc, in the same way as one might consider the arc of a storyline. We have sometimes achieved this consistency by collaborating with a particular band or artist to provide all the music for a show. Working with the band lamb on *Peepshow* we were given access to their entire back catalogue plus stripped down versions of songs. These alternative versions are incredibly useful in being able to develop musical recurring themes throughout a show. We had eight versions of one particular track, 'Gabriel'. By associating the track with one of the couples in the show, we were able to map out their relationship in musical terms, using the full original version at the start of the show and then a pared down, strings-only version at the end as their relationship had unravelled. Even in the event of not having a single band or artist to source music from, we have still made precise choices on the type of music we intended to use. For *Sell Out* we used many tracks that featured piano and strings and also electronic tracks in a minor key in an attempt to locate those examples of electronica that somehow melt the heart. In the case of *Underworld*, we looked for tracks that were predominantly rich in percussion or strings. In creating the arc for the piece, we placed a track in the very middle of the show that acted as a kind of keystone. The track was the theme tune from the film *Unbreakable* by James Newton Howard and was used to backdrop a physical sequence in which all four female characters experience violent nightmares over one night. The track itself is a grand cinematic blast, full of menacing strings and snarling brass with possibly the creepiest break in soundtrack history, topped off with a thundering finale with quivering cellos and explosive percussion. Everything prior to this moment in the show in terms of music was building towards this apex, starting slowly with the pedestrian simplicity of Goldfrapp's 'Felt Mountain' track. Everything after this point was an exercise in progressive distortion, each track becoming more and more ominous and degraded now that the dam had burst both musically and dramatically. In this way, the score for the show genuinely has its own arc.

We have used the musical idea of the overture and translated it into a visual form. In music, the overture is the opening section that introduces themes used in the piece about to commence. The opening of *Underworld* was an erratic, violent stab of images, bursting out of the darkness and disappearing as soon as they were established. All the images were taken from scenes to come but were presented in no particular order in an attempt to appear disorientating and nightmarish. In this way, our visual overture sets the tone and prepares the audience for what is about to come without acting as a kind of spoiler for the events. In *Rabbit* we opened the second act with a short two-minute piece where we picked out the various characters involved in moments that we imagined had occurred during the time the audience had been out in the bar sipping gin and tonics while we hid in the toilets. The visual montage formed a visual bridge between the two acts, wordless and economical and not without a slightly sinister twist, given the events that were about to unfurl.

Selecting music is always a very personal, subjective and idiosyncratic process and in many ways is true of a particular creative view or feeling at a particular point in time. There are, however, a few constants in our choices. Many of our music choices have been instrumentals. One of the reasons for this is that instrumental tracks still allow for interpretation by the listener in a way that songs with sung lyrics do not. A lyric adds a specificity to a piece of music and in some instances this can have a reductive effect rather than enhancing a scene. On the occasions that we have used songs it is precisely because we are looking to create that specificity with the scene. We also try hard to avoid using music that most of our audience will already know or recognise. In listening to known music, we often start to bring to it our own associations. There is a danger here for an audience who might suddenly lose their place in the piece. The music and the scene in this instance have to work very hard to claim precedence in the mind of the audience member. Our choices have often involved orchestral pieces as well as hard industrial techno, both forms that are very 'big' in terms of sound. Given our proclivity for loud volume levels during performances, we are firm advocates of the 'big' sonic experience but we are also wary of not allowing music to overwhelm the scene. In the same way that the actor-to-set ratio is an important consideration for the way in which the entire show is received, so the music should never be at a level that outweighs the action or event it is supporting.

The idea of truly supporting the scene or event is one reason why we are cautious about using music that allows too much space to the point where it is difficult to see whether it is having any effect at all. Despite being ardent fans of ambient music, we are deeply suspicious of the all too common use of the soundscape in theatre. Again, this is a very subjective area, but the vagueness of certain music can leave a scene floundering. As with the combination of text and movement, the combination of scene and music should never result in the scene suddenly being made strange. Music choices are not always about harmony (there is much fun to be had creating musical counterpoints), but each music track has to justify itself. Despite occasional attempts, a track has never appeared in a Frantic show just because we were in love with it at the time. (Oh, all right, well maybe there was the post-show playout track for *Underworld*, but it was just an unforgivably brilliant remix …)

Listening to music can be a highly effective shorthand in the rehearsal room. Arguably, we would never have come up with such creepy, disturbing, dead body material for *Flesh* without the Nine Inch Nails track 'Closer (precursor)'. It is hard to imagine a more menacing piece of music and it is no surprise that the same track went on to be used by David Fincher to accompany the seminal title sequence for his film *Seven*. While creating a duet for the Bare Bones dance company, we asked the two performers to listen to Bjork's 'An Echo, A Stain' as a way of describing the movement quality we were looking for. The track has such a distinctive production quality that there is no danger of there being radically different interpretations of the mood evoked by such music. The vocal quality of the singer Sia, as featured on 'Destiny' by Zero 7, was used by us as a mood reference point during the making of *Peepshow*. Note it was the vocal quality that was important here although the lyrical content was also pertinent with references to 'watching porn in my hotel dressing gown'. To not flag up the vocal quality at play is to miss a trick in understanding the effectiveness of the line. In rehearsals for *pool (no water)* we played the cast 'Hide and Seek' by Imogen Heap and asked them to pay particular attention to the amount of silence and stillness throughout the track. While improvising the scene where the four friends go to visit their hospitalised friend for the very first time following a horrific accident, we asked them to reference the same quality of silence and stillness. The result was a scene of very precise choreography that was as much about not moving – a reference to and reflection of the song which often reduces itself to barely a breath.

The dynamic structures used in music arrangements are also a precious tool for us. During a workshop session for *Othello* the company listened to Hybrid's 'Just For Today' and in particular, a section towards the end of the track where a particular kick drum is heard on the 2 and 4 count of the odd numbered bars and then the 2, 4, 7 and 8 counts of the even bars. This structure is repeated four times. The sound quality of the drum is hard and brash and we asked the performers to create a string of material that not only used the impact points of the count structure but also the savage, tight sound of the drum sample as a reference point for the movement quality.

We have no restrictions when it comes to sourcing musical ideas. We are purists only in the sense that the end point is to serve dramatic purpose. The music itself is as likely to come from the *Finding Nemo* soundtrack as it is to come from a rare remixed version of an underground European techno house classic. One of the most beautiful and fragile tracks we found for *Underworld* came from Brad Fiedel's otherwise industrial score for *Terminator 2: Judgment Day*. An open mind and an open ear are essential when searching for existent music tracks to work with.

One of the most progressive art forms over the last 20 years has been the music video. The marriage of music with images has become one of the most inspiring and invigorating practices, mini cinematic events that cram the epic into a four-minute gem. The visual techniques employed have been seminal in developing the ways that we read visual information and the editing techniques of directors such as Chris Cunningham are spectacular. In trying to understand effective use of music choices for theatre, it is probably best to look to music video directors such as Chris Cunningham, Michel Gondry, Jonathan Glaser, Mark Romanek and Spike Jonze. Of course, these artists are given the music track first and then look to create the scene around it but, in looking at the results they create, one can see the incredible outcome when music and images coalesce effectively.

Music sits at the very heart of our creative process. On many, many occasions, an idea has sprung from the conversation that starts with 'I was listening to this track and, I don't know why, but this image came into my head and ... ' Our relationship with music is an ongoing artistic development though there is a recognised Frantic-style track. We only know this as we have regularly had people tell us that they have heard a track and have thought it to be 'very Frantic'. It's pleasing to discover that, in most cases, they are absolutely right.

Stockholm Fight (and the Crooked Path)

We will use the fight scene from *Stockholm* (2007) to illustrate that the journey from idea to production is not always linear. It is often formed by mistakes and sometimes it is a deliberately twisty route that can lead to a much more complex and rich scene.

The process used is a good example of allowing a physical quality to permeate a production as it actually created three separate physical scenes.

This is not here just as an exercise in economy but it also serves to show how the meaning of choreography lies in the context in which it is presented. We have used the same or similar choreography to show the unravelling of a relationship over one intense night.

This process is similar to the approach used by a soundtrack composer on a film, creating motif and variations of a theme to highlight different levels of tension. Sometimes the music is familiar and comforting. At other times it makes us nervous and fearful.

The tension in *Stockholm* built up to a brutal and shocking fight between a couple that had charmed us and sold us a vision of their perfect life together. All their defences drop as they shatter in front of us. The intention was that these people would feel like our friends and while we are shocked and appalled by the nature of their destruction, there is still part of us that understands why they will forever crawl back to each other.

Socratis Otto and Leeanna Walsman in *Stockholm*, 2010, produced by Sydney Theatre Company in association with Frantic Assembly.

Photo: © Brett Boardman

We approached the making of the fight in a round about way. We did not engage the performers in any violent choreographic tasks. We wanted the violence to come from somewhere deep in their relationship and we did not want the violence to completely overshadow the love at the heart of this relationship.

There is a further complexity in that these are two people who love each other, yet frustrate each other. It is the quest for annihilation on one side and the denial of violence on the other. It is not all out war. There are different dynamics at work in there.

There were two major devising tasks that went into this scene:

1 Their Dance

This initial work was part of the research and development sessions and then carried into the rehearsals proper.

We set the performers the task of creating a beautiful and graceful dance routine bordering on ballroom and tango. We wanted them to possess a physicality that might not have been seen in previous Frantic shows. None of us were trained in those techniques so we were really looking at approximations. Being avid avoiders of any Saturday night celebrity dance competitions we aspired to developing a hybrid style of movement that could look genuine but was not necessarily stuck in any one style. The point was not that they were certain type of dancers, just that they loved to dance. It was to be beautiful. We wanted this dance to be a major part of how they expressed their love and joy for each other. We wanted it to charm us and make us want to be them.

Once we had made this string of tango-esque material we then created different contexts in which the performers could dance.

1   While dancing they had to say sorry to each other when it felt right. They had to keep saying sorry and build in intensity throughout. The results were very striking. The raw passion was amazing but it was never a simple presentation of increasing remorse. Sometimes the 'sorry' became very aggressive, the hold on the partner appeared to become crushing and the whole tone of the piece had changed from joyful to heart breaking or terrifying.
2   Again, keeping the same moves, they entered another scenario. We created a room using an old metal filing cabinet, tables and chairs and placed plastic bottles and knives and forks precariously around the place. The room was made as small as possible. Claustrophobic and cramped.

    The performers were asked to commit to the set moves. These moves required a much bigger space and would lead to the performers clattering into the furniture and knocking over the bottles and cutlery. They had to ignore the chaos they were creating and keep dancing.

What transpired were a couple oblivious to the end of the world. Or was this a couple causing the end of the world? Did their love transcend this chaos or was it the root of it?

3   This time we arranged a room of tables and chairs. It was set out roughly like a kitchen with lots of worktop surfaces. Again the performers were to stick to their choreography where possible but it was all to happen off the floor, across the tables and chairs.

Here the moves quickly became dangerous. They also became a challenge and a ritual between two people as they tested each other's commitment, careering across gaps and teetering on precipices.

The three scenarios above brought out a lot of the potential in the movement. The interesting thing to note was that it was the setting or theatrical context that was crucial to this potential meaning rather than the choreography itself. The moves ultimately bent under the weight of the context but the joy of seeing them exist in one context and then struggling to exist again in another context was fascinating.

The beauty of their dance was an important part of the portrayal of the couple in *Stockholm*. It was crucial to get this right to suggest the couple were capable of such beauty as well as the carnage of their later scenes. It was this dichotomy that gives them depth as a couple and makes their predicament painful and tragic. We never wanted to dismiss this couple as just hateful and violent.

The exercises opened some interesting possibilities about how we could use their dance. Having achieved the beauty it was extremely useful to see how dark and disturbing the same choreography could become through a change in context. The dance moves could then become motif and pliable to the retrograde and expansion employed by any dance company worth their leg warmers.

This extract from one of our notebooks shows how the dance was already becoming a vital part of the storytelling:

Does the dance break down?
Does it become exhausting?
A ritual? A symbolic act?
Bullying? A reluctant partner?
Is it performed in increasingly smaller spaces? On a podium? Dangerous?
    Perilous?
Risk – To stop is to fall off – metaphor
Along the top of the kitchen?

A desperate, exhausted act...

Or a passionate act of apology...

An attempt to recapture something?

A definition of their relationship that bears less relation to reality the more they do it? E.g. Man leads – woman follows but outside the dance he is losing all power?

2 Push and Pull

Recognising the many dynamics that exist and conflict in this complex relationship we set the performers off on a simple choreographic task. (Remember, we have not told them that this has anything to do with the fight or their characters.)

Using Round/By/Through (page 125) as a base we asked them to create a string of material exploring the transference of control and a push pull quality. This would mean moving their partner but stopping them before the move is complete, e.g. pushing away but suddenly stopping them. Pulling them and then blocking them. They had to try smaller moves too, e.g. throwing a partner's hand up and then stopping it dead.

It was simply about push and pull, start and stop but the control would constantly swap back and forward between partners after a few moves.

As this was billed as an exploratory exercise it meant it escaped any declamatory and fighty quality. It was just a sometimes simple, sometimes intricate exchange of manipulation and control. One partner would provoke the other into a move but would stop the move before completion, as if to emphasise their control. They might push their partner away and almost instantly pull their partner back under their control.

Once the choreography was secure we could test it through slight directorial adjustments, just like Their Dance, to see what more it could offer us.

First we brutalised it. The performers could use more force and speed but had to retain the precision. Their touch would press harder and deeper into their partner's body.

Then we stripped it of all the sharp and confrontational quality and softened the moves. This became a very tender and playful string of material. (More on this below.)

We now had a wide range of complex physicality to draw on. We drew on the dance and push pull material, using some of the moves from the 'dance' and then arrested them with the 'push pull'. We wanted the fight to have this depth and physicality and felt that it would not have been possible to have shades of love mixed with the struggle for power if we had simply approached the scene looking to make a standard fight.

That said it had to be brutal and we worked hard on this quality once the performers were comfortable with the choreography. If we had worked on the scrappiness of it too early it would only ever have been scrappy. By taking something secure and at times beautiful and then making it scrappy it retains and hints at some of its former quality. This is literally what we wanted the fight to do; present something brutal that suggests a connection to something beautiful.

The final stage was to take the choreography, all of which had been made off the set, and put it onto the set. We used the same route around the kitchen as Their Dance and then embraced any moments the set itself offered. By placing it in its context we could make the adjustments necessary to make sure we were not just expressing the fight through dance. It had to feel just like a fight but have the heightened physicality of dance. Placing it on the set was the last step in making it real.

A by-product of this approach was the creation of the Tea Towels scene. Midway through the process we explored a tender and playful version of the choreography. We took this quality and improvised with it.

This quality actually first surfaced during the development workshops. Here we took the choreography and then gave them tea towels and got them to tidy up the kitchen while still committing to the choreography. At times the top half of the body was busy denying the existence of the choreography the bottom half was playing out. At other times they were moving each other around the room with a matter of fact physicality.

We played with the potential of this. Could the couple use the moves to make up? To say sorry? To say I am still pissed off with you? To say you don't get round me that easily?

What emerged looked like a semi-willing game. It had a complex sexiness to it as one partner would submit to the physical commands of the other and then instantly switch to dominance. We got them to try to make each other laugh during it as the intensity built, or whisper something to each other.

Again the journey matched that of Their Dance. The finished scene was a charming game of cat and mouse, of trying to apologise and trying not to be put off by the other person. It was a lovely scene where one tried to resist the other working their magic upon them and failed miserably and beautifully. It was joyous to watch.

That did not save it from being cut though! The scene destroyed the rhythm of the show and had to be excised.

Here was a scene born from a pseudo ballroom/tango dance and the desire to create a complex and terrifying fight. It contained many of the moves and most of the same journey but it was a million miles from either scene.

The thing to take from this is the simplicity of the processes (Their Dance, Push and Pull) and the potential they have to keep offering more and more meaning.

Possibly more important is the route taken to create choreography that was in turn provocative, sexy, violent, abusive, reconciliatory, flirtatious, cheeky, disturbing, brutal, funny, etc. These qualities emerged without us really asking for them explicitly or exposing the performers to give us their sex face or their abusive face! They never felt that they had to edit moves and offer what they thought we were looking for. They just stayed true to the task and let these things happen.

This ultimately led to a violent scene that had disturbing and heartbreaking echoes to a love scene. Not only did this suggest the couple's warped cycle of mutual destruction for the audience but it also gave a resonance to the performers. That memory of the loving embrace and flirtation around the kitchen, the memory and beauty of 'Their Dance' was still warm as they found themselves tearing each other apart. This gave that moment a tragic depth that could have been easy to forget.

Do not underestimate the importance of this crooked path. It is not just about discovering depth with experienced performers. It can be extremely useful when working with the inexperienced and younger performers.

Remember that it can be entirely natural for any well-meaning performer, when told we are going to make a scene about a domestic fight, to go to the part of their brain that says 'Domestic Fight' and pull out the applicable moves. This will give you a very small palette to work from. It will probably not present you with something you could not have thought yourself. Remember, that is the aim behind so many of our devising processes. To expand your potential palette and offer a world of possibilities you could not have thought of. To achieve this you might have to withhold some information from your participants.

Another important reason for the crooked path concerns the participants themselves. Most plays are written by adults about the complexities of the adult world yet young people find themselves grappling with the issues and performing those roles all the time. If you look at Headsmacks (page 155) as an example it unearths a sensitivity, a sensuality even, that was never mentioned in the devising process. Even though the result presents something mesmerizingly sensuous, no one was ever asked to achieve it. As said above, no one was asked to show his or her sex face!

This is a crass example. It is not about sex. It is about subtle complexities that can be apparent from the outside, which you do not have to burden the participant with the task of having to find. That can be exposing and paralysing and can be unfair. Headsmacks and Stockholm Fight show that there can be a really fruitful and safe way to get to complex and challenging material without burdening the participants with the complexity or suffocating them with the challenge. It is not always the quickest way but sometimes it is worth taking the crooked path.

Dance Face and the permission to perform – working with dancers and actors

We are lucky enough to work with both actors and dancers and are impertinent enough to ask actors to dance and dancers to act. The demands we make on our performers do of course depend on the production but we have recognised that besides offering brilliance from within their area of expertise both actors and dancers can offer something surprising and invaluable when asked to explore the other's area of expertise.

This is not about exposing people's limitations or putting 'bad' actors and 'bad' dancers on stage. There is something about the process that each has to go through that can be exhilarating and enlightening.

To be fair, we are mostly in the business of getting actors to move rather than getting dancers to act but we have often included a dancer in a company for their physical ability to rub off on others, for their work ethic, for their bravery and willingness to try things. All of this has a positive effect on the company.

One of the more surprising events occurred on a development week for *Othello*. We brought together a team of predominantly actors but included long-term collaborator and dancer Eddie Kay. We rehearsed in a pub with the express desire to root the text in the mouths of the people that would frequent that pub. (Our *Othello* took place in the pool room of a Yorkshire pub and was inspired by the race riots of 2001.) We felt the pub location would help the actors find an earthy authenticity and refrain from that Shakespearian voice that can be heard booming from nearly every production you have ever seen.

Our performers launched into the text, leaving Eddie looking a little lost and out of his depth. At this point Eddie had very little experience with text, let alone Shakespeare. Around him performers were tipping knowing winks and lascivious looks as they worked with the text. They laughed and protested in all the right places. It was soulless and fake. It was just what we were trying to avoid. We were utterly unconvinced that the actors really knew what they were saying but they certainly knew how to make the sounds and shapes that gave the pretense of them knowing it. It was horrible and part of our conviction about tackling *Othello* started to wobble.

Then Eddie threw a spanner in the works by saying, 'Sorry, can we stop for a minute because I don't think I can say these words as I am not sure I understand Shakespeare?'

Jimmy Akingbola and Charles Aitken as Othello and Iago in *Othello* (2008). Image by Manuel Harlan

Charles Aitken as Iago in *Othello* (2008). Image by Manuel Harlan

It was a moment of startling honesty that gave us the conviction to challenge the actors and their delivery. It meant that we had to break down the whole process. If the performers were to attain the authenticity of a gang of hard cases in a run down pub then they had to have the words in their bodies. The words could not just skitter around their mouths like an academic exercise. They had to be owned by the actors. They needed to be spat and hurled with conviction. They needed to be fragile, fraught, honest and brave. They needed to have a fire that came from the gut.

This might seem obvious but it was a necessary stage that the actors were prepared to skip, such was their fear of being exposed as being underacquainted with The Bard. To be fair, this was in a three-day development workshop. We are not questioning the rigour of the actors' process. We are absolutely sure they would not have done this if it were actual rehearsals. We share this story to illustrate that, in this instance it was fear that inhibited the actors from really embracing the text. It was the dancer's ignorance of the text that gave him the freedom to make the obvious statements and bring honesty and authenticity flooding back into the room.

Putting the peculiarities of this story aside there are many advantages to getting actors to move. There are many pitfalls too, but ultimately the greater effort can be really worth it.

Firstly, it takes longer. You have to introduce the actor to new physical skills. The upside of this is you have an actor who goes home from rehearsal every day having achieved something they had thought was beyond them. Do not underestimate the psychological value of this! We have developed a whole warm-up ethos based on this and it continues to reap rewards. (See 'Why warm up?' on page 91.)

When the actor rehearses the choreography we have found we have to work really hard to remind them that it is only rehearsal. It has to remain a technical exercise as we explore detail and potential. Sometimes 'Dance Face' can descend as the actor adopts a Valentino mask, acting their socks off. This might be a mask used subconsciously to cover up the obvious deficiencies of their early attempts at movement. There is really no need for this, as we have not reached the point of performance.

This is a major difference between the actor and the dancer. The dancer is ready to explore and break actions down. They are secure in their clumsiness and mistakes are part of the process. This is where they feel at home. Conversely this is when the actor is most exposed and wishes to get through this process as quickly as possible. It should be noted, though, that the dancer is not immune to Dance Face. It can take a slightly different form. Maybe a slightly tortured look into the middle distance. Maybe an air of frustration and angst. Either way they need to be challenged as a default attitude is a mask and stops an audience really engaging with the dancer on a human level.

Working with actors on any choreographed violence is nearly always fraught with danger. This is because the actor does not want to be exposed to be working through a mechanical process. He wants to make it seem real, to shock the audience with the reality of the violence. We have found we are constantly reminding actors to slow it down, to stop acting, to just go through it step by step. This is something the dancer does not need reminding. It can be a very frustrating process for the actor. It certainly was with the fight in *Beautiful Burnout*.

This was a highly choreographed eight minutes of stage time involving an awful lot of boxing. Each punch and slip had to be painstakingly rehearsed. We could see from the actors' faces that this was a demoralising experience. Every time we would say 'slow it down' or 'just walk through the moves' they seemed to think they were moving further away from the moment they would wow the audience rather than taking methodical steps towards it.

Adrenalin and the desire for authenticity in the skill and violence of the boxing became our ally and worst enemy. It meant that we all probably wanted to run before we could walk but we had to stick to the process to keep everything tightly choreographed and safe for the performers. The resulting scene is one of our favourite moments in a Frantic Assembly show.

To achieve this level of choreographed complexity you simply have to drop the story for a while. Stop acting and don't be afraid of treating the scene as a mechanical exercise. The time to perform will come. But not before we are ready.

If this is only a problem for the actor then why don't we use dancers?

The point to remember is that we use both. It is in these frustrating moments for the actor that the reassurance from the dancer is invaluable. They become the ones that let the actor know that it is going to be ok. They can guide and advise from within.

Having taken the actor through this process you might find yourself getting them up to a standard that they probably had never thought possible. This has certainly been the case in our experience. But there is more to be gained than taking an actor to a point where they are a more than passable dancer. Having got the choreography down you now have the particular pleasure of reminding the actor that they are an actor and they now have permission to perform! They might actually have forgotten this! By this we mean the movement is in their muscle memory and that there is now headspace for all the complexity of thought that the actor can bring to a role. We have found that it has to be in this order if you are looking for precision and set choreography. Of course it is very interesting to take formed characters into improvised physical situations. This can be exhilarating and utterly enlightening but it does not really lead to set choreography. Remember, it is the actor that needs to rehearse. It is the actor that does these moves night after night. The character only does the moves for the first and only time each night! That is why the actor might need to drop the character for a while until invited to bring the character back into play.

Giving the actor the permission to perform is a brilliant moment where the choreography really takes off. It explodes from its context and has a depth that few dancers can find. This is what actors can bring you. This is why it can be so worthwhile to take the long route with the actor.

The importance of space

Notions of space are integral to our understanding of the creation of theatre. In order to illustrate this, the following essay will look at this key element in five distinct but interrelated sections:

1   Rehearsal space
2   Performance space
3   Textual space
4   Space between performers
5   Space to interpret

Rehearsal space

Our initial rehearsal periods often took place in what might appear less than ideal spaces. Car parks, dilapidated school halls, filthy carpeted rooms in run-down arts centres, corridors of strange council buildings, etc. Needs must and you are thankful for them! We have already pointed out how the transition from these quirky environments to the pristine, custom-built dance studio did not necessarily assist the creative process. In 'Accidents and creativity' (page 20) we talk about the struggle of creating in that void and how the idiosyncrasies of certain rooms have helped us discover defining moments. Nearly all discoveries in that section were afforded by the room we were working in.

There is an obvious thrill to find yourself working in a proper dance studio after years of rolling around in detritus and pubes. They were pristine and white walled. They had built-in stereo systems. They had sprung floors. There was a cafeteria. We would be working next door to Matthew Bourne and Adventures In Motion Pictures. On the contract it actually said the words 'Dance Studio'. It would be clean every morning on our arrival. It was in Central London! We had, surely, arrived. We were serious. We were rehearsing in a space that we imagined as the creative requirement for all proper, serious artists.

The problems were almost immediately apparent. We could not play our music as loud as we needed through their stunning sound system. (That was just a tease to boys who only ever wanted to turn it up to eleven!). The fact that Adventures In Motion Pictures were rehearsing next door had moved from being a matter of pride and inspiration to being a matter of resentment. The neighbours didn't like our tunes!

Then we found we could not afford to eat in the café. This might seem like a small point but what it seems to say is you don't really belong here. That is exactly the opposite of the message we were hoping to embrace while working there. None of this is the fault of the building or the management who have remained absolutely supportive of the company! It comes down to our naivity about the importance of getting that creative space right for the project.

It was affecting the work. At the end of week one, we hadn't really made very much material and, apart from two exercises (Hymns Hands and a sequence of contact work), we had very little that we actually liked. We had never been so slow in creating material or having ideas that latched onto other ideas that latched onto further ideas. The cleanliness of the walls became teflon. Nothing would stick. What we realised was that the rehearsal space we thought we needed and had yearned for over a number of years turned out to be a huge mistake. We needed somewhere a little gritty. 'Hymns' was a show about emotional darkness – how did we ever imagine creating such a piece in a room that suggested anything but?

Since making this discovery, we have since sought to create conditions within the rehearsal space that best accord with our practice. You can adapt the conditions to get the best out of your performers. Try an evening rehearsal and see if that invigorates or refreshes the experience. Move your desk to a different place in the room. You have to accept that if you only sit in one position you will only see your work from that perspective! And make sure there is space to escape! Escape can mean different things. On *Dr Dee* it meant a table tennis table. On *Curious Incident* it was the space to play games with a tennis ball. On *Beautiful Burnout* it was a rugby ball. Just find that something that can help people switch off for a moment, have fun, and find themselves refreshed and ready for more work!

Performance space

As a touring company, one of our main concerns is the creation of work that moves from home to home, sometimes over a protracted period of time. Early Frantic tours lasted for up to 12 months of pretty much constant touring, where anything over a one night stand in a venue was a rare luxury. When this is the situation, it is not just the size of the stage itself that becomes crucial. Wing space and the way in which the audience sit in relation to the stage are equally important. Even the location of the dressing rooms in relation to the stage can be critical (and there is a winning 'Spinal Tap' episode we were guilty of one night in Ipswich during the *Tiny Dynamite* tour that means we speak from experience here...). For the period that we are resident, that space belongs to Frantic but the consideration of performance space begins long before this moment. Is this the right venue for this work? What is the pricing policy at the theatre? What is their average demographic? What regions in the UK are we touring to? Is this a good spread across the country? Given our drive for generating new audiences, are we being diligent in presenting the work in the areas where theatres need this the most? Though in the early days it often felt anything but this, it is important to remember that this is always a choice. This choice takes many forms – it is social, economic, artistic and strategic all at the same time.

Textual space

The idea of textual space is crucial to our work. This might suggest work where there is some form of air, a sense of absence or a place where another (physical) language might be allowed (or best placed) to speak eloquently. It is about the moment where that audience might lean forward in their seats to engage with what is *really* going on and not just with what is being said. It is probably why we are such happy collaborators with writers such as Abi Morgan and Bryony Lavery – two writers who share a love of the spoken word but are also fine advocates of what is left unsaid or what cannot be said or what one might refuse to say. With such eloquent writers, the task in the rehearsal room can be to create the glue, the unifying visual and emotional current that will substantiate one moment following another (see 'The Events' on page 203). They recognise the process whereby the text is but one form of address, that as a collective, we are relying on the backbone of the spoken word but that the point of any particular moment might be delivered by a lighting cue or the considered movement of someone's hand.

Many unsolicited scripts sent to the Frantic office were of no use to us. If we were merely expected to employ a given physical language to capture the event in a play about, say, abseiling, we would find we had no interesting entry point. Shows about football were not in themselves bad ideas, but often the placement and application of the physical event within the structure of the play allowed for no play, no discovery. Often we were being suggested to produce the play because we were 'physical'. What this can mean is that our physicality can be seen as a way of solving the problem of capturing the context of the play. We need more than this. As we have often said, physicality works best and offers more when it can be seen to illustrate the subtext rather than the context.

There is a beautiful tension in the space between language being uttered and the understanding of an audience. Caryl Churchill is the most exquisite example of how this makes for remarkable theatre. Like all great writers, plays such as *Far Away* and *A Number* demonstrate a strident, beautifully crafted narrative arc that simultaneously plays with the actual form of language. Where such strength meets such invention and interpretation, we are at our happiest – and also our most challenged. We actively look for the 'gaps' in a text. Without them, we are never the best people for the job of bringing it to the stage.

Space between performers

The space between two people is an epic point of dramatic tension. We are not the first to be obsessed by its potential in art. Michelangelo's 'Creation of Adam' is the most obvious. John Keats 'Ode On A Grecian Urn' is arguably one of the most profound examples. Even the work of sculptor Cornelia Parker draws on this spatial dynamic, without the use of actual bodies at all. Put simply, it is the final moment of 'what if?', the second before it becomes what it will always be. It is found in many spheres. It is in the moments in judo where, with firm grips on one another's judogi, the two combatants move towards the decisive action that will commit one of them to victorious status and the other to that of loser. It is the airborne moment of the ballerina as, her body in flight, she remains held only by the air and the possibility of the successful grip of her partner. A circus acrobat troupe play on these moments of beauty and fascination over and over again. It is the commitment before knowing the outcome. It is where possibility is at its most intense – on the brink of its obliteration as the consummate act is decided upon. Regardless of the outcome it is the moment that precedes this, that split second, that possesses the most intoxicating quality. Without the active engagement of the audience in the various potential outcomes of any moment, that moment is effectively dead. The life of the moment exists in the space around it.

In the rehearsal room, we are always on the lookout for opportunities that are missed with this truth. Performers of all manner and type are often eager to get to grips with one another – literally. This can be out of overt enthusiasm or just to overcome an embarrassment of physical proximity. Either way, it is a missed moment. One that we are always calling to the attention of our performers and their sense of themselves as physical beings that we are watching. To acknowledge the power of the space between two bodies is to recognise how we observe ourselves on a consistent and subliminal level. Such intensity is not just the result of almost touching. In Pina Bausch's version of *The Rite of Spring*, the point of extreme tension is where the sole female figure stands in one corner of performance space while the brooding mass of the entire company bristle at the opposite diagonal corner. So much space affords us no respite from the palpable tension. But it is particularly in the creation of duets that we consistently push for this way of thinking. All too often we find ourselves bored by the lack of intensity in duet work between even the most dynamic dancers and physical performers. Without the space between them being taken into account, they are a continuous fait accompli. Their predicament is a visual done deal that will, at best, only sustain rather than develop the moment. In all other forms of art, the sustaining of interest is the mark of success for an audience. If this is to be believed, then surely when we take bodies in space, we should look to the same tools in order to warrant their presence at all. This is not to say that full contact is uninteresting, of course not. But the constant presence of space that keeps appearing, returning to the mix, creates the tension that keeps the moment alive. It might be why the standard waltz makes for bad theatricality and why the Argentinian tango is mind-blowingly good on this front. The dynamism of proximity is only ever truly known or interesting by also considering distance, space and time. By that we mean that reminder we find ourselves giving in the rehearsal room that there was a world that existed before the touch and there is now a world that exists after the touch. The touch must change the world. Touch must never be a given unless that is the point you are making (see 'Fluff' on page 144). This tension is crucial to any dramatic arc in movement.

Space to interpret

Finally, there is the space to interpret and perhaps this is the most straightforward. It is the understanding that, in moments of inspiration, what has been created is a source of interest, sometimes so interesting that it makes it feel like your heart is breaking or that your life has been understood and explained in a single moment. Even when as profound as this, what has also been created is the space to take this forward, to move it on. But to do it with what you yourself know, feel and think. Not a wholesale smash and grab but a first step, having had the pleasure of that moment where something clicked into place. Such moments might be found in this book (we would hope that there is something of value if you are this far into the book). It might be in the colour scheme of the uniform worn by the air hostess serving you a suspect risotto on the Lufthansa flight. It might be in the middle eight section of the Elbow track you never got round to really listening to in detail. It might be the opening pages of Bill Bryson's *Short History of Nearly Everything* but it could just as well be the daily choice of cute pet featured in the free newspaper you scooped up from under your bum on the bus that morning. All are valid and all operate along the same lines. The moment is possible anywhere. The point is to take it forward yourself. To relish the space where the artifact or moment once was and where you might land it yourself. Maybe not on the first attempt. Maybe never. But to relish the challenge of this is when theatre making is the best job in the world.

chapter two

Scenes and their creation

This chapter highlights scenes from Frantic Assembly shows, describing the devising process behind each of them. These scenes have been performed hundreds of times and have taught us much about the processes behind them and how we might have developed them. More importantly, this chapter suggests how you might develop them.

To facilitate this, each scene will be looked at from three perspectives:

- The Idea – the inspiration behind the scene and what we wanted to achieve.
- The Process – how we created the scene.
- The Development – how you might develop the process. Any process is not forever linked to the end product. It can be adjusted and reused. This section explores the future potential of the process.

Each scene is named as it was in the production. That in itself is a clue to our devising history. Each scene was named because the structure of the production was up for grabs. Initially we were not making work from a script. Each scene needed a name so that we could refer to it quickly when trying to work out the order of the production.

The names are personal. They just emerge because of the scenes' association with the music used (Lullaby) or the sheer hell of making it (Headwrecker). They were our code or shorthand.

Refer to the Anthology section in the Introduction (page 6) for more details on each production.

Lullaby   *Hymns 1999/2005*

This scene is called Lullaby after the music track used ('Lullaby' by lamb from the album *Fear of Fours*). See 'Accidents and creativity' (page 20) for more details of how the track came to be used.

The idea

The set for *Hymns* consisted of five chairs and one strong metal table, surrounded by a construction of ladders. Four men sit around the table. Previously they have laughed and joked their way out of the funeral, through several bottles of beer, and now find themselves with very little to say. This is a moment of introspection after the macho bravado of their reunion.

Lullaby is about time passing and not a word being said. A friend has died and all that has been shared are jokes and beers. We wanted a scene that captures the extended introspection of the hours following the funeral where the information of the day slowly starts to sink in.

Karl Sullivan, Eddie Kay, Joseph Traynor and Steven Hoggett perform Lullaby in *Hymns* (2005). Image by Scott Graham

THE FRANTIC ASSEMBLY BOOK OF DEVISING THEATRE

The process

Lullaby is a series of opportunities for connections between the four guys sitting in chairs around a large table. At times their actions attract each other. At others they repel. As one person moves forward to possibly speak, address, or even touch their mate that person is pushed or feels compelled to move away. Why? What do they fear from those connections? What would the touch mean? What can of worms would it open?

The first thing we played with was stillness and potential. This had to be a scene where the tiniest movement could be explosive, so we had to start from stillness rather than action. From the stillness the performers were asked to find fairly naturalistic but precise moves that involved resting their arms on the table, resting their heads, touching their face, looking at their hands. They were insular and fairly abstracted moves.

When one performer moves it has a physical consequence on the other. It might push or it might pull them. They do not touch but what makes them connect is the feeling of the move. More specifically it comes from starting and stopping at the same time even though the moves are different. For example, one character might brush dust off his trousers and fold his arms while another might be compelled to look at his hands and then place them on the table. If both characters' actions start and finish together, it empha-sises not only the actions but also the return to stillness. The stillness is once again filled with potential. The sense that the men want to connect but are terrified to do so, or be seen to be trying to, returns.

This is the choreographed scene in its simplest form. We then started to play with the focus of the audience. Instead of all characters stopping together we tried one character continuing on their own and found that they now com-manded all the attention. We played with connections across space. We had one person sit back in their chair as their connection with another character opposite appeared to pull that person forward in their chair. We played with levels of action. We went from the focus of a single hand moving across a table to the frenetic readjustments of all the characters in their chairs and then returned to a perfectly timed stillness. All of this was then shaped by the par-ticular and peculiar rhythms of our choice of music. This dictated when we used the material that we had found. It was the structure that the physicality was placed on. We also found moments of focus on each of the characters and the lighting picked them out accordingly. This allowed the scene to present a group unified in grief but also individuals lost and alone as they con-template their friend's death and the newly forming dynamic of the remaining friendships.

The development

The basic task within this process is to find connections between people's movements. We opted to keep it mostly small and slow. This fitted our theme. The process itself could support other themes and contexts.

The process highlights tension between people. Tension can be a positive or a negative. Within *Hymns* it was about people with emotions to hide, desperate to avoid being asked to talk about them. The process could just as easily portray sexual tension. It is all about changing the context.

Try following the process above and choreographing a scene between, say, two potential lovers. Run the material created to make sure they are secure in their knowledge of moves.

Decide on a piece of music to accompany it. Get to know the music and begin to tie down the moves to the music (you are not necessarily changing the moves. Maybe just noting when they happen within the music).

Now create two rooms and place the two characters in a room each. Instruct them to sit oblivious to the presence of the other in the next room. Run the scene and see whether their physicality can still connect while they are separated by the 'wall' between them.

What if the characters were aware of each other, longed for each other but could not be together? Run the material again to see whether the moves have a greater or different resonance.

Headwrecker   *Hymns 1999/2005*

The idea

Headwrecker was a physical sequence that followed the line 'We could just talk' as the four friends who have come together to mourn the passing of their mutual friend struggle to genuinely connect. The idea was that each of them, on hearing the request, slips into the kind of conversation that men might find easy. Such language would be incredibly informed and detailed but reveal little or nothing about the speaker. To 'just talk' is easy. To talk about what matters and be prepared to listen to the uncomfortable truths contained is another matter.

The process

To start with, the four performers were each given one of four conversational topics – car maintenance, stereo technical specifications, traffic directions and commentary on a football match. Choreographer and director Liam Steel then developed text for each of these topics before the four of us were introduced to the track 'Petite Fleur' by Chris Barber's Jazz Band. We were asked

Steven Hoggett, Joseph Traynor, Karl Sullivan and Eddie Kay having their heads wrecked in *Hymns* (2005). Image by Scott Graham

to sit the entire text within four bars of music. For some of us, this meant talking at an incredibly rapid pace while for others, the tempo was far more laid back and casual. The point here was to refrain from using the strict rhythm of the music track to inform the rhythm of the spoken words. Instead, we were to make the words sound as casual and natural as possible. This very simple step took a considerable amount of time. Counting the bars in order to fit within the four-bar limit instinctively led us to create weird rhythms and inflections that took some ironing out.

We were then asked to create a gestural string of movement to accompany our words. The moves were to be quite heavily influenced by the music and its count structure. In being a gestural string, the emphasis was on the hands, arms and torso with the feet remaining fixed. We were also asked to remain facing the front for the duration of our sequence. Finally combining the two, words and gestural string, was possibly one of the most frustrating periods of any Frantic rehearsal. We were at the end of the rehearsal period and all very tired and bruised. Our brains were full of counts, lines and motivations and this sudden, seemingly simple task proved too much for each one of us at some time or another. As frustrating as it was, this period was also a formidable bonding experience as the remaining three would pick up the wailing boy from the floor where we all at one time collapsed. The result, however, was absolutely right. A fluid combination of words and text that taught us much about the steps required in combining the two. The tight, detailed choreography sat completely at ease alongside a very casual, believable delivery of words. Knowing that this was within our grasp we spent every spare second (there were about eight of them we think) practising together – in the bathroom, in the canteen, walking to work.

Just when we thought we had it nailed, Liam then introduced a collective task. This was an eight-bar text that looked at the comparisons between the body of a woman and the body of a car along with a whole new gestural sequence. Upon realising this was the request, it's possible that most if not all of us wanted to take hold of a large hammer and cause some serious damage. However, an interesting lesson is the human capacity to push the limits of their self-imposed restrictions. In suddenly having a whole new section to worry about, the previous section no longer seemed like the problem. Simply thinking this turned it into a reality – it really wasn't the problem and it instantly stopped being one. Our capacity to get that third count right in the sixth bar was extraordinary. As for the new section, the first few attempts brought fresh tears but we were on a roll now and in one afternoon we had something that, while not being presentable, was at least respectable.

Liam pulled the same trick the following day (and to repeat some of the comments made between the four of us would do some serious damage to what continues to be a very loving and respectful relationship) but the effect was exactly the same. The Car/Woman section was forced to fall into place as the new section – a combined and fractured combination of all four narratives – took precedence. The following day (the day before the show actually opened), when Liam added in a new unison section, we were so attuned to the demands of the task that we had it down in 20 minutes.

Having completed the sequence, we thought it fitting to give it the name Headwrecker. Even well into the tour, Headwrecker would feature the most spectacular mistakes. In presenting the scene, the four of us would climb onto a small table with two at the front and two close behind. The interweaving individual sections were underpinned by moments of extremely tight unison, not least of all spatially. Any errors up there were glaring and Headwrecker always required maximum concentration to get through the four minutes without suddenly getting eye contact with someone who you had never spotted before doing that move. One tiny error and suddenly somebody's spark plug move was swinging into your humpbacked bridge moment. Climbing down off the table after a clean run of Headwrecker never failed to be a moment of pure collective joy.

The development

An obvious development of this exercise is to suddenly introduce language that does have emotional weight and resonance. What might this do to the movement? Does the leaking of personal, internal thoughts lead to empowerment or does the realisation that the truth is flooding out lead to something like a breakdown? Does the body resist in an effort to shut down this unravelling?

There are many themes and ideas that might be used in place of the textual ideas we used for Headwrecker. Looking at the characters specific to the piece being created will dictate the kind of text that might be used for this exercise. Our decision to sound like our dads is a very simple one at heart. The perceived notion of how difficult men find it to communicate is not so simple an issue, but in looking at a simple starting point we work our way closer to the central idea of the scene.

As ever, play with pace and rhythm. Try different music once you have the material down. Consider the flippant, blokey atmosphere Headwrecker created. What would the effect be if you had one of the characters, separate from the others, going through his lines and moving quietly on his own? Does the group scene become undermined? Is it a moment of unity or is it a tiresome practised ritual?

A perfect example of devising to the end?

Headwrecker came late into the rehearsal process for a reason. Director Liam Steel did not keep it tucked up his sleeve just to cause pain in the production week. We were already at a point of running what we thought was the complete show when we all recognised that it was getting stuck in a mire somewhere in the middle. The pace became turgid. The mood became excessively heavy. It felt indulgent. This was a crime, not only against theatricality, but against the subject matter. We were determined that if we were going to make a show about men grieving and not feeling like they have the platform to air their real thoughts, then it must never seem indulgent. This would see the whole theme dismissed by the audience and would make the show pointless.

Headwrecker came about through the need for light relief. We needed something to break the tension, to make the audience laugh and feel refreshed. We also needed the characters to believe that their flippancy had got them off the hook ('we could just talk') for a moment before their world comes crashing down again later. Otherwise the show was all one rhythm.

This is an example where we got the judgement right. This is not always the case (see 'Stockholm Fight and the Crooked Path' on page 32).

Heavenly Legs

The idea

The audience have their perspective changed and look down on three men sitting in a waiting room in Heaven. The audience feel they are watching the men from above. The men are on a sofa and their mindless twitching and bored adjustments becomes a choreographed dance for legs. It was a light-hearted observation of the patterns of behaviour the three men adopted as they passed the time and tried not to get on each other's nerves.

The process

The process should have been simple but it caught us at a bad time. We were exhausted and our brains were in meltdown. We sat in three chairs placed in a row. We improvised some playful choreography with our legs crossing and uncrossing, draping them over and flicking them off each other, kicking them out and twitching them. We filmed these doodles until we could cherry-pick moments that were funny or clever.

We already had a piece of music in mind so we started placing our rough material within the track. We decided to match the dynamic of the music quite closely at times and more so towards the end. The choreography should initially appear accidental and haphazard but then become more and more Esther Williams. We hoped this would achieve a comic effect.

There was a crucial third part to the process. The intention of the scene was to present a new perspective for the audience to observe the characters from. To do that the action must take place on the inverted sofa placed 10 feet up the back wall of the set (as shown in the image of *Heavenly*, in the colour plate section). This was a mirror illusion of the sofa on the floor. To achieve the illusion of gravity we had to perform it on our backs with our legs in the air. We had to keep our necks very straight and maintain little naturalistic looks and gestures. We started by inverting chairs until we had the 'luxury' of trying it on the set.

This was one of the most painful and gruelling physical scenes in any Frantic Assembly show. During the tour our stomach muscles became defined and our necks bulked up with muscle. Not once did anyone ever show appreciation for the physical strength and stamina involved. That was because the illusion was so successful. It really did look like we were just sitting in a sofa larking around while the audience watched from above us!

The development

The initial idea and process shows quite a bit of creative development. To explore the further theatrical development we suggest that you take it back to chairs sat on the floor and play with the context within which the choreography is presented.

Give your group some time to create their material. Remember that people will normally give you more than you will need so stress with the participants that they should only use their legs (think *Riverdance*) and not set out to tell a story. Keep it fairly simple and have around 18 moves between the group of 3. Avoid predictable patterns and rhythms and make sure they are not working to counts.

Now show the material. Is it fast enough? Do they know it well enough? Is it clear enough? It needs to be slick and well practised. Ideally they should be able to loop the material until you want them to stop.

At this stage it is only choreography.

Now give one group three newspapers to read so that we do not see their faces. Choose a music track and run the scene. Does a story emerge?

Tell another group to rest against each other as if asleep. Play a different track. Let their legs spring into life as they sleep on the chairs (park bench?).

Get another group and ask for a volunteer to walk around the room staring at them. The three have to stare back at the walker as their legs carry on the routine. Change the music. How has this changed the story? Is it provocative? Flirtatious?

Now for a more complex development. Get a group to sit in the chairs, preferably a group we have already seen. It is always useful to see our opinions of the meaning of choreography change in front of our eyes!

Ask them to go through their routine as slowly as they can. Make two of them stare at one of the performers sat on the outside of the three. They should look right at them throughout but the third performer must keep looking straight ahead. That is, until a single moment when they can fleetingly return the look to their colleagues. The colleagues must maintain the look throughout. Try a new track. Or try one you have already tried. Does it or the choreography become redefined by the new direction? What is the story? Is it more complex? Is it a love triangle? Is it bullying? Is it funny? Is it scary?

Try presenting the choreography in a more literal context. The initial intention to show subconscious patterns of behaviour in moments of tedium can relate directly to many literal contexts – a dentist's waiting room, a tube train, etc.

The animated audience

There is another way to create work through a similar process. This time let the groups of three create a string of material that does not involve physical interaction. It can also involve the top half. It is about creating unison and you can use the literal physicality of the waiting room as a starting point. They can cross legs, uncross, adjust, lean forward, back, fold their arms, pick fluff from their clothes, clean their glasses, stretch, etc. The task is to turn it into a creative string of choreography.

If you have bleacher seating or any kind of raked seating, you can now place the whole group randomly around the auditorium. They are all now watching a show. Their focus must express this but they continue to perform their string, still aiming for unison with partners they are no longer next to.

Place yourself on the stage opposite them. Film them if possible. Play with the dynamic. Is it best slow? Or a freestyle mixture? Is it just a mess or is the camera picking up some happy accidents? Have the relationships been blown apart or do they still exist over space? Are there new relationships and fleeting connections being formed? You can share these discoveries with the group and quickly try out new dynamics.

This exercise creates a large group scene without having to manage the whole group. They have been broken up into bite-sized groups and given simple tasks. You then bring them back together and shape the overall choreography.

Select Delete   *pool (no water) 2006*

The idea

Select Delete marked the final act of atrocity committed by four would-be artists upon their hapless one-time friend. In terms of text, it consisted of the words 'select delete' repeated 47 times as the characters deleted one image after another from a computer file and, in doing so, ruined the creative efforts of their ailing fifth member. After a variety of read-throughs, a turning point was established by introducing the Imogen Heap track 'Mic Check' to sit alongside the scene. Previous attempts to unravel the repetition seemed to fail – probably due to the heavy, malicious intentions we were playing with. 'Mic Check', with its slick, playful, jittering rhythm patterns, set us off in a completely new direction – to find the joy in wanton destruction.

The process

Each of the four actors were asked to create a simple eight-count gestural sequence, using only their hands, consisting of four imitations of the action select delete. To start with, these versions were to be fairly realistic, using notions of screens being wiped, disks being plucked and chucked, information being clutched and then vanishing into nothing. Once each performer had their eight, they were shared and learnt by everybody else. In order to ease the process, initial rehearsals used a different music track with a slightly slower tempo (Crazy P's 'Lady T – Hot Toddy Mix' for those who really want to get personal ...). This stage took some time to learn. As with all challenges of this nature, it needs to become an exercise in muscle memory before it is possible to start playing with the detail and intention of the movement. On any given day, somebody who was incredibly confident with the material might suddenly fall apart. The non-progressive nature of exercises like this can sometimes lead to very frustrated cast members.

Once everybody was confident with the material we then set the cast the task of creating a foot pattern to accompany the material created for the hands. The instruction was to not move with every gesture but to pick out the more energetic gestural moves and move the body accordingly, freeing up the feet to side-step, shunt, step, pause – whatever the hands seemed to suggest. In making the feet and body correspond to the existing hands sequence, the entire movement vocabulary remained in the world of quick, neat, economic qualities that stayed in keeping with the music qualities we knew that 'Mic Check' would provide. One of the performers was also asked to create a further 16 Select Deletes which were to start pretty mundane but become more and more flamboyant as they progressed so that the hands began to operate with flair and, like a magician or card trickster, to defy logic and gravity. Selected objects might be flicked up into the air to remain there or tossed over shoulders or under armpits.

From here, the scene was a matter of structure and for this we turned entirely to the track we had chosen. We often find it inspiring to allow a music track to dictate structure, particularly when it is as challenging and original as something like 'Mic Check'. Of course there were elements within the text which suggested structural set-ups. To begin with, one character alone starts to select and delete, hence the solo of 16 movements he was asked to create. From there, the rest of the group are drawn into his actions as the movements become more and more extravagant. As the track began to fill out, so the entire group fell into a unison that itself became more and more effervescent. During a break in the track, the team also take a break, pinpointing images that remain, lining up for a final onslaught. Then, as the track reinstates itself, the group launch into the final onslaught, except this time the gestural sequence is at double speed and includes the feet and bodies material before a final coda that bursts into a whole new set of Select Deletes that sees the team now flinging their entire bodies into the air in jubilation.

The development

In many ways, scenes such as this are very simple constructs. One area of development would be to experiment with the music track or count structure as it plays such an integral part in the scene if created in this way. For example, in 'Mic Check' there is a section of the track where there are nine descending notes followed by the first three of those nine notes being repeated twice. The whole structure is repeated four times. By numbering each note and then attaching a particular gesture to each of these numbers, the choreography is attributed a structure that is totally at the mercy of the music track in terms of tempo and incidence. By listening to the note structure of any particular track it would be interesting to tie movements to notes or even phrases and to see what choreographic results emerge.

This type of creative exercise might also be useful in the early stages of combining text with movement. Any two words might be used. A binary opposition would be a good starting point.

Scribble   *Beautiful Burnout 2010*

The idea

Appearing at the front end of *Beautiful Burnout*, this sequence was notoriously difficult. It is named after the Underworld track that was used as the score. In terms of narrative, it was the point at which the owner of a grotty, urban boxing gym, Bobby Burgess urges his would-be pugilists to go through a succession of training exercises. Setting a clock ticking, he sets in motion a challenging, exhausting set of movements that reflect the dynamism of the training undertaken by any boxer the world over.

The process

In many ways, Scribble came to represent a textbook event for us at Frantic, resembling all the trademarks of everything we had learnt thus far. For whatever reasons, it was a sequence that allowed us to cram in a number of principles, practices and ideas that form the heart of what we do with physicality.

During the early stages of development for *Beautiful Burnout*, we had the privilege of attending boxing training sessions at a number of gyms around Scotland. A few elements seemed to be universal. One was the camaraderie that existed in every gym between the boxers regardless of age, gender or race. This extended to us, a humble pile of bodies sat on the benches at the sides, alert and blinking in the often harsh strip lit halls and gyms. Another shared element was how music was used to drive the energy in the room.

Taqi Nazeer rehearsing Scribble in *Beautiful Burnout* (2010). Image by Johan Persson

More often than not, this was provided by a loud, scuffed, distorting stereo system on a windowsill. The music of choice tended towards the trance and techno end of the musical spectrum (at which point, we realised our decision to procure the services of the band Underworld to work on our show was a stroke of unwitting genius). In addition, and this might seem the most obvious point, we realised just how *hard* these boys and girls were working. We have often been given the credit for creating hard and brutal material that is physically draining and extreme for our performers but they now seemed like octogenarian bridge players compared to these real athletes. Scribble was our love letter to that realisation and those people that turn up on cold, wet nights on the outskirts of big, ugly cities at the end of long, thankless, tiring days and somehow find it in their bodies to become invincible.

Scribble was always going to be a challenging section of the show to achieve, purely because it has the fastest bpm (beats per minute) rate of any track used in any Frantic show ever. This was always something we knew. We have often used music that clocks in over 120 bpm (this being the standard bpm rate for the modern western song). As performers ourselves in shows such as *Hymns*, we were only too aware of what a difference just a few bpm's can make to levels of accuracy and stamina over the duration of a track only a few minutes long. Scribble clocks in at a formidable 172-ish bpm – that's fast, folks. But this was always the ambition – to have a sequence that raised the bar in terms of capability, a reflection of the frenetic but controlled ability we had witnessed in the gyms. Just watching a boxer take control of a speedball was enough to inspire us to go for something outside our comfort zone. As a music track, it was always an obvious choice – a skittering but disciplined piece of electronica that has a light but driving energy and a youthful exuberance.

The initial sessions to create the material happened some way into the second week of rehearsals. We knew we wanted to draw on the physical regimes we were using as warm-ups for the show. Each day we all partook in an intense hour-long session that incorporated a little yoga and a lot of stamina and strength training as well as exercises specific to boxing techniques. Add to this some extreme cardio exercises and we had quite a lot of physical exercises to draw on. Because we knew the tempo would be so fast, we talked about the idea of a sequence where nothing was quite as full as it should be – as if the exuberance of these young hopefuls in some reflected their eager minds. Minds that are yet to be fully disciplined and so the focus often shifts and diverts away from the task at hand. Not through any laziness, more out of a constant search for the next physical moment or challenge.

We asked each of the performers (even those not playing the roles of boxers) to create a string of material lasting 16 counts. Within this phrase, we asked them to take our known and existing physicality from the warm-ups and in some way fracture it, as if attention got diverted part way through the motion. This might take the form of only one half of the body completing an exercise or move that would normally involve both sides of the body (a star jump for instance). It might be that the mid-point of a motion or action might slow down or drift – again as if the mind suddenly went elsewhere and corrupted the move. In all instances, we asked for there to be a level of corruption to a known physical event. At this early stage, we were very careful not to use the Scribble track in the background. Instead, we used tracks that had a much more hospitable bpm so that the company felt comfortable, creating material that was attainable.

As ever, our company created beautiful, innovative, dynamic material – our older non-boxing members creating the most complex and interesting sequences of course. We strung the various sections together in a way that felt impulsive more than anything else. So at this stage we have a cumulative string of choreographic material of a substantial length that is new to all of the performers in terms of actual content as they have broken the physical convention of the originating material to create something slightly skewed, slightly off. At this point we introduced Scribble and the next few weeks we allowed time each and every day for the slow process of trying to achieve full expression of movement as had been set, but at a much higher speed. This is an exercise in endurance, perseverance, humility generosity and determination. On any given day, we had to be ready to clear up the mess left by sweaty bodies under pressure – and on certain days it was a spiritual mess that we had to handle as the company struggled with a relentless tempo. In a few rare moments we allowed for the adaptation of a few moves when we realised that the human body might just not be able to make that turn or execute that half-punch that fast. But for the most part, we urged and encouraged and bit by bit, the sequence began to get faster and faster as their bodies began to recall the sequence at this new level of difficulty.

Once the actual sequence was well under way, we began to work with the material from a choreographic viewpoint. We both had the pleasure of spending a few days in a studio with the esteemed choreographer Javier de Fruitos earlier that year. Javier had, very generously, spent those days demystifying the choreographic process, showing us the known tricks of the trade and some basic principles. As practitioners who only ever learnt on the job, some of these were shockingly new for us. The set for *Beautiful Burnout* was a raised square platform. In rehearsal this resembled nothing so much as a square of red tape marked out on the floor. It looked very academic, which suited us just fine. We took all the standard choreographic patterns and then applied them one by one using the five performers who were part of the sequence. So we started with the five bodies occupying the four corners and the central spot. They moved across onto hard diagonal lines. They gathered as a tight huddle at one corner. They swept across the square from the front to the back. And vice versa. They formed a single line behind one another in the centre of the square. That line splintered to both sides then reformed as another diagonal, this time on the opposite angle. In truth, this was entry-level mapping but given the speed and intensity of the material, it became intoxicating as the performers moved at intense speeds in their spots before swiftly morphing into another formation. The hard angles and lines we selected were regimental in essence, something that was palpable in every boxing gym we sat in.

After creating a rough version of sequence plus choreography, we then went back to the track to find elements of dynamism. Listening to the musical details of Scribble, we found rhythmic shifts, clicks, accents, stutters, crashes and hits that we then matched using both the physical material and the movements around the space (and sometimes both) in an attempt to match the complex nature of the music.

So, in many ways, the creation of Scribble seemed like an indicator of all that we are when it comes to the creation of physical sequences.

Music track as starting point? Check.

Creation of initial material by taking identifiable physical actions as a source then distorting it? Check.

Taking the choreographic string and placing it within the space to test choreographic possibilities? Check.

Music track as a source of guidance for speed and intensity? Check.

In addition, there is the priceless material created simply by watching a group of applied and willing performers undertaking a simple task and coming up with thrilling material – even on the days when their bodies are aching and tired or when their body is willing but the mind is several steps behind. Sometimes it is in these states of being that we find some of our favourite physical phrases or ways of executing movement. In our very privileged position on the outside, it is our job and our duty to ensure that we stay alert to these moments. Even in meltdown, the performers were still giving us great material – the key was to keep looking at it in this way.

The development

How might we develop Scribble further? In some ways, this was one of the most meticulous processes we ever undertook. We threw everything at it to the point where we tried and tested it in a way we have never done before. It was a rigorous and extensive event. The development on this was massive. Our performers might give a different account. One development they would have loved was to try this exercise with a much, much slower music track to dictate the tempo. How slow would these actions have to be before they become almost unrecognisable as warm-up moves?

The action of warming up is very often a solo physical experience. What would happen if people were paired together and asked to run the same warm-up action? What kind of shapes could be created by wrapping one body around another while attempting to touch your toes or commit to a full stretch star jump? What would the result be if the two performers were attempting to execute two very different warm-up moves? This is assuming the moves are executed fully. Another version to try would be one where, like our exercise, each move was in some way fractured or incomplete.

If slowed down, taking a string of warm-up sequences or moves could be developed by way of introducing qualities that are not normally associated with fast, ballistic movement like this. Try a stuttering version. No, we're not sure what that might look like either but it might be really interesting.

Split the group in half – one half will run the sequence the group has devised at full throttle. Give the other half those little wipe down towels and see what kind of sequence emerges when the towel group is given the task of intertwining themselves with the workout person and trying to dab the most intense bead of sweat from the appropriate part of the body given the move that the dynamic person is executing. Take this further. Does the towel become the third partner in the choreography? Can it be used as a lasso or weight-bearing device?

… then speed it up!

Or take the existing material you have created using this process (you do use this book, don't you?) and place your performers with their left hand side against the wall. This will root the left side. It is not to move. You could set them the task of using the existing vocabulary and trying to stay true to it but only performing it on their right side. Some of this will be impossible but they should try to get as close as they can to it. Once they have done this they could try it on the floor lying on their left side. Then try it standing up in the space with as little movement on the left side as possible.

This might go nowhere but they are ways of reinventing existing choreography and trying out ideas on performers without asking them to make new material.

Arrested Punches   *Beautiful Burnout 2010*

The idea

This scene is from *Beautiful Burnout* and is an attempt to get inside the super fast reaction time of the boxer, to articulate the thought process that allows him/her to assess the intention and arc of an incoming punch and evade or

Stuart Ryan gets caught by Taqi Nazeer in *Beautiful Burnout* (2012). Image by Scott Graham

Margaret Ann Bain as Dina in *Beautiful Burnout* (2012). Image by Scott Graham

counter with their own punch. It comes at a point where two boxers have to fight it out for the opportunity to face another opponent in a lucrative championship bout. Each boxer is keen to impress the watching coach and convince him that they have learned from him and have what it takes to succeed. They try to convince him through their skilled actions but we also get access to their thoughts as the fight continues.

The process

Having watched countless hours of boxing to accumulate moves to choreograph it struck us just how often we had to 'rewind' a particular flurry of action and still struggled to break it down into its component moves. Boxers move and think lightning quick. Bodies weave to evade the punch before it is even thrown because they recognise the options open to their opponent. It is like chess. In their head they can be several moves ahead of the move in action.

We decided we wanted to freeze the action mid flurry just as it appears a punch might land. As the puncher freezes the other boxer steps out and assesses all his options. Can he dip to the right? Will this free up his left hand for a counter punch? If he slips to the left will this expose the ribs of his opponent? Can he bring up his gloves to make the punch glance off them? Can he cover up and absorb this punch? Does he find there is no way to avoid this incoming punch? Does he find his body cannot quite move as quickly as his thoughts?

We wanted to explore many of these moments within each freeze. When he makes a decision he returns to the exact position he was in when he stepped out of the action. His opponent is still frozen. After another split second the action returns and the punch is thrown and we see the decision in effect. The boxing continues.

It was important not to think about the stopped moment but to initially create a string of choreographed sparring that seemed genuine and realistic. The frozen moments would only have their surprising power if the audience could get sucked into the danger of the moment. The fresh and thrilling perspective offered by the frozen moment, the discombobulating juxtaposition of boxer caught mid punch and the other boxer detached, pacing, calculating, would not have the same force if the scene was not set up as a naturalistic fight.

We worked on about six sections of boxing. No one boxer was vastly superior to the other and it would take a trained eye to tell who was the superior boxer and more worthy of the chance on offer.

This was a slow and meticulous process. *Beautiful Burnout* required the boxers to make contact with their punches. We had to work hard to develop a safe way to pull these punches and absorb their impact. We had to create a culture of safety first, and practice, practice, practice! It is difficult when your ambition is to create something that aims to be brutal and insanely quick, to capture something that looks, feels and sounds like boxing, to stick to such a slow process. The performers were crying out to unleash and feel that they were boxers but until you create a precisely choreographed string of material that you know is completely safe you cannot start to pick up the pace. That means a long process of marking the material and adding much shorter strings of movement together like this…

A jabs with his left as B weaves to his left
Practice
Practice a bit faster
Repeat but now A adds a left hook that B ducks under
Practice this string
A bit faster
(When ready) B throws a right hook to the body of A
Go through it all slowly without contact
Mark where the contact will occur
Choreograph the movement of the defensive boxer – the movement of the gloves and elbows to create safe impact
Put it together and slowly build to the point where contact can safely be made and safely repeated.

It is a dance. The performers had to remember this. The problem is this goes against the credibility the performers are desperate to attain. It is all a reminder of how unreal it all is, how limited we are as boxers and how we are all just 'acting'. The key to it is to make sure they commit to that restraint but are also made aware that every rehearsal of a sequence takes them closer to the point where they can unleash and look and feel like boxers.

This is also clearly in their interest! The choreographed sequences involved moments where a punch would stop, ideally, a couple of centimetres away from the boxer's face. This helped the performers stick to the process. No one wanted to have their Spotlight entry altered from leading man to character actor with one wayward punch!

We did not want to turn this into a textual scene despite the complexity of the boxer's situation and thought processes. Text was used but the physicality had to dominate. We wanted to show the boxer exploring the options available to him physically. We see him weave or cover up or prepare the counter punch. In this moment we are presenting a very different timescale. We present the situation of a particular nanosecond in a boxing bout that we were witnessing in real time. We are suggesting that the boxer has these complex thoughts in the nanosecond presented. Once the boxer has made a decision we wanted the return to the normal timescale to be brutal and exhilarating. Gloves smack into flesh. We see the importance of getting the decision absolutely right in this expanded, hyper-reality.

We wanted the audience to get an idea of the options open to the boxer rather than just admire their skill. Within the scene this freeze happens five times and the intention was that it should bring the audience closer to the mind of the boxer, not to alienate them with his brilliance. He should remain vulnerable and liable to make mistakes. This makes the moment dangerous and both boxers are in danger. Ultimately the intention was to take the audience to the point where they share the boxer's dilemma and might see some of the options available to him even before the boxer does. This trains the audience to appreciate the speed of thought and movement but also brings them closer to, in fact almost inside, the action.

To help this dissection of the art of boxing, to give the audience that scientific eye on the 'sweet science', we placed the action on a revolve imbedded in the set (the set looked like a boxing ring, minus the ropes and pillars, but actually contained a few tricks). In the moment the action froze the revolve would start, creating the illusion that the audience was circling the boxers, forensically inspecting the action, noting the balance, the coiled potential ready to unleash.

A further device we employed in order to get the audience 'inside the head' of the boxer was with the music track we used during the sequence. We had been particularly impressed by a moment in Matthew Vaughn's directorial debut film *Layer Cake*. At one point, one unfortunate character is enjoying a bite to eat in a greasy sandwich shop when the hapless chap is brutally attacked. Smashed to the ground, he is subjected to a barrage of kicks to the head from men in large boots. Prior to this moment, the radio in the cafe is heard, playing the Duran Duran song 'Ordinary World'. In a stroke of genius sound design, as the man on the floor is having his head kicked, the sound we the audience hear is the one we imagine the man on the floor hearing as his head and ears are battered and kicked. The sound of the Duran Duran track begins to muffle, with pockets of air being heard between the kicks that land on his head. It is an effect that is both nightmarish and thrilling. The aural experience of having your head kicked in has never been so well committed to film. Taking this line of thinking, we found an Underworld track ('Dub Shepherd') that already featured a rather muffled vocal and rhythm track. This was played from the start of the boxing sequence. At any point where we went inside the head of the boxer, the physical action acted as a trigger for the sound desk to hit an effects cue. This added a wash of reverb to the track that gave the impression of time emptying out, slowing down. It also suggested being deep inside the mind of the afflicted pugilist, supporting and signalling the idea that here was a moment where time was being spliced and stretched.

By keeping the cues of this sound effect tied to the split second of the physical act (a process which took up many hours of very patient technical rehearsals), what was presented was very clearly the sound as heard by the boxers onstage. It was, arguably, one of the most successful moments within the show. How an audience hears an event is often overlooked. To see how brilliant sound design is used, check out the fight sequences in *Raging Bull* and note what genius is at play by way of sound effects in telling us what is happening externally and internally to the fighters.

The development

The important thing to take from this is the delicate baby steps that were taken to achieve something physically dynamic. This applied to all of the boxing within *Beautiful Burnout* and at every stage we had to fight the impulse to get ahead of ourselves. This urgency to leap to the end result too soon often appears when working on stage combat. The problem is that everyone has a picture of what the end product should look like and wants to achieve it with total credibility. As stated, the process means parking this for a while.

There are three important elements to the creation of this scene. Context, time and space. It started by looking at the action of boxers sparring. The components were broken down and recreated with performers. Then different time realities were introduced where one figure effectively freezes while the other expresses, in real time, the many physical and mental calculations necessary to respond to the punch. Thirdly, the environment the boxers were presented in changes. Importantly, it alters in a way that makes the audience think that it is their world that had changed. This gives a new micro focus on an action we often see in macro, as spectacle.

You might choose to use these three stages to focus on another subject. We have already alluded to the chess-like quality of the boxing mind. Maybe you would want to look at chess itself.

Context (the reality)

What you have first is the task of setting up the realistic context. Just as in boxing this involves two people facing each other, trying to pre-empt and counter each other's moves. Between the chess players sits a clock that measures the time they take for each move. There are many moments of stillness.

Time

You can play with the time. Does the clock tick loudly? Does it slow down? Do one player's nervous ticks and adjustments speed up into a frenzy while the other player slowly reaches out to move a figure? Does this suggest the player moving the chess piece has taken an absolute age to do it, in which time the other player has adjusted and readjusted, looked away, scratched his head, got up and adjusted his trousers, etc.? Does this make the move itself more powerful, ominous or decisive?

Space (how we see it)

During this move, as the hand moves towards the chess piece, do we, as the audience, know which one he will touch and what the move will be? Do we see the pattern of many possibilities played out in his head and rejected for this one move? Is there a way of seeing into their mind? Does the nervous player actually see the killer move that will destroy him before the player taking his turn? Do we hear the blood in his brain creating a screaming cacophony? Do both players spin, like the boxers, offering us a way into their tension? Do the pieces slowly explode away from the board as the player completes the checkmate? (Difficult, I know, but where there is a will there is a way!)

The three stages outlined are there merely to get you to think about the potential of a naturalistic moment. Any naturalistic moment can have a vastly different resonance depending on the context. Inserting the keys into a car and starting the engine might be the start of an ordinary day. It might be the most decisive moment of a life so far as someone commits to leaving the life they have known. It might be your last act as it sets off the bomb wired to the underside of the car. The act itself can be shrouded in vastly different intensities for the audience. The three steps above help exploit the potential of these.

Lovesong Bed   2011

The idea

This is a scene that sets out to capture some of the secrets that a marital bed holds. It has seen every aspect of a couple's life played out on its surface. As a terminally ill old woman faces her demise we wanted to find a way of her summoning some of these memories.

The process

Again, it is worth noting that, to start with, this creative task was a very simple one and that the actors were given no immediate emotional context to work within. The act of creating and then running the material meant that all four performers brought very different emotional states to the exercise and we were then able to make instinctive choices based on what moods seemed to resonate the most with the physical storytelling.

Edward Bennett, Leanne Rowe, Sam Cox and Sian Phillips in *Lovesong* by Abi Morgan (2011). Image by Scott Graham

In order to prepare the actors for the exercise, we ran the rolling exercises explored in *Suggestions for Constructive Warm-Ups*. In addition, the performers were introduced to the idea of the body being suddenly stopped by their partner.

For the exercise, we taped out a white square on the floor and during the day, each of the performers were given a period of time to work on the floor in this space. Given the rehearsal schedule for *Lovesong*, each of the performers would be creating material while other scenes were being rehearsed in the room but the square was located off to the side of the main space so as to allow them a certain level of personal space.

The actors were asked to remain floor-bound for the duration of the exercise and to remain within the confines of the taped out square. The first task was to work with two ideas. One was to imagine that the partner that you have shared the bed with for all this time is no longer there. The task was then to create a physical search for the body of the absent lover and to play with varying states of wakefulness. We also asked them to play with the idea of scooping up and gathering memories from the surface of the square – a rather more abstract strand of exploration but one which we hoped would yield interesting results and to prevent the performers from falling into stretches of mime – a territory we are always keen to avoid. Initial try-outs with soft music backtracking the exercise began to give rise to ethereal physicality, which seemed inappropriate and wistful so we took note and started to work with more driving music tracks. This music would remain 'aural wallpaper' for the performers – our way of saying don't play along to the music, let it be in the background of your exercise. This began to prove very exciting and soon all four performers had some substantial material.

We referred back to the rolling exercise that morning where each of them had experienced the sensation of having their bodies stopped or arrested mid-action. Using this very real physical sensation, we asked them to replicate this quality to their own solo sequence. This time there would be no outside individual stopping them. Instead, they were asked to cut movements off before they were completed, to cauterise the physical action. It was made clear that this should in no way change the sequence or order of movements that they had created. In some respects, part of the task is about trying to get from the beginning of the sequence to the end, while at the same time, being prevented from executing the full physical event.

For the next stage, we paired the performers up randomly and asked them to try to run their solo in its entirety while sharing the same space as another performer. This kind of exercise subscribes wholly to the belief in 'happy accidents' – choreographic moments that could take hours to actually construct but will happen of their own accord given the right circumstances. From the outside we were looking for moments of connection and where they might lead. We were also looking for moments where the action of one performer seemed to bring a sudden halt or arrest to the other performer. Again, the task was to keep driving at the sequence so the task of getting from the beginning to the end, no matter how inhibited, became very real. Again, we were careful not to insist on any emotional context at this stage.

A few days later, we revisited the same material but putting the actors on the bed that formed part of the set for *Lovesong*. This time we attempted putting three of the performers on the same bed and repeating the task of trying to complete their physical sequence in all its fullness, negotiating the physical limitations and restrictions. Once again, from the outside we were looking for any moments of connection, near miss or stoppage between any of the trio at work.

Finally we spent a session working on linking entrances and exits. No one would ever step away from the bed though. They had to be memories that were pulled from the bed itself. We had a custom made bed that had a hidden slit running from the head to the foot of the bed, allowing the characters to melt into the bed and also to emerge from within it. Putting the actors in no specific order, we tasked them with finding a way of allowing one another to appear and disappear into the bed. In each instance, the remaining character would be instrumental in assisting the disappearing or emerging character in some way. This created a varying palette of holds, lifts, pulls, pushes, stretches and releases as the four performers sought ways to keep the bed a constantly shifting landscape of bodies, melting and emerging.

Next we listed what we had created. At our disposal we had four solos, seven duets, one trio and something like six linking moments. We decided that the sequence would be about the older version of Maggie remembering her entire life in this bed. We started the sequence as her solo, attempting to pull all the memories of the bed and all that had happened there into some kind of reality. In doing so she might be able to locate her partner who had just 'melted' into the bed. From here the sequence built as a number of duets leading to a trio before a final section with all four of the characters, a younger and older version of the same couple, meeting and merging on the bed before the younger version melted away, leaving the older couple, Maggie cold and racked with pain, Bill holding her in his arms, unable to alleviate her agony. Each section was seen as a continuation and build on the intensity of the previous section. The linking sequence we had created was taken apart and used as the glue between any two sections.

The final part to the sequence was to go back to the originating idea of stoppages. Looking at the physical sequences, we shaped, crafted and nudged it so that each individual stoppage (initially self-motivated) was now the result of a strategically placed hand, foot, crook of elbow, neck, and ribcage. Implicitly, this forced us to change certain shapes and angles of the physical material in order to truly honour this rule. In doing so, we created shapes and movement that would never be instinctive. It also began to give rise to some truly sumptuous interactions when we began to apply it to the trio and the quartet sections. The intensity of trying to achieve your own sequence in the face of such physical adversity became the emotional context of the scene. It also served to expressed the desire for each character to hold on to a memory, to make it real again, even for a moment, before it faded back into the bed.

Maggie's impossible task of retrieving the past, the physical history of her union with Bill, the lost youth of their physical bodies, the imminent demise of their physical selves, all this was a very simple addition to the now fully choreographed sequence. The use of the track 'Last Night The Sky' by lamb only added to the intensity with its thudding, driving rhythms. The surreal activity of melting into and out of a bed immediately signalled to the audience that we were entering into Maggie's fevered imagination – at which point we have given ourselves the license to enter a world of impossible physicality – to pull former and future selves into existence. Their impossible presence was alive in the clear physical dynamic that no move or gesture ever reached its full fruition. Moves ached to run their inevitable course. Future and former selves could delay for a second but could not stop the memories fading and returning to the bed. The bed was left telling its final story with the clear and now very real image of Bill holding Maggie as she cries in pain.

Development

It is hard to talk of the development of what might have been for this scene, or where it could possibly go. That is because it was so reliant on the custom-made bed. But that was our version of this process. How can you apply it to your needs? We urge you to see beyond its application in *Lovesong* and break down the process into its important stages.

Think about the importance of the warm-up and how it primed the performers.

Think about the space and how it was limited.

Think about how that space, being just a floor with tape on it, afforded a freedom for the performer. Although the context of a bed was mentioned, the actual bed was withheld from the performers until there was a substantial amount of choreography created.

Think about how one person's material gets challenged and reinvented by another's. Think about how 'happy accidents' present potentially clever choreography.

Think about how all of this creates complex choreography that can then be applied to the bed. It is much more important and useful to get your performers applying what they created with more freedom to a situation that now has limitations. If they had only made material in the bed then the movement would have been defined by the limitations of the bed. This way presents potentially much more complex and daring physicality.

Think about how the bed then defined the possibilities for movement. The simple rule was no one should exit the bed yet people had to disappear and appear. This meant the complex choreography was now totally applied to the bed. The context is never diluted. The tyrannical instruction led to much more creative problem solving.

Think of these stages apart from the context of *Lovesong*. Do they offer a blueprint for something? Is there something in simplicity building to complexity? The relationship between freedom and limitations? The creation of a space for accidents to occur?

Returning to our version, every body that emerged from the bed was a composite whole. What kind of effects and material might be created if several performers attempt to represent the arms and legs of a single body trying to emerge from under the bed through the mattress? What bizarre and twisted forms might be suggested in this version?

What happens if everyone has to emerge from the hole in the mattress using a different body part? How do they overcome this very distinct physical challenge? What does it look like from the front? What if you try this with the bed on its end, essentially making the audience feel as if they are watching from above? Does this present new possibilities? Is it possible to stay true to your original material?

All of the above make for intimate, sweaty, claustrophobic working conditions but such conditions can also give rise to odd, off-kilter physicality that enforces performers to commit to movements outside of their habitual patterns. The simple task of emerging through an aperture demands this. In setting further tasks beyond the simple 'get up, out and onto the bed', we open up a wealth of possibilities and, admittedly, struggles. But even to struggle is a worthwhile and often stimulating experiment as we have found ourselves.

The Club   *Little Dogs 2012*

The idea

This scene is from *Little Dogs*, a co-production with National Theatre Wales and was based in, and partially inspired by, Swansea. It was also partly inspired by 'Just Like Little Dogs' by Dylan Thomas, and by our time living in the area. We focused on sexual awakening among the rampantly hormonal youth in Swansea (ok, partially autobiographical!) and the tension that exists around the unexplored territories of each other's bodies.

Hannah Good and Darren Evans rehearse for *Little Dogs* (2012). Image by Scott Graham

The club scene from *Little Dogs*. Image by Farrows Collective/National Theatre Wales

Remy Beasley watches Berwyn Pearce and Matthew Trevannion kiss in *Little Dogs* (2012). Image by Scott Graham

Sian Phillips as Swansea in *Little Dogs* (2012). Image by Scott Graham

This was our return to our originating roots after some thirteen years and we made the brave decision to create the piece in the style of our younger selves (although we did grant ourselves the luxury of a couple of development workshops). What followed was an unapologetic, rough and ready, dance theatre piece.

The deliberately short, intense rehearsal period and performances happened in the Patti Pavilion, a huge hall that would allow us to make a promenade piece where the audience would be led to various sites throughout. This effectively brought the outside to the inside.

We knew we needed to include a scene from a club in order to truly honour our love letter to Swansea. Many of our breakthrough discoveries were made in Swansea's clubs. Our affinity with the music, the structure of the DJ set informing the structure of our early shows, the heaving choreography of real people...

The problem was club scenes are often done really badly. Within this scene we wanted to specifically capture the throbbing energy of the mass of bodies and then focus on one individual's thoughts from within the moment. Deep from within the club these thoughts would emerge and soar, intimate and unique.

This scene was not without obvious problems. Technically, presenting a convincing club would be a real challenge. The individual and the group are contradictions. So too the noise and the thought. It was our fascination with the individual within the crowd, the weakness within the strength, which spurred us on.

The process

Our first decisions were purely spatial. Creating vast open spaces would only highlight the limits of ten people trying to create a mass. So when we looked at the plans for the hall, we assigned a tiny corner of the space that would be delineated by two stand-alone units containing fluorescent tubes, marking out the territory as 'dance floor'. This was just enough room for our performers to fit into and the audience was encouraged to wrap around this area to create a further level of enclosure. In an open space behind our dance floor we placed a huge sub speaker that faced the audience directly (that's the one that is responsible for providing all that bass that you feel in your sternum in a good club). The audience's bodies literally became the wall that we blasted the bass at.

Once we were in the rehearsal room, we began to think about how we might create this energetic mass of bodies, free yet seemingly bound to each other. It needed to be faithful to the clubbing experience and yet do more. It had to compress those four exhausting, wanton hours into several bars of music. If that proved successful we then only had to achieve the impossible – zoom in on the individual thought strands of the clubbing collective.

We needed a way to pull focus to the individual. We had originally looked at the way, in rugby, that the back row would lift a jumper in a lineout. The mechanics of this move are laid bare and they rely on a jump and at least two extremely strong lifters. It presented the focus we were looking for but we wanted to hide the mechanics and make it much smoother. This was going to need many more lifters. We were trying to get our team of lifters to squeeze in on the lifted person and for the lifted person to push down initially so signal the moment to smoothly squeeze and lift. We were struggling to put across the technique as we were suggesting it should not rely on strength or a jump (Completely the opposite of the original rugby inspiration. It was a particularly unhelpful analogy!). Then came the most absurd moment of brilliant inspiration! One of the performers simply said, 'you mean, like a Calippo?' (The ice-lolly that you squeeze from its tube, allowing it to rise majestically!) This *was* the principle we were trying to explain all day to the *Little Dogs* company. At this point the performers all murmured an instant understanding and we wondered why we had ever bothered trying to use anything else to describe it. The 'Calippo' lift was born. (Other iced lollies are available.)

The quality we wanted was one of weightlessness, the feeling that these internal reveries that the individuals were experiencing was taking them out of their actual earth-bound bodies and assuming an almost angelic-like form, floating above the throbbing mass. Reminding the cast of the genius of the 'Calippo' principle consistently eradicated any wobbles or strains. The process demands equal pressure all round to create the smooth upwards motion. The effect was so startling that the lifted person would often scream or shout out as they headed for the ceiling. They needed to be reminded to stay calm. Panicking shifted their weight around and meant that the lifters would end up using strength to compensate. This was completely against the ambition of the scene. Harnessing the Zen power of 'Calippo' allowed the lifted person to relax and concentrate on being strong and firm. The result was far more heavenly.

A structured movement sequence was then created in our favoured way, each performer being asked to create four bars of physical material. The task was to make a string of moves that were very much about the driving physicality of a dance floor but all the while to be observational about what body parts were moving. We asked our performers to push through a tight crowd and note the shapes and positions they were forced into. This might mean being knocked off balance or dropping lower to find a crevice to work into. They were asked to focus on shoulders and hips rather than hands when making their way through the crowd. This exercise gave the performers a movement palette. It gave them new and unnatural shapes to draw on. This is a crucial element behind much of our choreographic devising techniques – the need to make new or strange. Otherwise we would always draw on what we think our body is capable of and this is an extremely limited palette, even for experienced performers.

As the performers were in individual spots around the room, we asked several of them to include a moment where they would check a body part or section of clothing, a moment of conspicuous investigation among the physical jubilation. Does my skirt just about cover my arse? Have I got sweat stains in my armpits? Did I just step in something? Has that girl behind me noticed me yet? I've lost the back of my earring! With others, we asked them to include physical moments of 'bullet time', those blissed out seconds where time slows down and stretches as you bliss out on a certain word or note you are hearing or savour the last second before that chorus finally, finally kicks in. We asked some of them to feature adjustments of clothing as they danced, preening and priming so that their physical attributes were at their most resplendent while they moved.

Our sequence now involved a long, unison physical sequence that combined all the individual sequences strung together. Threaded throughout this were moments where individuals would float up from the centre of the group, Calippo'd skywards. At these points, each individual had a moment where they spoke about their internal thoughts at that moment, a brief snapshot of the private thoughts inside that clubbing mass. Sinking back down into the club, they assumed their rightful place and joined in with the choreography, a blend of hard-hitting moves as the group pounded away to the rhythm, but consistently dropping into physical moments of self-examination or internal private bliss.

Development

Again this was a scene where we identified a desire for unison but recognised that the creative process must possess individuality and personality if it was to create interesting material. It would be easy to give a group of clubbers a few gestures to repeat that would suggest that they are all the same. This does not capture any of their idiosyncrasies or particular desires and thoughts. Remember this scene was about trying to find the individual happy to be absorbed within the crowd. The choreography had to be a celebration of all of the individual foibles. It was about acceptance and strength in numbers. Seeing a muscle-bound clubber searching for the back of an earring or adjust a high heel meant that they belonged in the group of mini-skirted girls who are doing the same. It was not to diminish his own identity. Similarly, said girls flexing muscles and adjusting their crotches was not to send up the actions of the clubbing boys. It was to claim it as a group. This is who we are and this is what we do!

To achieve this we needed the variation in the palette we were going to work with. This led to the giving of the detailed individual tasks outlined above. This was not a trick that we kept sitting in the bag, waiting for the right moment to pull it out. This came from observing the work we were making and seeing it fall into all the traps we wanted to avoid.

This is an important part of the creative process. You have given your cast the freedom to create but you now have to respond to this creativity. Not all of what has been created will be brilliant but just watching the work will show you possibilities that would not have been apparent to you earlier. Now you can be that outside eye and shape the choreography. It is now much easier to make technically difficult demands on the performers now that they have mastered the original, simpler instructions. You can throw every choreographic cliché at it if you want. Ask your performers to do it faster, slower, backwards, canon, whatever, the point is they have something secure and yet malleable for you to mould. This approach allows you to try things out, to change your mind many times without degrading the source material or detonating the brains and goodwill of your performers.

This scene was ambitious in that it wanted to throw power and energy at the audience (the sub speakers, the intense choreography) but it also wanted to offer a glimpse into the mind state of the characters – be that bliss, euphoria, anxious or confused. We quickly realised that there was no way a non-amplified voice could compete and be heard among this noise. Using microphones would have been difficult due to the sweaty contorted nature of the moves but the potential for feedback and just amplifying the ambient sound ruled that out. In the end it meant that we had to record the voices and imbed them into the soundtrack.

The jury is still out on whether this was a satisfactory conclusion. It certainly freed the physicality. It also explicitly made the words out to be thoughts rather than exclamations, as the actors did not need to move their lips. This was a definite bonus but maybe the rushed nature of the process meant that the result was a little rough around the edges. Maybe we made our discoveries a fraction too late to really nail the scene.

The scene still worked though. We definitely found the individual within the crowd, isolated and unified in the same moment. Looking at the creative structure and timescale that we set up for *Little Dogs*, if you ask for 'rough and ready' maybe you get 'rough and ready'. Nothing wrong with that, once in a while!

Richard James-Neale and Charles Aitken in *Othello* (2008)

Image by Manuel Harlan

Socratis Otto and Leeanna Walsman in *Stockholm*, 2010, produced by Sydney Theatre Company in association with Frantic Assembly.

Photo: © Brett Boardman.

Socratis Otto and Leeanna Walsman in *Stockholm*, 2010, produced by Sydney Theatre Company in association with Frantic Assembly.

Photo: © Brett Boardman

Socratis Otto and Leeanna Walsman in *Stockholm*, 2010, produced by Sydney Theatre Company in association with Frantic Assembly.

Photo: © Brett Boardman

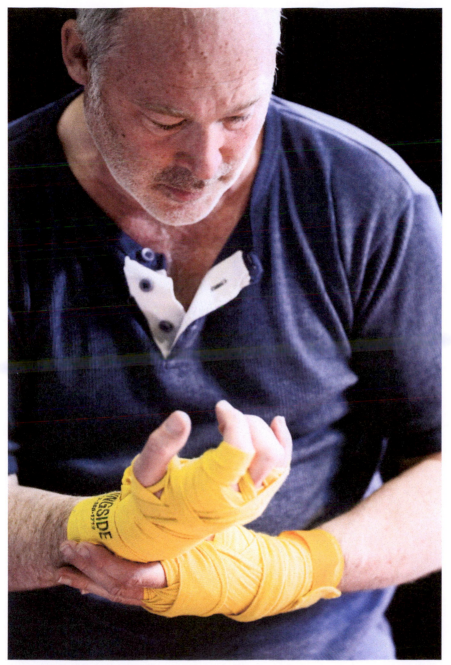

Ewan Stewart prepares for the warm up on *Beautiful Burnout* by Bryony Lavery (2010) Image by Johan Persson

Sam Cox and Leanne Rowe in *Lovesong* by Abi Morgan (2011)
Image by Johan Persson

Sam Cox, Edward Bennett and Leanne Rowe in *Lovesong* (2011)
Image by Johan Persson

Leanne Rowe in *Lovesong*
Image by Johan Persson

Kevin Guthrie, Eddie Kay and Taqi Nazeer in *Beautiful Burnout* (2012)
Image by Brett Boardman

Kevin Guthrie, Eddie Kay and Taqi Nazeer in *Beautiful Burnout* (2012)
Image by Brett Boardman

Sian Phillips and the girls in *Little Dogs* (2012)
Image by Scott Graham

Sian Phillips and Darren Evans in *Little Dogs* (2012)
Image by Farrows Creative/National Theatre Wales

Darren Evans gets lifted above the clubbers in *Little Dogs* (2012)
Image by Farrows Creative/National Theatre Wales

Luke Treadaway in *The Curious Incident of the Dog In The Night-Time* (2013)
Image by Brinkhoff/Mogenburg

From the Ignition 2013 production *From Me To You* (2013)
Image by Helen Maybanks

Luke Treadaway is lifted by Matt Barker and Rhiannon Harper-Rafferty in *The Curious Incident of the Dog In The Night-Time* (2013 cast)
Image by Brinkhoff/Mogenburg

part two
practical exercises

chapter three

Getting started

Initial movement sessions

In the early stages of rehearsal we may ask our performers to improvise using rolls and lifts without ever coming off the floor. Smooth contact work looks at taking the effort and conflict out of physical contact. They are instructed to continually move across the floor taking each other's weight and momentum, 'listening' to their partner's physicality and learning how their partners operate. This stands the performers in good stead for when they have to work quickly together to make material for the show. These initial sessions are all about opportunities and possibilities.

This is also a development towards a strong, grounded performance quality and to make sure there is never an element of 'waft' in the physicality. It is not full of meaning or emotion at this stage. The performers are working very hard to explore and retain a particular truthful quality.

When setting up a session like this, always look out for students/performers overly emoting during movement, embellishing their moves with earth shattering importance. It is important to aim for something more naturalistic. Movement can be a heightened reality and can be rooted in everyday situations and, most poignantly, be performed by everyday characters. Encourage your performers to use their personalities within movement and not to lose themselves behind a physical theatre mask. Allowing your own personality to come through moves is the first step to allowing your adopted character's personality to be expressed and developed through movement.

Don't rush things

Remember the importance of *building blocks*. Keep things simple and move on once you have mastered them. Do not rush things no matter how excited you might be about the possible outcome. Be prepared to change direction if the moment calls for it. These early stages should be about creating a culture of success. Keeping exercises simple and then adding complexity adds to this. This applies to initial movement sessions and warm-up games as much as it does to the creative devising processes.

Trust

A massive part in creating a conducive environment for producing good work is achieving trust. This should be a major priority.

This is NOT about ingratiating yourself.

This is NOT about dated and cringeworthy trust games.

This is NOT about telling your participants your deepest and darkest secrets within the first 20 minutes of meeting them.

This is NOT about plying them with cake and biscuits.

It is NOT about being everyone's best mate.

This IS about breaking down inhibitions.

This IS about setting high standards and keeping to them.

This IS about leading but also listening.

This IS about reading body language and group dynamics.

This IS about having a plan yet being prepared to throw it away.

This IS about motivating, encouraging and praising where necessary.

We have always found that people can do more than they think they can. They can be pushed to surprise themselves. But you cannot just expect someone to fly without giving them flying lessons. Confidence and trust go hand in hand and should be worked at.

The importance of rules, time frames and limitations

The little details – owning the space

A conducive environment for your participants is more than a creative process. It is a first impression when they walk in the room. It is the temperature, the smell, the lighting and the music playing. It is the atmosphere. You can go a long way to dictating the mood and success of the session through controlling that first impression.

Pushing it a little – you are the boss

We have found that people produce their best work when they are hot and sweaty through exertion, when they are focused and committed. This, of course, creates a hot and sweaty room. Wherever possible resist the temptation to throw open all the doors and windows, the fire escapes, to let the fresh air in. Believe us, something more valuable will escape! As soon as the outside world crashes in with its noises and smells, the world you have created dissolves. The focus is gone.

Give breaks when needed. Look out for exhausted participants. Put their welfare first. But don't submit to the first request, for they do not always know what they are losing. When we deny requests for the window to be opened we always explain exactly what we will lose and we have never had any complaints. It helps to explain the dangers of warm muscles cooling down rapidly and then being asked to move again. There is real risk of injury here.

Improvisation rules

Of course some rules are there to be broken, but so far we've preferred to stick to the 'one track' rule when improvising.

The 'one track' rule came about when we realised that we could remember nothing from the endless physical improvisation we had just been through. It had felt great and we were sure there had been some wonderful moments, but there was no way we could detail them. So the 'one track' rule limited the improvisation to the length of the music used to accompany the exercise.

This was symptomatic of the way we worked back then. Being in the shows and trying to direct and/or choreograph is a difficult situation. We are not in the shows any more and the use of the video camera in the rehearsal room has softened the rule slightly, but we feel it still serves us well in the rehearsal room. It stops improvisations becoming indulgent and allows us to quickly get our heads together, find out what we all have learnt and try it again or something new.

The structure of the week in rehearsals

This is something that has been 'acquired' from the Australian Dance Theatre. It is common sense really but it has shaped the rehearsal process for our last few shows.

We now make sure that we work our performers hard, physically, for only two days in a row. The third day is for recuperation and will be focused on text or gentle physicality. The 'two days on, one day off' rule helps you structure your rehearsals in advance, with your performers' welfare in mind. And you will hopefully not be surprised or obstructed by tired performers.

This is the basic structure of the week. You can also structure each day in advance. We start every day with a warm-up (even the calm third day). Physical work dominates the morning and text tends to dominate the afternoon. Immediately after lunch we play a game to sharpen, engage and enthuse our performers. Too many afternoons have been scuppered by the post-carb collapse. Rehearsing in the afternoon can feel like hard work, especially if the muscles have cooled down over lunch and the lactic acid has started to build up. A fun game can be 20 minutes well spent if it gets everyone active and alert again.

Always forward, never backwards

This is such a simple mantra but it has been so useful in all aspects of our work. Specifically with young groups it is expressed as our company maxim, our commitment to always striving to do something better than before.

Young groups may be suitably fascinated by a creative devising process, but the repetition and polishing needed to make any scene ready for performance might be a new demand upon them. It can also feel dull and unrewarding when all they want to do is work on new things.

By applying the maxim to the rehearsal the targets are clear. It must be smoother than before. Or faster than before. Or cleaner than before.

It may not seem very theatrical, but if you need a physical scene to speed up to match the perfect piece of music, then share that information with the cast. Get the stopwatch out. The goal of the perfect timing becomes clear, shared and attainable. The maxim makes it clear from the outset that you will not settle for anything less than improvement each time.

Morning warm-ups – teamwork and personal attainment

Warm-ups should be tailored to what you are about to do. That seems obvious enough but they can be much more strategic and important than that. It is a time for building strength, confidence and camaraderie and all of these elements should be considered when constructing a warm up.

Why warm up?

This is a question that is not the singular right of the tired and over-worked performer. Believe us when we say that, despite nearly 20 years where almost every working day has begun by taking an hour-long warm-up, there have been plenty (and we mean *plenty*) of days when this question has been just as readily formed on our lips, even if it remained unsaid. So we speak from experience when we say, with utmost confidence, the following edict – *Because you must.*

There are a variety of reasons why.

There are endless books that cover this issue very well. In fact, there are many books that cover this and only this. When researching possible approaches to creating and rehearsing a show that involves boxing, we were presented with literally hundreds of books that are solely about ways to warm-up before a boxing session. Most of these books go into great, often pictorial detail about the behaviour of muscle groups, bones, tendons, tissue, respiratory systems and the like. We have rarely been in a situation where we have had the time or resources to be able to convince a room full of tired people in this way.

One analogy that is both simple and obvious is that of the squash ball. On entering the squash court, the players are reliant on the squash ball. On first appearing on the court, the squash ball is 'cold', by which we mean it is unwieldy, moves slowly and without conviction, responds to stimulus very badly and is prone to cracking. So the ball is 'warmed up' – the players take a few minutes to whack the ball around the court, generating not just heat but also pliability, responsiveness and all-round suitability for the job at hand. Admittedly, the example above, and much of the available literature is focused on sports and the essential nature of warming up before any game or match. This gave rise to one infamous episode in our early days when a disgruntled actress, following a typical warm-up, stormed out of the hall, but not before bellowing the immortal line 'I'm an actress – NOT an *acrobat*!'. True enough but dammit, even darts players flex their fingers before a match.

Frantic Assembly makes work that is essentially physical in its creation and execution. Our experience of being able to do this has always substantiated what we knew from day one – none of this would have been possible without warming up each and every day. It ticks three boxes – all of them essential.

1   It makes the creation of physical work possible.
2   It makes for great results.
3   It ensures safety.

Each point is obvious enough but it's worth making a few points in each area.

Just like the squash ball, your body is not always ready or aware of what is about to happen to it. And why should it be? If your body has its own consciousness, our lives would become very complicated so let's be thankful that this is not the case. At the same time, respect the fact that we are the sentient beings that hold the information and a sense of what is about to happen. It is not whimsy that leads us to say this – your capacity to make physical work relies heavily on your capacity to be in touch with your body. You absolutely need to be able to think physically. This is not a connection that is in place at 9.30am on a wet Tuesday morning – this is why all dancers take a class at the start of their working day. We don't expect people to behave like dancers but we would be ignorant and idiotic not to take the lead from those that must connect their brain with their body in order to achieve what they are required to do. Creating this connection between mind and body is the essence of every warm-up. It is what unites all warm-up techniques from Capoeira and Kung Fu to Tai Chi and Curling. So before we even get to the idea of the muscles being flexible, the blood running sufficiently through the veins, the respiratory system being called into action, the skeletal form being in some form of alignment, the balancing systems being switched on, the capacity to subconsciously know that you are body occupying space, all of this is secondary to creating the essential relationship between mind and body. All of the others listed here are, subsequently, vital but they are only possible by creating the correct mindset in the first place. Now admittedly, your body and mind are connecting from the moment you open your eyes at the start of the day. It becomes more and more proficient even with the innocuous task of swinging your feet out of the bed but the point is, in order to achieve something more than ordinary, this state of play between body and brain has to be the very best it can be. Here's where warm-ups come in. They are an act of generosity – not by us, though we do get thanked regularly for them. They are the necessary introduction into the realm of possibility. Swinging your feet out of bed does require thinking (can I get away with delaying this action for another 20 minutes?) but it does not test the realm of possibility. A creative session of any kind is only going to work if this IS the intention.

A room full of warmed-up people leads to amazing results. This is not a term we use freely or easily but it is one that is absolutely applicable here. We have had the pleasure of watching a huddle of wet, bleary-eyed students traipse into a cold hall on early October mornings, knowing nothing about us and caring even less. Two hours later they have not just executed, but created physical sequences and material and solutions to tasks that they genuinely did not know they were capable of. And this happens A LOT. This is only partially due to the exercises we have run (and why we wanted to write this book). The essential element? Yep, the warm-up.

It turns a gaggle of individuals into a collective. A team.

Actors returning from their days off frequently comment on how they feel they have already connected with the acting company before they meet on stage, simply by having warmed up in a room together. A warm-up connects a company in a way that even an actual performance cannot surpass. It involves everybody, all the time. A warm-up has no regard for who is the best actor or the best dancer or the best looking or even the strongest. In many instances it levels the field. It also operates on a glorious principle – what you put in, you get out.

Point made? There is more

You don't need to prep a biology lecture in order to convince a room that this is both necessary and worthwhile. There are other long-term benefits from a warm-up and not all to do with simply preparing the body for the immediate task in hand.

The warm-up is the time to introduce new skills. The body is pliable and the mind is not fixated on and limited by the world of the play. You can play games or go a bit left field with the movement. It can be silly and fun but all the while it can be building technique and strength. During rehearsals for *Hymns* director and choreographer Liam Steel would make us learn a Ricky Martin routine! For people with very little experience in movement and even less in the joys of Ricky Martin this was a period of initial embarrassment and clumsy failure but Liam persisted and eventually, after much swearing and laughter we started to get it. We are not saying we would ever convince a crowd of adoring Latinos but were stringing together some choice moves and having a good time doing so. In retrospect the genius of this approach meant that we had applied all our feelings of inadequacy and failure to the Ricky Martin routine that would finish the warm-ups. We had also seen those inadequacies diminish over time, the fluidity of our movement increase and our ability to retain movement expand hugely. All of this set us up beautifully for the task of making the actual choreography of *Hymns*. We had done all our failing in the warm-up. We had overcome in the warm-up. All because we were disposed to do so. We were relaxed and it did not matter if we failed because it was the warm-up. It was just silly fun. But we came out of it with new skills and a new confidence without ever compromising the creation of the choreography of *Hymns*.

The warm-up can be where you build your team ethic. (See Lessons Learnt). It can also be where you address potential issues that might be problematic further down the line. Young performers might be wary of touching or embracing others. This might be personal or cultural and can often seem quite entrenched. Talking about such things publicly can often exacerbate the problem, as people can feel exposed and uncomfortable. We are firm believers that in most cases it is not the touch itself but the context within which the touch happens that can be problematic (see 'Games – a selection of crowd pleasers'). We just play games that necessitate touching and embracing and put a bit of competitive heat under them. By making them fun and competitive you replicate the environment of a football match or the playground. Areas where that level of contact is a given. Once you have that, harness it, and your group will not take a step back to the squeamish non-touching days.

The warm up can set the tone for the whole rehearsals. We have experience of working on someone else's show where, because of their sensitivity to the delicate and dark nature of the play, the whole experience became dominated by an oppressive hush. They had blacked out the windows of the ground floor rehearsal room because there was an extended section of the performance that required the performers to be nude. This meant there was no daylight. The cast of two had nowhere to escape to. Nothing else existed apart from the play. This may sound like a good idea but it presented a crushing atmosphere of negativity. We are all for focus on the work but at what cost? Our warm-ups are about personal and group development. They are designed to present a challenging situation but also a promise – 'you will get better at this'; 'we will make you feel fitter and stronger.'

For example, we often make everyone do press-ups. On day one, we can guarantee someone will say they cannot do any or will try to do girly cop out ones with their knees on the floor. Within reason, we insist that everyone tries full press-ups. There is no shame in only managing one. It means that you will double that tally next time. Invariably, what we end up with is a company of fitter, stronger performers pumping out press-ups like athletes. You might ask, 'what has this got to do with making theatre?' The answer is not much unless that show requires you to move in any way, catch, hold, lift embrace, etc. but it does have an awful lot to do with a group of people experiencing incremental success every day, achieving something they had not thought possible and generally feeling better about themselves and each other. We find a positive and fun rehearsal room will want to go the extra mile no matter what the subject matter of your show. The rehearsals room for *Lovesong* was almost constant laughter and jokes despite the weight and sensitive nature of the subject matter. This was not about a lack of respect for the subject matter either. It was about a respect for the need of all involved to let off steam and our need to create a room that was full of creative possibility and not one defined by the heartbreaking and inevitable conclusion of the play.

During an extended run, the warm-up before the show reintroduces all the ingredients together, especially if stage management can find the time to take part. (Do not underestimate this! A company that respects and includes its stage management team will be a happy one!) These component parts will be the ones calling all the cues, handing you your props, lifting you above their heads, catching you as you drop, managing your quick change, etc. It makes sense to come together to focus. It serves to appreciate each other's input.

Even on a show with no obvious movement, even the briefest physical warm-up can work wonders. There was a first night of such a production where a nervous young cast all had that far away look in their eyes. They had spent a fantastic rehearsal time making great connections and now looked like frightened individuals, capable of throwing all that hard work away. In the five minutes we had together the only option was to introduce them to the thrill of the Calippo lift (see The Club). For those brief minutes they were achieving something seemingly impossible. They could only do it by connecting and working together. The person being lifted felt the adrenalin buzz from what their company members were capable of together. Once they all had a go at being lifted they all looked much more energetic and skipped off to their dressing rooms looking much more like the team we had created in the rehearsal room. This may seem a little trite and clichéd but it really did work a treat and reminded us that sometimes the way to bring back that focus is not to engage with the performer intellectually – they know what they *should* be feeling – but to give them that visceral shot, the distraction, the harmless reminder that we can all have fun here, the reminder of how far they have come together.

Lessons learnt

If you are creating a show that looks into a particular subject matter, e.g. club culture, prostitution, boxing, the world of high finance, etc. you may want to immerse yourself totally within that world. You might want to get a feel for how its inhabitants tick, what thrills them, what pressures inspire them. You might devour all of this greedily, pouring it all onto your production, giving your work the authority it needs. Experience has shown us that this immersion offers so much more than a credible production. There can be priceless lessons to be learnt from this intense observation of another world that can extend far beyond the run of your latest production. This was certainly the case when we looked into the world of boxing to create *Beautiful Burnout*.

We went into *Beautiful Burnout* wanting to know as much as we could about boxing and the world that surrounds it. It felt crucial to learn its vocabulary, its physical palette. Everything we would learn would shape what we create and give it an element of truth so missing from many depictions of boxing on stage and screen. (This aspiration for 'truth' was at the heart of the desire to create a show about boxing but it was further bolstered by our conversations with the boxing community. They had felt constantly

Vicki Manderson in rehearsals for *Beautiful Burnout* by Bryony Lavery (2010). Image by Johan Persson

misrepresented and they were as adamant as we were that we should present a truthful depiction of their world.)

(There are similarities between the worlds of boxing and theatre, not just in both of their need for an audience. Both worlds are inspired by their ghosts. A walk through the corridors of the National Theatre is a bit like walking into any gym in the country. Just swap Judi Dench for Mohammed Ali. They inspire from the walls. Both worlds are reliant on someone who is pretending to be someone he is not. He has to do this convincingly otherwise he is tragically exposed. For all his skills he can be reliant on the objective eye that can direct him to better results, i.e. the director/the trainer.)

It was clear that a large part of the potential success of *Beautiful Burnout* would rely on the perceived authenticity of the project, both from a theatre audience and from the boxing world we drew so heavily on.

Everyone knows that boxing is a strenuous and exacting sport that probably demands more of its participants than any other. We know that it requires strength, fitness and speed. We also know that it involves sweat, adrenalin and pain. Everything about our understanding of it is linked to the visceral. How can a production conjure all of this and maintain the precision and restraint to be presented night after night?

While we developed all kinds of tricks to give the impression of clubbing blows and fierce connecting jabs we realised there are things that you just cannot fake. The actors had to look like boxers.

This meant paying for the performers to attend boxing gyms three months before rehearsals, to learn technique and get fitter. We also decided that the performers should bring the training and fitness regimes they learned in the gyms back into the rehearsal room, with a different actor leading the warm-up each day. This meant subverting what we had come to believe as best practice in theatre/dance warm-ups. The boxing warm-ups that each of us experienced had very little recognised stretching at the beginning. There was a light loosening up but very quickly became intense aerobic work.

(A trainer we spoke to talked of muscles as elastic and how his boxers needed that elastic to retain its snap, its speed. To stretch it would be to diminish this. You can see the logic of the image.)

Warm-ups were intense and contained punishing circuit training. They contained technique work too, with each performer encouraged to share what they had picked up in the gyms. This meant the rehearsal room was filled with weights, skipping ropes, hand wraps, boxing gloves, medicine balls, towels, punch bags, practice mitts, etc. Without really thinking about it we had transformed the room into a gym. It did not look like the place where you might pick up a script. And good luck even trying to while you are wearing boxing gloves!

This created a room where anything less than the authentic stood out.

There were some startling implications and revelations because of this transformation.

The initial implication was about the script. As many of the scenes would require boxing gloves, skipping, etc. it became very clear that we could never work with scripts in hand. Scripts *had* to be learnt. It was imperative that the performers felt and looked like boxers and as a result this illusion was rarely shattered by having to fumble with a script. We spent many hours working on the grace, balance and confidence of the performer and did not need that work undone by them fumbling with a script while wearing boxing gloves. The impressive and potent becomes ridiculous and comical very quickly.

Through our initial observations in gyms you could not help notice how boxers help each other adjust gloves and equipment. They have to because the gloves make many things impossible. They unscrew bottles of water for each other for much needed rehydration. They hold weights for each other. They help each other through the ropes. They shout encouragement at every correct opportunity. Performance and effort is praised. Slacking off not only lets yourself down but also lets the team down. The importance of the team mentality within the gym is all the more startling for what is one of the loneliest sports. In the ring you are ultimately on your own with nowhere to hide.

Our relationship with boxing changed slightly. We wanted to observe it, reflect it, and see it anew. Having got deep inside the world of boxing and met people with the drive and discipline to get things right and make a difference we wanted to emulate it.

We noticed this team mentality was replicated in the rehearsal room. This was no considered effort. We just noticed it and then leapt upon it! Our circuit training warm-ups were brutal and there were days where the only things that got us through them was the encouragement of others and the desire not to let anyone down. While our bodies screamed in pain during endless press-ups and sit-ups we were always on the look-out for others drooping. A word of encouragement would always revive them. Circuit training had various stations, each focusing on strengthening a different part of the body. We moved around the station in twos so we always had a partner to push us on. If there were an odd number we would opt for a three rather than having someone on their own. It meant that a rehearsal room that could easily have been filled with respectful silence reverberated with encouragement and support. This approach to warm-ups helped create the team mentality but also presented each with personal goals. Every day gave the opportunity to do something better than the day before. The repetition gave us something from which to measure growth. So often in a rehearsal room actors feel lost and insecure. This approach at least gave them an indicator that every day they were getting better, that things were moving forward. Insecurity will always find its way into a rehearsal room but we had performers (and directors and stage management) that would start the day feeling good about themselves because improvement was tangible. And that only really happened because we were all in it together, looking out for each other in the moments where we struggled.

The room

There were other subtle (or maybe startling) discoveries. This approach, the set-up of the room and the very clear aspirations for the show meant that during tea breaks you would often find the actors back at the weights, or skipping, or working on sit-ups. Normally actors would seize the opportunity to have a cigarette and bitch about their agents. Not here!

The importance of how the room is set up became perfectly clear on the making of *Lovesong*. *Lovesong* is, of course, a very different beast compared to *Beautiful Burnout* but the actors still worked hard physically and enjoyed the sweat and aches that accompany such activity. The problem was that the set for *Lovesong* was a table and chairs and a big bed. It proved almost impossible to keep the actors off the bed in their breaks! This made getting back to work much harder. *Beautiful Burnout* offered no soft edges. There was nothing welcoming about its surfaces.

We took this awareness into *The Curious Incident of the Dog in the Night Time*. Luckily that project presented a naturally hard-working cast and hard unwelcoming surfaces. Perfect for avoiding that soporific slump after lunch or tea breaks. Still, this was to be an ensemble that had to work long hours together. Many of them were not used to creating and rehearsing choreographed movement and the aches and strains that it brings. We felt they needed something to offer security and reward. Rather than take the actors through a dance warm-up that would highlight many of their deficiencies and insecurities we opted for the circuit-training model developed on *Beautiful Burnout*. We decked the room out with skipping ropes and weights and designated certain areas of the set as constant circuit stations. Familiarity with the structure and routine of the warm-up helped. (Downstage right will always be 'abdominals'. Upstage left will always be 'legs'.) This gave them a structure from which they could recognise development and success. They could feel it on their waistline. They could feel it in the muscles that came back to life. They could feel it in the ability to do one more press-up than yesterday. It made success palpable. It created a positive atmosphere of hard work and constant improvement.

Our delving into the world of boxing on *Beautiful Burnout* taught us the power of hard work and the subtle ingredients that build respect and a team mentality. Do not underestimate the love that can flow towards someone who places a cup of water under your lips when you are dripping with sweat and, because of the boxing gloves on your hands, are incapable of holding that cup. Giving our cast a taste of that world paid massive dividends. As we all sweated we were losing weight but gaining muscle and respect. Those mornings of pain, Underworld blaring through the sound system, were moments of massive endorphin rushes. We felt privileged to be in this room together, to be aiming to emulate a fraction of what the boxer puts him/herself through.

Every show requires a slightly different approach but the *Beautiful Burnout* experience, coupled with what we learned from *Lovesong* and then applied to *Curious Incident* has taught us that people thrive off the feeling of hard work paying off. Even the initially resistant to the idea of hard physical exercise went home and said, 'guess what I was doing today!' with pride. That quickly became 'Look what I can do now!'

If that sounds childish then maybe we are in danger of forgetting how child-like we are in our needs. We need rewards. We need fun. So often theatre process can become dark and insular. It implodes in on itself. It appears to be giving itself a hard time to justify its existence. By giving actors a glimpse of the world of the boxer they see the level of dedication, focus, generosity and respect needed in his/her world. It is fun to dip your toe into that world and there are many rewards in doing so but it also reminds the actor that this acting lark is not a bad world to be working in. So in addition to rewards and fun it can be useful to offer perspective. It helps keep feet on the ground. There was still time for plenty of actor/director process but we were warily on the lookout for those processes that were divisive and which were inclusive. Which ones should remain homework for an individual and which ones brought value into the room.

When you are lucky enough to be researching such a rich area of life as boxing, just be careful not to merely dress up in its clothes. In doing so you might miss something fundamentally important that only that world can teach you. Be on the lookout for the values it holds dear. Can you emulate them? Replicate them? What can you learn from them and bring back to invigorate the rehearsal room and the processes that live there?

You might find that the warm-up is where you get to implement these new discoveries.

SUGGESTIONS FOR CONSTRUCTIVE WARM-UPS

The following exercises are useful in creating a more relaxed and fluid physicality. They do not replace more formal stretches, especially if the group are about to embark on some strenuous lifting, but they can play a crucial part in introducing the group to very important concepts needed in the more energetic work. They are very important building blocks that can and should be referred to in the creative choreographic processes.

Rolling 1 and 2, as you will see, are relevant to contact processes like Round/By/Through. Push Hands is usually our first building block before embarking on any lifting choreography.

These exercises are both warm-ups and fundamental training processes.

Rolling 1

This is a seemingly very simple exercise that is well worth taking the time to get right. Principally it is rolling across the floor, but there are very specific rules and instructions that lead the participant to a much better understanding of how their body moves.

It is also a gentle way into much more vigorous exercises.

Start by asking for a volunteer. It is very important that the group are observing each other as the success or failure of the following tasks is instantly visible.

Ask the volunteer to lie on their back with their hands above their head at one end of the room. You are going to get them to demonstrate rolling down the room. (You are going to manhandle them here. It might be best to warn them and make sure they are OK with this. What you are actually about to demonstrate is a moving technique similar to that used by nurses when turning over a patient.)

Crouch by the side of your volunteer making sure that you are on the side leading into the room. Ask your volunteer to raise their knee furthest away from you. Their feet should still be on the floor. There should be no effort here; the key is to stay relaxed.

Place your hand on the raised knee and quickly but gently pull it towards you, across their body. This will turn the volunteer over onto their front. Make sure you guide the knee to facilitate this.

A successful demonstration of this technique will show your observers how easily the body can be moved. Now ask your volunteer to replicate this move. Place your hand on their knee but do not pull. They must relax but just allow their knee to move towards the warmth of your hand. Again, if this is successful, you will see how the body leads with the knee, twists and allows the rest of the body to follow in a logical order until gravity takes over and completes the turn. This twist should be obvious to the observers. It looks like a ripple that runs up the body, meaning that the head is the last body part to complete the turn.

The next stage is harder but importantly works on exactly the same principle.

Your volunteer is now lying on their front. (Remind them to keep their arms above their head. They do not want them to get caught up in the rolling of the body.) Place your hand on the back of their head. They are to move their head towards the hand. The hand should lead them back onto their front by gently pulling away and across the body, just as you did with the knee. What makes it more difficult is that the volunteer will encounter a block. The head will feel that it cannot go any further, that they are stretching as far as they can. This is where you have to remind them of the natural logic we found in the first roll. Simply get them to have a think about this logic and consider the next part of their body that needs to follow the head. It is their shoulder. Is it relaxed? Once it is relaxed can it follow the head and send the ripple down the body from shoulder to hips, to knees, to feet?

Participants should always be on the look-out for this logic. They will encounter moments where they will feel stuck and will say they are stuck. Sometimes it is enough to remind them of the logic and they can release themselves.

Now it is time to put both rolls together. Get the volunteer to imagine the need to move across the room to the other side. This is the only motivation. The rules are that the body is being led by, alternately, the knee and the head. The volunteer also has to be encouraged to think about the next move just before the current move ends. This provides a fluid transition. Observers can see the ripple running up and down the body. (It might help to get the rollers to imagine the room is tipping away from them, assisting their roll.)

Be on the look-out for rollers getting carried away and rushing it. Rollers need to keep thinking throughout the exercise to achieve the ripple! When they get too fast you will notice that participants are rolling their hips. This mostly happens when they are trying to roll from their front to their back, leading with their head. If this is happening, then slow them down and place a hand on the small of their back and then their stomach to remind them that the middle of their body should be following and not leading. It moves when it logically needs to.

You can set the whole group off, taking turns, in twos, at rolling across the room. Encourage those waiting to look out for that successful ripple up and down the body.

Once you are happy that your group have got this principle then you may instruct them to try a freestyle run! In this they choose a clear body part to lead the roll. They should aim for the same smooth and fluid transitions and their choice of body part should be instantly apparent to any observers.

See how fast they can go while retaining the quality of movement. Never be afraid to remind the participants of the simplest form of this activity – the first building block, the knee and the head – if clarity and quality begin to be compromised.

You can return to this type of movement and start to play. Maybe the choice of body part could take them up from the floor briefly. Try placing obstacles in the way of the simple journey. How do they interact with these? Can they find a way of getting in and out of a chair placed somewhere en route and still maintain the fluidity and logic of the original task? Try placing other participants in their way, kneeling down, lying down, etc. These could be moving platforms to negotiate, but participants should understand that they are fleeting moments as the simple drive of getting across the room must not be forgotten.

This task is not just about helping people find a fluid way to roll across the floor. We sometimes use this exercise as a way into much more complex contact partner work. There are moments in such complex exercises where participants find themselves talking about being 'stuck' and unable to find a way out of a move. The rolling exercise is a good reference point for moments like this. Knowing how to continue with the flow of a move or using different body parts to lead can really help when creating contact work.

You can apply the logic you have found in the rolling to contact work. The rolling exercise is a good reminder of how someone can be active in a move even if they are being lifted. All it takes is to think about the exercise for a moment and apply a physical logic to the situation. The slight twist of the hips or turn of the head can open up loads of new possibilities for a dueting couple.

There is an interesting development to this rolling exercise. It uses alternate focuses of head/armpit and knee.

Use a volunteer couple. Get one of them to lie on the floor (A) and get the other (B) to stand above them. The one on the floor has to respond to the contact from the partner standing up. B has to lift or push the prone partner using their feet. They place their foot under A's knee and kick (push) it so that A rolls over onto their front with their arms above their head. Then B puts their foot under A's armpit and does the same so that A flips over onto their back, taking the impulse from the foot into the armpit and sending it spiralling down the body as they roll over. Repeat this making sure that A is still taking B's impetus and is not just rolling. With a bit of practice and an increase in speed and fluidity, the effect is of someone kicking another, rag doll like, across the stage. This can be quite a dramatic and startling effect.

Rolling 2

We have talked at length about the simple rolling exercises and their relevance to creating contact partner work while stood. This next exercise uses rolling but, building on the variation at the end of Rolling 1, solely involves working in pairs on the floor. We will also talk later about the 'log' and the 'rock' – two devices that help practitioners to visualise the kind of rolling movement they should be aiming for.

Ideally make sure your volunteer couple are of similar weight or build for this exercise. (It would be even better if you could demonstrate this exercise with someone.)

Both volunteers lie on the floor next to each other. They should start with their heads facing the same way and their arms above their heads. This time they do not have to think about individual body parts. They can roll in any way.

Make sure they are touching and ask them to roll the same way while maintaining this friction.

The person at the back needs to be thinking about this contact and this friction as they move across the room. They can use their arm, leg or head to make contact with such weight that they 'stick' to their partner and start to move over them. They need to concentrate on merely pressing down and not think about trying to roll over their partner. The effect we are looking for will not be achieved if the person moving over is actually trying to move themselves or throw their body over their partner's. They have to stick to the simplicity of the task and just let the move happen.

This successful connection through friction is sometimes called the 'hook'. Unfortunately this is misleading because if you were to actually hook onto your partner, then you would be liable to trap your arm under your partner as you both roll. You would also drop to the floor as you fall off your partner.

The person at the front just keeps rolling. The lifting is purely a consequence of their rolling. They will have to work hard on keeping the roll going with their partner's weight on them. As they roll, if a good connection is made, their partner will be rolled over their body. Think of the way ancient civilisations are believed to have moved large rocks by rolling logs underneath them. In both cases the item/person being moved remains passive. It just offers its constant weight.

When the person moving gets to the other side of their partner they smoothly make the transition from 'rock' to 'log' and continue the rolling momentum. As this happens the first 'log' needs to switch mindset to become the 'rock' and look for connections through friction (or hook). A successful couple can make several fluid transitions across the room.

There is always a chance that the transition will not happen straight away, but it is better for the couple to roll across the room together and for the transition to happen once properly rather than faking it repeatedly. Any observers on the outside will immediately spot a successful attempt. The effect is of a body surfing a wave but it is not bodysurfing. Bodysurfing tends to rely on the 'surfer' being rigid and moving over several people rolling as 'waves'. This exercise can be done slowly with both participants relaxed. When it works, the transition of one body across the other is tender and magical.

Things to look out for include:

- *Participants not sticking to the simplicity of their task.* Encourage them to just roll, or just to try to connect and let it happen. Watch they don't throw themselves over their partner!
- *People gripping with their arms, making a literal hook around their partner.* As we have warned, this will make an effective connection but once they are moving, that arm will become trapped under their partner, they themselves will come crashing down on the other side as the roll completes, and they will then have their arm trapped under their partner as they begin to roll!
- *People being scared about giving their full weight.* This will happen and the result is often that they inadvertently concentrate their weight into smaller areas by lifting their head or rushing the move and trying to get off quickly. This results in them pressing their weight into their partners in a painful stiletto effect. Remind them that an equally distributed weight is easier to handle and that this exercise demands total relaxation and giving of this weight.
- *People just rushing through it without mastering the technique.* If they are doing it properly, they can do it at any speed.

Once this is working, have a play …

Place the rest of the group at the opposite end of the room and ask your volunteer couple to maintain eye contact with them as much as possible through the exercise. Try different types of music. Try different speeds. Ask them to assume the 'log' position with their eyes open, the 'rock' with their eyes closed. What theatrical contexts emerge? Is there a relationship between 'characters'? What if you gave them text? How does this challenge and reinvent the text? (And the movement?)

Rolling around on the floor with a partner is fun of course, but like the Rolling 1 exercise there is method in this. It is relevant to general contact work.

The person who is the 'log' is taking their partner's weight and slowly moving it. They are responsible for how that body gets moved and are in control. It might be useful to point out to them that they have done this without placing their hands on their partners. The momentum and strength has come from their core and not their extremities. Similarly, the 'rock' has made this possible by giving their partner their weight and not denying it. It was this that made the contact possible.

This is a fundamental lesson to learn.

Push Hands

This exercise was adapted from a Tai Chi exercise and may be familiar to many in one form or another. Here it helps participants get used to the notion of non-verbal and essentially physical communication between performers.

Get the group into pairs. One partner puts their hand out, palm down, and the other partner places their hand on top of the other's hand. The person with the hand below pushes their hand upwards slightly so there is a gentle pressure between the two hands. The person with their hand on top is now in control. They can lead their partner around the room keeping their hand flat while their partner follows, trying to keep their hand flat and the pressure between the two constant. They can take their partner on a journey exploiting all levels without actually ending up on the floor (look out for people slipping their thumb around their partner's hand and thereby 'gripping'). To achieve this you have to relax your body and really concentrate on the signals your partner is sending through touch. As you may be asked to go all the way down to the floor, or walk quickly forward or backwards, you have to have your knees bent and be physically prepared to go anywhere.

It can be a group's mistake to interpret this exercise as an attempt to outwit your partner. It is important to stress that this exercise involves two people working together in an attempt to build a physical understanding. They should be working together to get better at it. With this in mind it helps to instruct the practitioners to be truthful and just stop and start again if they are losing the plot! Make sure they are being honest with each other about who is actually leading. Stopping is good and to be encouraged. It helps establish the limits and parameters and keeps the task simple.

Stop this exercise after a while. It may be that the room is experiencing varying degrees of success. Now instruct the person who is being led to close their eyes and concentrate fully on the touch of the hands only. Run the exercise again.

Debrief the group to find out if there was a greater success this time. Initially there may have been chaos until the followers could trust the leaders, but in our experience this exercise yields greater success when the eyes are closed and the focus is purely on the touch.

It should be pointed out that this touch and ability to communicate physically is the absolute bedrock to any contact work between partners. This simple exercise is applicable to all abilities and provides the perfect starting point or introduction to many more advanced exercises outlined later. It is a perfect example of a *building block*. Much further down the line, when contact work breaks down, you can quickly get participants back on track by asking them to refind the qualities they discovered through Push Hands.

GAMES – A SELECTION OF CROWD PLEASERS

These games are used within Frantic Assembly workshops to animate and energise the room. Workshops can be intimidating to participants and we try to introduce the idea that this is going to be fun as well as challenging as soon as possible.

Some of the games have been picked up and adapted along the way. Others have been created to satisfy a need for energy, focus or training.

As with the constructive warm-up ideas, each one is used when we think they will complement or offer something instructive to the rest of the workshop.

Marcia Takedown

This incorporates an exercise introduced to us by Marcia Pook, a performer in our production *Underworld*. We think she originally picked it up from her time working for V-TOL Dance Company, but it may be one of those generic exercises that all dancers will recognise from their training. Here it is expanded to create a dynamic and exhausting exercise that quickly tests technique, builds trust and animates and energises the group.

Step 1

Split the group into pairs. One partner closes their eyes and trusts their partner from here on. The other partner places a flat hand gently on the back of their partner's neck and leads them around the space using the slightest pressure possible to indicate directions and speeds. Both partners are communicating through the area of contact, as in Push Hands.

Once the group are comfortable and showing signs of trusting each other, open the exercise out again. Allow anyone to take control of a random partner for a short time as they walk around the room before safely letting them go free again. Once this is working insist that the partner who is being guided closes their eyes the moment their partner takes control. They should think of this moment as liberating rather than frightening. They are not required to make any decisions but purely to concentrate on the minute fluctuations in touch from their partner's hand guiding them around the room. When the controlling partner wants to release them they give a small squeeze on the back of the neck and touch their shoulder. This is the sign to open their eyes and carry on walking normally, looking for people to take control of so that the relationship is constantly changing.

Try increasing the speed when the group appear to be working well. Instruct the group to cut down the duration of contact and make those moments more fleeting. This allows for many more moments of contact between different people. When they are almost at running speed you should notice how quickly people can turn from looking around the room for a victim to a completely trusting, passive partner with just the slightest touch on the back of the neck.

As with all exercises make sure this is advanced in very clear stages. If it is not and people start banging into each other, then any group trust will be lost. At this stage you could try the hand on different body parts. Aim to use more difficult connections, possibly not with hands. Try shoulders or hips.

Step 2

This next stage moves on from a trust exercise to a contact exercise. It is a very useful way to get the group thinking about how to work with people's weight, about using their own weight when moving people and not relying on strength.

The basic set-up of the previous stages still exists. The group walk around the space and anyone can place their hand on the neck of another. This time they only lead for a short time before giving their partner a squeeze on the neck (both partners keep their eyes open for this stage). This is the signal for the squeezed partner to gently take themselves to the floor and lie on their side.

From here they need to be rescued. The rules and technique of this engagement need to be clearly set out before this stage commences.

The person on the floor waits for someone to rescue them. To do this anyone can slide in behind them, spooning into them and placing their free/ top arm around them, pulling themselves in as close to their partner as possible. This contact is crucial. Remind the practitioners that this contact is still the point of communication, as it was in Push Hands and in the stages above. The 'rescuer' pulls their partner towards them and rolls onto their other side, taking the partner with them. They keep this going and the partner rolls away once they reach the other side, then up onto their feet to resume walking. The rescuer keeps as fluid as possible and rolls away and gets up to carry on walking, awaiting the squeeze on the neck that will send them to the floor or looking out for people to rescue. Everyone in this game is a potential victim, everyone a potential rescuer. They have to work hard to keep the game alive with the emphasis being on rescuing.

The group may encounter some awkwardness in this exercise. People may be reluctant to give their weight, thinking they are crushing the person that they are rolling over. Similarly, if the rescuer does not concentrate on the contact between their stomach and the victim's back, then the move runs the risk of being an uncoordinated act of strength. If the victim senses this, then

THE FRANTIC ASSEMBLY BOOK OF DEVISING THEATRE

they are even more likely to withhold their weight. It needs to be pointed out to the victim that withholding or apologising for their weight can mean that they rush the move, throw themselves over the rescuer, or lift their head and legs up during the move. If they do this, they create a stiletto heel effect where their weight is given to the rescuer over a much smaller body area, thereby increasing the pressure on the rescuer. The only way to help the rescuer is to make as much contact as possible and move with the impetus they offer through the contact between back and front.

It is worth emphasising that we have thrown nothing away from the previous stages. We should not forget what we have learnt. We are just applying the same basic principles to more complex situations.

Step 3

This step is useful for all levels of ability. In Step 2 we can crank up the pace so that it becomes an intensive physical session. In Step 3 we have no choice. It is fast and furious.

Split the group up. If, for example, you have ten participants, split them up into two groups of five or groups of four and six (this will make it slightly easier; groups of five will be very hard work). The group of, say, four are now the victims. The group of six are the rescuers.

Take the group of six out of the space. Line them up and make them form a queue facing into the space. The group of four walk around the space and can randomly 'die', taking themselves to the floor and lying on their side. It is the task of the group of six, the 'rescuers', to storm into the space and rescue anyone dead on the floor as they did in Step 2. They are to spend as little time in the space as possible. The person at the front of the queue must do their duty and get out again to join the back of the queue, leaving a new person at the front of the line ready to go into action. As the victims choose to 'die' randomly it means that the rescuer at the front of the queue must be prepared to act quickly. Indeed the random nature means that it is possible for all the victims to 'die' at the same time, meaning that the first four rescuers in the line need to race in and save them and then race back to the queue. All through this it helps to shout, cheer, encourage, etc. from the sidelines. If you have a large group and therefore have spectators, have them roar at the 'savers' to react to the 'dying' and to get back out of the space as quickly as possible.

This can be an exhausting exercise. What we are looking for here is a commitment to the techniques already explored and mastered. If they start to panic, then it will all collapse. If they relax and don't think too much about it, then their contact can and usually does become much more fluid and dynamic. It is all a balancing act of technique, energy, adrenalin and confidence.

Step 4

Follow all this exertion up with a debrief session. It is very useful to ask whether people found it easier when they didn't have time to think about what they were doing or worry about being polite about where they are putting their hands! We often notice a marked improvement in the application of technique from this stage onwards. It should also be an opportunity to remind the participants of the simplicity of the route taken to this point, how they had to take little steps along the way. It is important to recognise these steps as time and time again that process of mastering bite-sized chunks will stand them in good stead.

Quad

This exercise is a Frantic favourite and is useful in getting people used to count structures. We are not sure where we picked it up. It is probably a generic theatre game, but we constantly adapt it to suit the groups we work with.

Firstly, the group should be placed in a grid formation or as close as possible to a grid in the event of having odd numbers. Everybody starts facing the same direction, which we shall call the 'front'. For the purposes of this book we shall imagine that there are 16 people, with 4 rows of 4.

Set a tempo by means of a music track or a simple count or rhythm and ask the front row to bounce on the spot eight times in unison. These should be small, light jumps with the shoulders and hands relaxed. The feet should be relaxed and we suggest that, when in the air, the feet should hang down towards the floor in a relaxed manner rather than tense and held with the toes pointing straight ahead. On the eighth count, the front row jump around through 180 degrees. We suggest that everyone turns in the same direction, e.g. clockwise. If all is correct, the front row should now be face to face with the second.

On the next 'one' count, the second row do the same thing, bouncing on the spot eight times, turning through 180 degrees on the eighth count. The third row pick up on the next count and repeat. When the count reaches the 'back' row, in this case the fourth row, they too take the next 'one' count and bounce on the spot eight times, turning clockwise through 180 degrees on the eighth count. As the back row they then continue, using the next 'one' count and bouncing on the spot, except that this time they turn back clockwise on the sixth count, at which point they are face to face with the third row. The third row copy and so on along to the front row who, after bouncing on the spot six times, will end up facing the 'front'. Using the next 'one' count, the first row then bounce for four counts before turning. This continues through the grid until it reaches the back row that then turns after just two counts. This moves through the grid to the front where the first row bounces twice before facing the front and immediately turning back on themselves after a count of just one. The other rows all follow.

Put simply, the group stand in grid formation and, using a simple bounce, turn after a count structure of 8, 6, 4, 2, and 1. This count structure could be adapted, e.g. 8, 7, 6, 5 or, for a more advanced group, something like 5, 3, 8, 3, 3, but we would suggest keeping it very simple to start with. Some of our most accomplished performers have fallen foul of what would seem to be the simple logic of this exercise. Even in using the basic count structure above, the group are still working with a complex rhythm, which is particularly apparent if using a music track in 4/4 time to accompany the exercise. At various points, the group will be counting 'across' the bars of the music, which always requires a little more focus.

Once the group seem to have the hang of the basic structure and counts, you might then introduce specific events on particular counts for the jumping group. One example might be to throw the right hand up into the air on the count of two. It is probably necessary to point out that this does not mean throwing the hand on every second count, only on the two itself. It is also important that this additional move should, like the feet, be relaxed; the hand should have weight in it and should feel like a hearty fling into the air before returning to the side, all within the single count.

Other events that might be thrown into the mix are a handclap, bringing the feet together while in mid-air on a given jump, or a shake of the head. You might even choose to bring in some vocal events. Putting the events on the same counts as the turns means that during the sequence, participants now have to manufacture a turn AND the prescribed event. This might influence the type of events you choose to add in.

An advanced version of this is an event for the standing groups. For example, on the count of 3, the 12 standing bodies are asked to sweep their right foot behind their left heel and then return to their standing position all within a single count. (Due to the visual nature of this event, we like to call it the 'Cat Litter Tray' move.)

In making the exercise more complicated, look out for shoulder tension in both the jumping and standing groups and also point out anyone clenching their fists. Often during this exercise you will witness the phenomenon of the body turning through a half turn and the head seeming to arrive a second later. This is not uncommon and we take it as a good signal that the body already has a rhythmic sense of the exercise and the head has yet to catch up.

(Note: We always suggest that all turns are made in the same direction, turning over either the left or the right shoulder. For some reason, the physical instinct seems to be to turn over one shoulder one way and then the other shoulder in order to return. In keeping it in the same shoulder, even the simple task of turning requires a little bit more thought and concentration.)

Feeling confident? As this exercise is all about building on success and pushing the participants further, many variations of Quad have emerged over time.

Different Frantic Assembly practitioners put various spins on it. Some of them change the turn from 180 degrees to 90 degrees. This means the side of the group becomes the front of the group for the next round of numbers and then passes that responsibility on to the people who started at the back. They then pass it on to the people who originally started at the other side of the quad.

One of our practitioners has even dispensed with the formality of the quad and has the group walking around the room for eight counts but on that eighth they have to jump and turn to face someone. Immediately they set off around the room, walking for six counts and on the sixth they, again, jump and turn to face someone else. This continues through the sequence. It is a short, sharp energetic sequence that tests concentration, focus, counting and spacial awareness. They have to read the movement in the room, keeping an eye on the direction of others, to ensure that they have someone to face on their final count (the 8 or 6 or 4 or 2 or 1).

Quad is one of those exercises that you can keep adding to as the performers master more and more complex tasks. You might find that the better they get, the more cluttered the choreography becomes as you try to give them something that will stretch them further. There might be another way of taking Quad forward that might just melt their brains for a little while and give them a new challenge.

Quad Negative!

Think of the basic Quad bouncing sequence. Strip it of all the embellishments, of moves on certain counts, etc. Think of it in negative. By that, we mean when the group have been still then they should now be bouncing. When they have been bouncing they are now the only ones who are still. That means that at the beginning the whole group, with the exception of the first row, will be bouncing for eight counts. The first row will be still until the eighth count when they jump and turn and pass on the stillness. The first row then jump, with everyone, apart from the second row, for eight counts. The second row remains still until the eighth count when they jump, turn and pass the stillness on.

This is a much more energetic version as everyone will spend by far the majority of their time bouncing and counting. In the original version you can sense the relief in a row when they have done their counting and have passed

Ankit Giri is lifted in rehearsals for *From Me To You, Ignition* (2013). Image by Helen Maybanks

the movement on. In this version there is no rest, as they will have to count throughout and turn on cue in the still moments.

Once (if) they master this you can go back to the embellishments. They will thank you, maybe even love you for this. (Probably not.)

What this presents is stillness as the focus. That stillness becomes powerful and that in itself is a useful lesson for students and performers. You can, of course, play with this stillness. Maybe instead of stillness it is a naturalistic conversation that just happens to exist over eight counts and ends on the eighth as they turn sharply to face the next group (who then burst into conversation). And play with the numerical sequence too. If the stillness or whatever you use is interesting then maybe it gets impossible to read it once you get down to turning on the two and one count. It is not a hard and fast rule that you stick to the 8, 6, 4, 2, 1 sequence. It is a suggestion. You can adapt accordingly.

Quad Jump

Like many of these exercises, Quad Jump can start simple and be taken a lot further. It works best with a group of 8–12 people. You could always split larger groups into two and have one group watch as it is fun to observe.

Consider the four corners of the room. Place all of your group in the bottom right corner. Number them, e.g. 1–12. The first person sets off from the bottom right corner running towards the bottom left. They turn sharply and head towards the top left corner (they are running around the room clockwise). At this corner they have to create a manoeuvre that accomplishes a sharp 90 degree turn to the right. They then move on to the top right corner. Again they have to negotiate a turn of your choice. Having done so they then head back to the group in the bottom right corner.

Here the group have assembled themselves into a rough horseshoe shape to welcome the runner. As the runner runs into them they are lifted by the group high into the air, held for a second then returned to the ground and the second runner sets off on the same route.

The key to the group lift is the runner thinking about pressing their weight down into the hands while also thinking about going up. The lifters need to know where they are going to place their hands and absorb the energy of the inbound runner and transfer that horizontal energy into a vertical thrust that lifts the runner high above their heads. They should lock their arms at this point and ensure the weight is evenly distributed through the group.

The runner needs to know that they are aiming to make contact with one person at the back of the horseshoe. They plant their hands on that person's shoulders and press down. When they are up their hands should still be pressing down completely vertically, sending their weight down the body of this person. This person has their hands on the front of the runner's shoulders. (You can build towards versions where the runner just balances when they are up above the group and they do not press their hands down on the person at the back of the horseshoe. It is crucially important that the supporter has a good connection with the runner, however.)

The runner has to help with the lift. They do this not by jumping but by sending their weight forward rather than up. As they lean forward they should lift one leg behind them. This allows part of the group to get hold of it. As soon as the runner feels this leg lift off the floor they need to press down into it to allow the other leg to lift. They also need to imagine their backs being lifted or pulled up to make sure they do not sag during the lift.

Once they have been held for a second they need to be safely let back down again, feet first. The group need to negotiate their way through this.

The person at the back of the horseshoe should change for every runner and they all need to keep alert to know which number runner is setting off and if they are next!

Start slow and steady, making sure everyone is confident and clear what is being asked of them. Warn against adrenalin taking over. Allow a couple of pedestrian rounds so that people can settle into it. As they do you can start to crank up the speed. Give them an exciting, pumping music track to help them. Things should improve quickly, but point out any tendency to jump or stall their momentum as they approach the lift-off moment.

There are a couple of ways to turn this into a more advanced exercise (and a much more exciting one too!).

Instead of waiting for the first runner to complete before the second runner sets off get the second runner to go when your first has reached the top left corner (the second base). This means that there are two runners at one time. This puts pressure on both runner and jumper to get it right and get it over with. The group must also organise themselves in such a way that someone who is crucial to the lift is not suddenly obliged to set off just as a runner is about to reach them! The group have to continually re-form and reorganise.

If your group are advanced and disciplined enough, you could turn the lift into a proper leap. The group still have to absorb the energy and translate it into a high lift. They have to be careful and adjust to the different forces exerted by different runners. The more confident and capable they are, the faster and further away the leap becomes. The dismount can be more choreographed too if you ask your group to find a route out of it that can serve the speed and precision of the whole Quad Jump task.

Clear the Space

This is a variation on what we are sure is a generic exercise that has been around for years. We include it here to show how we have morphed the exercise to fulfil the needs of a Frantic warm-up. This version has gone through many variations over the years and in some ways is at its best when used to respond to a space. The version here contains the most reliable elements we have found, but the simple nature of its form means that it is highly adaptable. We often use this exercise at the very start of a session in order to help participants get a sense of the room they are working in. It is also useful in breaking down physical inhibitions as the instructions come fairly rapidly, giving people no time to worry about contact with other bodies in the space!

We advise describing all of the instructions *before* starting this exercise in order to allow it to flow once begun.

Start the group off by asking them to simply walk around the space for a minute or so. Ask them to imagine that regular pedestrian speed is 100 per cent and, for the sake of this exercise, all walking is at 105 per cent. Even the simple task of walking has a little bit more energy involved, a little more intention. This helps to charge the room and raise physical awareness among the group as they negotiate their bodies in space. They should be asked to consider just what it means for this number of people to be moving in this particular space and at this particular speed. Once the group seem comfortable with this, start to throw in any number of the instructions listed below. At first, the rate of incidence should be kept fairly low, not least of all for the sake of safety, particularly if the room is quite small. Once the group show signs of confidence, increase the rate of the instructions to the point where some-times one instruction might not yet be complete before the next one is given. Allow each instruction to occur a couple of times before adding in another one. All instructions should be carried out as *quickly* as possible. Once each instruction is complete, say 'go' to signify a return to walking (which should be maintained at 105 per cent speed).

Clear the space: The whole group must move to the outsides of the room and place both hands on a wall surface. It might be necessary to limit this instruc-tion to certain sides of the room, for instance if one wall is all windows which might be open on a hot day!

Centre: Having established a centre point in the room for the group, they have to stand as close to one another as possible in the centre spot. Once in place, the group rest their head on whoever and whatever is nearest. It is important to point out the two-part nature of this instruction. The group need to come together as closely as possible *before* resting their head. The reverse might lead to some serious floor cleaning issues. Check that the group are respond-ing to a single 'centre' of the room. The collective huddle should not look like a string of people but one single 'blob', with no satellite groups hanging off.

Fold: Participants take themselves down to the floor in a fluid spiral motion and pull themselves into the foetal position, resting their head on the floor. For this, the group must make good use of the room and be aware of the proximity of each other. In simple terms, they should get themselves to the floor as quickly and efficiently as possible, taking care to avoid impacting the elbows and knees on the way down. Use the instruction 'Unfold' to get the group to reverse this and get them back to a standing position. In unfold-ing, participants should use the same idea of a spiralling motion that takes them from the floor to standing.

Look: Everyone stands completely still and looks directly into the eyes of any other member of the group. It does not matter if the gaze is not met. They should remain fixed in this way until another instruction is given.

Favourite: Ask each participant to choose a favourite part of the room. This should not be another person and needs to remain a constant. On hearing the instruction 'Favourite' they must come to a complete standstill and, using their right arm and first finger, point and look directly at their own favourite part of the room. Push for the response time on this particular instruction to be as sharp and fast as possible.

Person: On this instruction, each participant grabs the nearest person and pulls them into a hug. They should only embrace in pairs here, not least of all to provide an incentive not to be the one person who remains hug-less if the group are an odd number. In hugging their partner, each person should be seen to be pulling their partner's back in towards their own front and effectively squeezing the air out of the space between them. There should be no chance of seeing daylight between their bodies at all. They should also keep squeezing throughout, sensitising their fingertips, which should be pressed into the back of their partner. Don't let people off here. Make sure they commit fully to the hug. If you make sure they do the first one properly then, when the game speeds up, they will be doing it properly without thinking about it.

Stereo/Teacher: This instruction should make specific use of an element in the room – the LED display on stereo equipment or the eyes of a teacher who may be sat at the side of the room for instance. On hearing the appropriate instruction (we'll use 'Stereo' for this example), the entire group should run towards the element and sit together cross-legged as close as possible with all their eyes focused on the stereo. Like 'Fold', this instruction needs the group to pay particular attention to one another and the space provided by the room.

Once the group have a solid understanding of the different instructions and have a good, quick response time to each one, it is then possible to be creative with the order in which the instructions are given. One example is to give the instruction 'Fold' and then, once the group are in full contact with the floor, give the instruction 'Favourite'. In order to achieve the instruction with maximum economy they should not return to standing but shift from the foetal position and twist themselves into a position that allows them to see and point out their favourite part of the room. This added task of economy in following one instruction after another might also be exercised by following the instruction 'Stereo' with either 'Favourite' or 'Person' – a combination of all three in various orders is always a good finishing point.

Advanced versions of this game might involve the instruction 'Different Side Clear', which should only follow a 'Clear' command, at which point the entire group need to choose another wall to make contact with. This instruction sees the entire group pass through the space and requires some spatial negotiation. 'Different Person' works in much the same way, following a 'Person' command. To advance this instruction even further, there is the instruction after 'Different Person' to then return and find the person you were hugging just prior to the instruction. We have yet to give this instruction a permanent title. Any thoughts here are welcome via our website (www. franticassembly.co.uk/ p127.html).

This game should be both energetic and precise. Instructions such as 'Person' should be closely monitored to ensure that the group are committing to full body contact. The 'Person' instruction also works best if the group are an odd number. By stressing that the instruction means that people are only allowed to pair up, there should always be one person left out. Asking the group to make sure that they do not become the one left out is a good impetus for creating a room full of people desperate to grab hold of a body, any body! By stressing that nobody ought to be the one left out more than once, you only heighten this effect.

This game is a superb building block for team work and breaking down physical inhibitions. Often students can be quite uncomfortable about the prospect of the contact that may be required in a physical theatre session. Young men can be particularly uncomfortable about this and yet they will happily jump all over each other when one of them scores in injury time. This is the atmosphere you should be looking to tap into. Serenity and reverence might not be your best friends when trying to coax teenage boys to embrace. Our point is that it is all about context. They are not averse to the act. Just its connotations. The game should be rowdy and boisterous. It should be disarming. That way you will find you have a room of young students willing to hold and be held without anyone ever bringing it up as a problem.

Relays

We often include relays in our warm-ups with large groups. These can be simple shuttle runs to a point and back, handing over to the next person to do the same, or they can be more complicated.

The relays are very useful. Often when we are working with a large group for the first time, they can be nervous, apprehensive about what they are going to be doing. They might think that the session is going to be serious and exhausting. They might have all kinds of preconceptions about us, theatre, or physical theatre. The relays quickly introduce an element of fun. Once participants realise that fun is allowed they are generally much more relaxed.

The first relay

We always start with the simplest version. We split the group into teams. Getting them all to stand in a line and then going along the line numbering them 1, 2, 3, 4, 1, 2, 3, 4, etc. will provide four teams of number 1s, 2s, 3s and 4s. This also splits friends and same-sex groups up.

Place the groups at one end of the room and place an object (a book, a trainer, etc.) opposite each group at the other side of the room, leaving plenty of space from the wall.

Tell them this is a race, but most importantly lay out a couple of clear ground rules:

1 You must touch the object.
2 When you return you must touch RIGHT hands with the next person. This means that the person running back will always pass on the right side of the person setting off. It means there is little chance of confusion and collision when the adrenalin is pumping and everyone is desperate to win.
3 You should make as much noise as possible when cheering your team on.

Create a bit of tension before the 'go' moment. It should feel like pure play but there are important things happening here. The group are focused and are about to be energised. They are listening to you avidly and are following clear instructions to the letter. They are about to start thinking like a team. They are about to feel as though getting something right matters.

The second relay

Things are getting more complicated and more physically risky here. By now they are usually hooked and energised and really want to know how this relay will differ from the first. They will also want to make amends for a loss in the first round or keep up their winning record.

It is best to demonstrate this exercise. Walk it through with a group of volunteers.

1 The first runner sets off and touches the object at the other end of the room. They run back and offer their hand to the next person.
2 They hold hands and set off towards the object but the first person is now running backwards, leading the second. The second person must instruct the first (who is running backwards) that they are approaching the object. When they get to the object they must both touch it. This is what releases the second runner to head back to pick up the third. (The first stays down the other end of the room with the object.)
3 The second runner connects with the third and then runs backwards, leading the third across the room. As runner 2 heads backwards as quickly as possible without losing contact with their partner, the first runner, now waiting at the other end of the room, waits to safely guide the second runner 'home'. Anyone left by the object has to remain active and safely guide the backwards runner home.
4 The relay ends when the last person has been led to the object and the whole group run together back to the side they started on.

Again they need to encourage each other and create some noise but they also need to remain active and aware. They are all working as a team, pushing each other along but also making sure everyone is safe.

This relay is such a simple way to get a group working as a team without them having to think about it.

The third relay

If you ever need to break the ice, this exercise is great at addressing that reserve in a new group.

Make sure that the object you placed at the end of the room has plenty of space around it.

1 The first runner sets off down the room and runs *around* the object.
2 They head back and when they reach the next person, the first runner turns around, puts their right arm through their own legs and reaches for the left hand of the next runner.
3 They set off down the room as fast as they can, the first runner hunched over but leading the second.
4 They run around the object.
5 When they head back they need to turn around so that the second runner can put their right hand between their legs and reach for the left hand of the third runner.
6 The three of them set off again. Continue.

The group gets longer and more absurd. They are not allowed to break the chain. If they do, they must stop, link up and continue again. They also need to find a speed that suits the whole group – the first runner cannot just run around corners at their own pace as centrifugal force would send the people at the back through the walls.

The relay ends with the whole group going around the object and making it back to their starting place.

Another relay

If your room and floor surface will allow this, try another relay (it adapts the first relay but should be used in addition and should not replace it).

For this you need to make sure the group can all slide on the floor on their thighs. They need to put a hand down onto the floor and push their hips forward, sliding on their hip/thigh while pushing away from the hand they put on the floor. They need to make good contact with the floor and avoid dropping onto knees or shuffling on feet. You should be looking for a smooth downward curve towards the floor rather than a crunch of bone and dancefloor.

If this is in place, the relay then basically involves participants running towards the wall and sliding to the floor as they arrive there, using their feet to soften into the wall and push off in the opposite direction. It should give them the propulsion a swimmer looks for in their tumble turn. Apart from this it is the same as the first relay.

Relay slalom

This relay is advanced only insofar as it requires people to have a good, solid grasp of spatial awareness in order to eliminate risk.

The initial set-up follows that of the first relay with the teams numbered in one corner of the room and an object some distance from the wall in the opposite corner. By number, each individual runs at a regular speed across the room, around the far object and returns to tag the right hand of the next runner as specified earlier. It might be necessary to point out the importance of efficient cornering around the end object, leaning into and over the object rather than out and away, to increase efficiency and time.

From here, a second object is placed to the far left of the room, about a third of the way along the route, and a further object to the far right, two-thirds of the way down. This time, each person should set off from the corner and run over to the far left object, passing along the outside. They then move across the space to pass along the right-hand side of the object placed two-thirds down the room on the right. To complete the slalom they then run towards the original object in the opposite corner, passing along the left-hand side of the object and around it before running straight up through the middle of the room to tag the next person.

An advanced version of this sees participants running down through the space at a regular speed and then returning up through the middle at a sprinting speed, i.e. as fast as possible.

A further version (and the one that calls on good powers of spatial awareness) is where, after the first person has set off and passed the second of the three objects down the slalom trail, number two sets off. Runner 3 sets off as runner 2 passes the second object and so on. This creates a sweeping field of running subjects, some moving at regular running speed and others at full sprint. It is a great exercise in testing the response time of a group operating at speed. Further versions might involve more slalom objects along the length of the diagonal or people setting off at even shorter intervals one after another for a really invigorating field of runners.

chapter four

Choreography

What we mean by 'choreography'

By choreography we mean any formalised movements that become set and can be repeated. This can be the dynamic and spectacular or it could be the minute and precise. It can be explosive and it can be introspective. We will not go into notation here (we film everything anyway) as what is important is the process behind the genesis of the choreography, not the choreography itself.

When we have visited schools, colleges and universities, or even when we have been talking to fledgling devising companies, the same question about creating choreography comes up. How do you get started? After further discussion we have usually found that people are overcomplicating their attempts to make choreography. They are often bogged down in attaching meaning to moves. This can make the creative process unbearably heavy. If you approach making choreography this way, you might find the process impossible.

This chapter aims to demystify the creative process. Each exercise tries to be as simple as possible and you will notice that meaning is hardly ever addressed. If it is, it is always at the end of the process and emerges through directorial manipulation. Our hope is that, as meaning is separated from process, you can take the process on to create choreography for new and different contexts.

Stopping Points and Connections

This building exercise was employed in the early days of the tenth anniversary revival of *Hymns*. It can be easily translated for your own needs.

The four performers were asked to pair up in the space. They were asked to move around a most basic set of randomly placed chairs. They could sit or stand or move in any way but they had to take the impulse for their starting points and finishing points from their partner's movements. What you have is performers listening closely to each other, using their peripheral vision to key into the quality and timing of their partner's moves. At no time do they mimic or mirror the actual physical movements of another performer. It is only the quality and timing of the moves that connect the partners. Both sets of partners share the space but never become aware of the other pair. What appears is a scene of four individuals whose physicality or body language is subconsciously connected. As one person moves, another might connect with them and move as if being pushed or pulled across the space. They do not touch but there appears to be a clear connection across the space between them. The small movement of a person's arm may appear to be connected to the completely different move of another person. It is important that they don't do identical moves but just try to discover moves that have a similar quality and dynamic. Very quickly little stories and connections appear and disappear like fireworks. It is very important to note this effect as already you may have found a key to telling complex stories through physical suggestion and not words.

This was a crucial stage in the development of the performers. They needed to get a sense of the potential economy of physical storytelling. By storytelling we mean the visual presentation of a complex emotional situation through simple physicality. The story at this stage is very much in the eye of the beholder and is an early example of how important the role of the audience is when we make our work.

As a result of this the performer learns to avoid the temptation to 'tell' the story with their moves, to only do sad or frustrated moves to show sadness and frustration. It is only your audience at this stage who are reading any story; the performers are simply committing to a physical task and are not trying to tell a story. Even when we get to that stage, we might find out that the character's understanding of the context may be completely different from that of the audience. It is a reminder that 'theatre' may well be what happens when performance meets the audience. Does it really exist without their consideration? Remember that the sadness of a scene may truly lie in the audience's reaction, in their judging it to be a sad situation. For example, a character who feels there is no hope when the audience knows there is none is sad. A character who feels hope when the audience knows there is none is utterly tragic.

We wanted to move on very quickly from here but we identified that if the performers were not to capture this quality of communication, then we would never be able to work at the rate we felt we needed to. As it turned out, the exercise can be made much more complex before the need to move on. This simple exercise may suggest a situation where the physicality of four performers would scream a whole spectrum of desires, needs, grievances without ever saying a word. As this was only an exercise and did not directly become a scene, it served to instruct the performers of the importance of body language in our work. It quickly unearthed an incredibly rich subtext.

It is very important not to think that we like to throw out deliberately obscure work towards our audience on the understanding that they will make something of it and that 'everyone will have a different interpretation anyway'. This might be a valid approach for some practitioners, but it is not a theory that we sign up to. Through our use of physicality and movement we found we are always inviting and guiding the audience towards our preferred conclusion. We don't have to spell it out for them in every action. We realised that it was so important to engage the audience and not just present what we feel they need to understand. This can feel like being battered around the head for an audience. We always try to imagine what will bring our audience forward in their chairs, what will send them reeling backwards. What is it that animates and activates our audience? In fine art terms, we are Impressionists rather than Surrealists. The Impressionist uses a variety of colours and textures to elicit an almost emotional response from the viewer but always guides the viewer towards an understanding of what is being presented, e.g. through the title.

> Try to make Monsieur Pissarro understand that trees are not violet; that the sky is not the colour of fresh butter … and that no human being could countenance such aberrations … Try to explain to Monsieur Renoir that a woman's torso is not a mass of decomposing flesh with those purplish-green stains.
>
> (Albert Wolff, art critic, *Vigztoon* 1876)

It was at this stage that we started to harness the potential of the exercise and move towards its possible use in performance. The exercise was carefully moved closer to the theatrical context of *Hymns*; of four men contemplating the loss of a friend and desperately wanting to say the right thing. The stillness of the physicality was now informed by the context; the subtext remained rich and full of possibilities; the performers were now clearly characters, complex in their silence. We found with this exercise that what the characters don't say is what they need to say and that the audience plays a crucial role in articulating the unsaid.

It was vital not to rush this transition from what can be considered 'play' into 'work'. It is worth noting that the temptation when working on your first section of a production is to 'solve' it rather than open out possibilities. The subtle blending of 'play' and 'work' liberates the performer from this expectation and allows them to explore freely while the director/outside eye helps collate and store all of this new information.

This exercise was very useful for the performance style that dominated *Hymns* but it serves as a much more general exercise too. Sometimes our attempts at naturalism can smother the more subtle body language. This exercise creates a dance out of that unconscious body language, revealing what we are screaming from the inside, and it is really important for us not to bury that physicality under extraneous movement. It serves to remind the performers that they are responsible for every move they make, that every move they make has a reaction or impact upon someone else, that a well-trained audience eye is looking keenly for the story beneath the surface. Within *Hymns* it meant that every moment on stage was considered. Moments are held. Physicality is awkward. It gives the impression of people physically and emotionally holding back.

'Listening' to each other physically

At every stage of working together we ask performers and students to listen to each other physically. We call it 'listening' but it is actually the use of peripheral vision, sensitivity to touch and just learning to communicate non-verbally with your fellow performers. This is the building block for all our physical work.

Round/By/Through

This exercise asks participants to create a string of material that has them moving all about and through their partner. It is simple and requires fluidity and balance. The words 'Round', 'By' and 'Through' are there to assist this process in that they offer a physical vocabulary to get started with and can be referred to if the couple (or three) become stuck or begin to over-complicate things.

This is one of a series of exercises that are useful in the initial stages of developing movement skills and material. As such, it should be considered in terms of providing a series of building blocks, both as a principle and as a practice. As a group of exercises they share a common principle, which is that, for the most part, they should be attempted as neutrally as possible. This means that they should only be infused with emotional meaning or character or relevant performance instinct towards the end. In this way, we keep the exercise open to possibilities. With exercises like this it is also useful to keep the end point out of sight and hopefully prevent performers falling into known patterns of physical behaviour. (By this we mean dance practices just as much as physical character practices – individuals should be equally discouraged from imbuing this exercise with flashes of contemporary dance styles as much as anybody demonstrating their 'person in lust' physicality.) The exercise works best in pairs but is also possible for groups of three. With this exercise it is entirely possible to have the start of a fairly complex looking duet up and on its feet within 20 minutes.

The partners stand opposite one another and choose A and B status. A is then given the task of changing the physical and spatial configuration between the two using any one of the instructions 'Round', 'By' or 'Through'.

The term 'Round' here is chosen to represent any move that involves passing closely around the body of the partner. From this initial position, using around as the principle for movement, A might move around B to a point where they are now back to back or where A's front is pressed into B's back or A is standing with their front pressed in at 90 degrees to B's shoulder. 'Round' will normally involve some form of rotation in the hips of the person moving and normally some degree of circular movement around the partner, however small.

'By' is a term that comes into effect as a consequence of the actions 'Round' and 'Through' where either one of these two actions has created a space between the two partners. 'By' is the means by which the space that exists between the two is constantly reduced to as small a space as possible. Partners are encouraged to squeeze the air out from between their bodies during this exercise, to work in close proximity. This proximity should be considered at all times and should never be so close that it inhibits natural or free movement. 'By' should feel like a 'slotting in' move that is neat and efficient, a linking device to produce flow and possibility between the moves being created.

'Through' is the idea of passing through the partner and for the most part should be confined to the use of the upper body and arms. (More advanced groups might try using the lower body and be particularly vigilant in avoiding stock physicality.) A simple example of 'Through' would be for A to start off by using first their fingertips to make contact with the inner elbow of B and create space between B's ribcage and arm. This creation of space should be as economical as possible, with just enough room being made for A to pass their body through. For their part, B should neither help nor hinder this moment. A should be able to feel the full weight of B's arm in attempting this part of the exercise. The variety to be found here lies in the various ways in which A might pass through the space created by B's body – whether the fingers and hand continue to be the first body parts to pass through this newly

THE FRANTIC ASSEMBLY BOOK OF DEVISING THEATRE

made space or whether it is another body part such as the back of the right hip that passes through, creating a sense of A's body 'reversing' into the allocated space. Other points to pass through first might be the shoulders or the back of the neck. Rolling the outer hip in towards the partner when passing through is a very different dynamic from when the body rolls the same hip out and away from the partner. With confidence, it might be that the creation of the space on B's body is not initiated by the fingertips but by the elbow or the shoulder or forearm. Again, it is important that the partner gives full weight to the body part being acted upon. In the event of A moving 'Through', B should also be seen to close down the space created by A as soon as possible, i.e. as soon as that space is no longer needed or useful.

As a structure, we would usually ask the pairs to create a string of material involving between 12 and 16 moments, with the responsibility for movement switching between the two partners. In the instance of A having created the first three moments, B would then start from the configuration point that the pair find themselves in at the end of those first three moments. In this sense, the exercise is a cumulative one. Be on the look-out for 'shifts', which is where, at the end of A's sequence, one or both of the pair shift themselves, sometimes very slightly, into a position that feels more comfortable as a starting point. It is important to point out that this is unnecessary and to encourage the participants to use whatever they are given as their starting point.

Once the string has been created, an important next step is to consider the entire sequence as one arc of events. Usually, due to the way in which this material has been created, when running the string there will be pauses (sometimes very small, sometimes not) at the points where the responsibility for movement switches from one partner to another. These moments halt the flow of the string and it takes particular focus and attention to remove these pauses and create a string that has a beginning and an end rather than three or four observable 'chunks'. This part of the exercise is important in understanding the flow involved in the transfer of energy and responsibility in both a visual and a physical sense.

Throughout this part of the exercise, it is important to remind the pairs not to imbue the material with intention at this stage. It is very easy, even at the first stages of this exercise, for the material to seem either 'fighty' (hands heavy, bodies seemingly flung into configurations suggesting aggression) or 'dancy' (hands floating delicately around the partner without making real contact or involving any true weight). Both of these types of event should be avoided.

The next step is to play with intention. One way for us came out of rehearsals for *pool (no water)*. During a development period, Mark Ravenhill observed us creating 'Round/By/Through' strings and then, in pairs, gave us slips of paper showing different ways in which to present the material. These pieces of paper contained words such as 'educate', 'protect', 'forget', 'insist', 'inspire', 'amuse', 'regret', etc. Adding this element is a great tool for starting to understand the communicative nature of movement. The observing participants were asked to guess what the informing word was and in most cases the group were correct or close without the rendition being ridiculously overt. It also asks the performers to bring into play their interpretative skills when performing movement – a delicate first step along the essential path of creating movement that has meaning.

The eventual scene we created never made it into the final version of *pool (no water)* but involved one of the performers (A) being acted upon by not one but three others (B's) who were all 'Round/By/Through'-ing at the same time, examining the 'patient' with inquisitive detail that became more and more intrusive. For this version, the patient remained pedestrian throughout. This development created some fascinating physical opportunities between the three B's, who often used the end of another B's interactive moment as the start of their own. This exercise requires an A that is physically very responsive and doesn't mind being pulled around the room for a couple of hours in a way that is far from hospitable.

Round/By/Through is one of the most important building blocks we use when creating contact work. It can be the first solid step towards much more complex choreography.

By squeezing the space from the string of material you have created you are introducing so many moments of touch. These moments are opportunities for communication, as demonstrated in Push Hands. That is why Push Hands and Round/By/Through are such useful building blocks. They are solid and secure in themselves but are also brilliant steps towards the much more complex. And as stated before, when the complex breaks down (as it will do) you can quickly refer to the simplicity and clarity of these exercises.

As the space gets squeezed and more opportunity for communication occurs, partners can find themselves sending signals about where and how they want their partner to move. This occurs through the touch. That friction also become the start of a lift. A partner finds themself in the right position to take the weight and the other feels secure to give the weight. Quickly Round/By/Through is presenting opportunities for lifting that feels natural, safe and (God, we hate this word in this context!) organic.

Sign Describe

We developed this exercise through working with Graeae Theatre Company, who are notable for their work with disabled actors. We collaborated with them on the production *On Blindness*, which featured a cast of six performers. Among the company there was one blind actor and one deaf actor. As part of the rehearsal process we were all given extensive training in British Sign Language (BSL) as a means of communicating with one another. For a company obsessed with physical means of communication it was an intense and invigorating period. For a start there was the practical procedure of there only being one person able to speak in the room at any one time so as to allow the interpreters to be able to fulfil their role effectively. It is only in circumstances like this that we come to understand the nature of a Frantic rehearsal room, which often involves multi-narrative events all over the room. At times this new mode of operation felt like a restriction and on other days it felt like the most focused process we had ever enjoyed.

As part of creating a way in which we might all communicate effectively, Jenny Sealey, Artistic Director with Graeae, ran an exercise on day one, which involved us creating a sign name for ourselves, which would then be used by the rest of the company. Jenny explained that it should conform to the standards of BSL, which meant that the sign name should involve the hands, and operate in a TV-sized space in front of the chest and stomach area. We were encouraged to 'make up' our own sign language, the focus of the exercise being to create a physical gesture that matched the individual. This gesture could be representative of a physical characteristic or gestural trait, a physical habit or even the way we felt that particular morning (more on this later). This creative licence became pivotal in us creating a system that allowed us all to connect over the rehearsals and beyond, into the performance itself and then further into our social modes of communication while touring. (There was something very refreshing about being part of a full company that were able to sign effectively with each other in even the noisiest of environments – our voices during that tour were on spectacularly fine form if our memory serves ...)

The following was developed from this period and is a great exercise in asking participants to physically 'get stuck in' to one another. In this way it is often used by us when encountering a new group for the first time – setting a strict task that forces the individual to explore another body in some detail. As with any exercise of this kind, observing the group is important and more often than not we impose quite a short time period within which the task must be achieved.

Split the group into pairs, with each pair assigning themselves an A and B status. For the next few minutes, A is to remain standing and should neither resist nor help B in their task. They should stand with their feet hip width apart in a comfortable stance with their hands relaxed at their sides and their eyes open throughout.

B has the task of discovering something about A that A probably doesn't know about themselves. In order to achieve this they are to examine the body using three categories.

Visual evidence

Using the eyes, B scans A's entire visible body, paying particular attention to the parts of A's body that A has probably never seen, e.g. back of the neck, behind the ears, behind the upper arm. They should also take in every part of skin that is visible, looking for distinct markings, blemishes, birthmarks, colourings and shadings. The visual examination should be thorough, checking minute detail such as eyes, hairline, earlobes, cuticles, inner elbows, etc.

Frame

B examines the body using their hands, paying particular attention to the frame of A. This might be shoulders, elbows, knees, ankles, hips – in short, any part of the skeleton – to check for any idiosyncratic details such as knobbles, bumps, lumps and smoothness.

Measurements

B takes measurements of A's body but not in any metric or imperial sense. Instead they measure A in relation to themselves. This might be with identical body parts, creating a direct comparison, e.g. whether A has a larger hand span than B. Alternatively, and perhaps more interesting, this might involve different body parts, e.g. measuring the width of the back of A in relation to B's hand span or the distance between A's eyebrows in relation to the digits of B's index finger.

We normally find it useful to place a time limit on this task, usually between two and three minutes, during which time B has to discover as many 'facts' about A as possible using all three methods of examination in the time allotted. At no point do they give any signal to A as to what it is they have discovered. At the end of the two or three minutes (usually a music track), the roles are reversed and A now attempts to make discoveries about B. By making the time short, participants are pressed into action and should consider the body of their partner as an object that has to yield as many secrets as possible in a very short space of time.

Once this stage has been completed, each participant is asked to choose just one of the 'facts' that they have discovered about their partner. In having several to choose from, A's and B's should be encouraged to choose the detail that the partner is unlikely to know about themselves. From this 'fact' each then needs to create a simple grammatical sentence in their heads that relays this fact, e.g. 'A's back is the same width as three of my [B's] hand spans'. Once this sentence is clear in the mind, everyone should then create a gestural string to represent this sentence.

The gestural string should operate in the same way as BSL – that is, using the hands as a means of communicating and spatially working within the TV-sized space in front of the chest area. Note that, like BSL, the string need only communicate the essential details. Given a sentence like 'A's back is the same width as three of my hand spans', the words 'is', 'the', 'as' and 'of' would not be translated. In this way, the string is truly economical in the information that it seeks to convey. In our case, in the absence of knowing what the exact sign language was, Jenny Sealey always encouraged us to be inventive and attempt what we might imagine the sign to be for any word that challenged us, on the understanding that this in itself would, more often than not, convey meaning, even if not entirely accurately. With this exercise, it is important to encourage inventiveness. It is not an exercise in seeing how close we might be to actual BSL or any other form of signing. Again, we often place a time limit on this part of the exercise of two to three minutes. This should be an instinctive, reflective part of the exercise using physical intuition. We usually suggest that it is important only that the string makes true sense to the individual.

The basic version of this exercise culminates in the group then demonstrating their findings to one another. This can be done in a variety of ways. We normally form a circle with the pairs standing beside one another. They start by individually running through their gestural string, communicating the physical information to the rest of the group. They then tell the group verbally what it is they found, speaking aloud the sentence they constructed upon which the gestural string was based.

The advanced version is a first step in tackling the difficult challenge of combining text and movement. A runs through the gestural sequence alone, communicating the physical information to the entire group. They then repeat the gestural string, except this time they also speak the sentence at the same time. Both the gestural string and the spoken sentence should run alongside one another, starting and finishing at the same time.

The very simple task of effectively combining text and movement is often the undoing of many a budding physical theatre performer. By 'effective' it is probably important for us to define what it is we wish to avoid. In many circumstances (and, unfortunately, in many public performances) the collision between text and movement results in a scenario where the movement does have quite an agreeable and logical flow, but as a consequence, the rhythm of the sentence somehow becomes tied to that of the movement, producing what we call 'physical theatre speak'. This is when the natural rhythms of any given sentence are suddenly lost and instead the line or lines adopt a broken, irregular sound with odd stresses, falterings and hesitancies. Of course this is the only possible outcome when the rhythm of the sentence is being dictated by that of the movement. For us, this 'making strange' of language is highly undesirable. The natural rhythms and cadences of language are what we aspire to so that the spoken and physical languages truly coexist in tandem alongside one another in what one might call harmony.

This is not a simple task at all and as a company we have spent years and years wrestling with this challenge. Even a simple sentence like 'A's back is the same width as three of my hand spans' can come undone quite spectacularly when run alongside what is also a simple gestural sentence. For the above exercise, we ask that the verbal and gestural run alongside one another, each unaffected by the other in terms of rhythm, with nothing 'made strange'.

Sign Describe is a great exercise for bypassing the common fears of physical contact among a group. The task should be brisk, lively and light. Music tracks used here should also embody these qualities. Pushing the task element can often be the key to the success of this exercise. What often results are fantastic, detailed insights into one another, new information revealed and startling personal discoveries. Pleasure is often found not only in the observations made but also in the gestural ways in which people choose to represent their findings.

Name Circle and Sign Name Circle

An offshoot of this exercise has been our adaptation of an old, well-worn theatre game. Name Circle has probably had a variety of different names for the numerous groups that have used it over the years. In it, the company stand in a circle facing inwards. One member makes eye contact with another member of the group and begins to walk across the circle in a straight line towards them, maintaining eye contact. The person on the receiving end of this has to name the person striding towards them. The receiver then establishes eye contact with a different person in the circle and starts walking towards them. And so on. In our workshops this is then built up to the point where people run as fast as they can and shout the names as loud as they can. In this case there is more than one runner which means that people have to be incredibly alert and responsive. It also very quickly energises the group involved.

Our further spin on this is to establish sign names for each company or group member so that it is not the name of the individual that is called out but instead the person on the end of the eye contact gives back the person's sign name. By sign name, we mean a short gestural action that has been created in place of a verbal name. Like Sign Describe, this was inspired by findings during rehearsals for *On Blindness*. On day one Jenny Sealey, as Artistic Director for Graeae, set up a session where we all created a sign name for ourselves so that we might communicate with one another. This sign name was to conform to the conventions of BSL in that it involves the use of the hands and operates in a space in front of the chest area. Jenny suggested that we made our sign name personal to ourselves but within that there was total freedom as to what that might take the form of. It might be the way one was feeling that morning; it might be a physical characteristic or trait you are known for; it might be a representative action of your behaviour. We were encouraged to be creative and true to ourselves. To be creative meant that we were not pulled into the dark world of mime and the need to be true meant that it didn't have to be anything too elaborate. Each sign name should last only a few seconds and be clear, concise and repeatable.

Learning every sign name in the circle takes some time and every participant should be looking to emulate and copy the sign name in all its glory – this means not just getting the left and right details correct but also looking for rhythm, weight, momentum and details. We would normally treat this part of the exercise like a building block exercise, i.e. learn three or four and then go to the first person and run through them all before introducing another three or four. With each participant, once they have physically demonstrated their sign name and the group have a good grasp of it, ask the participant to say why they created the sign name that they did. This is also a useful way for people to remember every sign name once the exercise starts and begins to build momentum.

Like the traditional version, start the game at a slow, pedestrian pace as the group get used to responding to one another in this physical way. Once the group get the hang of it, encourage them to jog across the space and then build up to a running speed. It is also useful to introduce the idea that the person being approached does not have to wait for the incoming person to be at their side before they themselves set off. As soon as they realise the correct response, they should set off into the space. The result of this is that the sign name they offer is an action that happens on the move. This is an interesting dynamic to observe.

If the group are confident working at full speed, then introduce a second person into the game. By this we mean that at any one time there are two people establishing eye contact and travelling across the space. This requires the group to make good use of their peripheral vision, as there is now double the rate of incidence and twice as many bodies crossing the same space at speed. In this version there is a strong chance, particularly with smaller numbers, that at times two people will find themselves converging on one individual. In this instance it is the responsibility of the two runners to recognise this and for one of them to switch their eye contact to another member of the circle at the last minute. This also requires the rest of the group to be extra alert too, in case they become a sudden choice by one of the two runners.

A development of this game is to introduce the spoken name along with the sign name. In this way, the game becomes a very, very simple exercise in combining words and movement. Any of the above versions are particularly useful when working with teams who are completely new to one another. It is surprising how often we have taught this exercise to university students four or five months into their course who have no idea what some of their fellow students are called.

Ways into Unison

Unison movement is fraught with dangers ranging from the creative process to the final performance. The results can be impressive but if it is not absolutely nailed it can be a law of diminishing returns as presenting unison movement does an interesting and potentially damaging thing to an audience. It trains them to find faults.

They do not mean to be critical but it is an inescapable fact that when presented with unison the eye will automatically be drawn to any moment of variation. The brain is not continually saying 'identical, identical, identical' but it will say 'different, different, different' every time it spots the tiniest variation. This does not happen with canon.

If you are working with groups of young students (or even professional performers) this ultra-critical audience could be the least of your worries. The process itself can be torturous and can test patience to breaking point.

If you are feeling brave and confident you can wow your audience with unison then below are some pitfalls and maybe a few tips to get you and your team through the process and remain friends. The examples are all based on a room where you have your group split into smaller teams teaching each other small strings of their own work to create a larger string of unison work.

The mirror effect

Not all rooms have a mirror and where they do we have mostly shunned them. They can make people very self-conscious and this can be counterproductive. You can also spend most of your time trying to break the mesmerised gaze of the vain or curious. You can often see performers craning their necks, mid move, for a glimpse of themselves as they fly through the air. This should obviously be discouraged!

The mirror could be a very useful tool in unison but only if the movement requires you to be facing it throughout. The presence of the mirror might actually shape your movement towards it, limiting its potential considerably.

Mirroring

Be very careful about how groups try to teach each other their strings of material. Many will make the very simple mistake of turning to face each other to teach and learn. This comes from generosity and a dash of naivety. What this invariably leads to is at least one member of the group mirroring the leader. It feels like they are doing the same thing but they are actually using the opposite side of their body.

They just need to be patient and turn away from the rest of the group and be prepared to repeat and answer questions about the important details. Which leads to...

Group tensions

This can be a frustrating process. Not everyone is a great teacher. Not everyone is good at remembering their moves precisely and enacting them consistently for others to copy. Not everyone learns at the same rate. Watch out for the tension before it erupts. Clearly state that this is a slow and meticulous process that requires patience and a group mentality. It might be worth laying down some useful ground rules.

Who is the leader?

As your group practice their moves you might see the more confident ones drive the movement on at a frenetic pace, leaving the others behind. You may also see the hesitant ones dragging the group down. They might have their moves down but what will hold it together as unison? Often they may perform it as a group and merely hope for the best, hoping that it might look like unison from the outside.

There is a very simple exercise that can help clarify things. Everyone can see when the unison is not working. For a moment, get the group to forget about the choreography they are struggling to perform together. Place them in a clump, not a line, with a bit of space between each other and stand in front of them, facing the same way. Get them all to use their peripheral vision to watch and follow you as you simply raise your right arm. Chances are all of them will raise their arm in time. Move it around and they will probably match you with the same precision.

What you are setting up here is the sending and receiving of signals. It might seem so obvious being stated like this but groups so often forget this communication while attempting unison. They have to really look out for the movement of each other. Similarly, you have to treat your own movement as a clear signal to the others.

Now you can address the problem of the fear of being at the front. Often people will find themselves at the front and keep looking back to see if everyone is in time with them. This does not help anyone. If the leader knows their material then the rest of the group need clarity and conviction from them, not hesitancy. Being in the front can feel like the scary place to be, like you are responsible for everyone else. The opposite is true. The front is the easiest place to be because your only responsibility is to set the pace and be clear. You should just move with the clarity that you have just demonstrated and the others can take their timing from you with confidence. But what happens when the group turns around and you are no longer at the front?

You might have noticed people at the back of the group moving faster than those at the front. This needs to be addressed. Stand in front of the group as before and clearly move your arm. The rest will follow in unison. Now turn to your right. You will find that you are not at the front of the clump any more. The new person at the front, who was behind and to the right of you, is now the leader. They should continue the freestyle movement with the same single responsibility as when you demonstrated from the front. This should not be a demonstration of passing the pressure. It should be a demonstration of how being at the front is actually liberating and how, if everyone is looking for the signals, unison can be easy.

The new leader can pass this on by turning to their left or right and another person will find that they are at the front.

So how do you know if you are at the front? How do you know if you are in control? The simple but important answer is if you cannot see anyone else then *you* are in control. If you can see someone else and they probably cannot see you then you should not dictate the pace. The pace HAS to be dictated by the person who cannot see the rest of the group. They need to realise that the rest of the group need them to push the pace on. If they do then the others can follow easily.

Simply, if you can see someone then follow them. If you cannot then you are the leader so push on with conviction!

Build up slowly

Now that we have sorted that out you will want to make sure the group does not run before it can walk. All of the little rules above need to click together before you can really fly with the unison. Always progress as a group. Make every moment about communication. Send the signal. Receive the signal. Don't forget these simple things as you speed up.

What next?

It is worth remembering that the first problem with unison still exists. The audience cannot help noticing flaws.

Now that you have your material you can test and play with it in all kinds of ways. Play with canon, or get the group to start separately and randomly.

Slow it down. Reconfigure the group. Try it as a duet with them facing different ways or differing speeds. Try it sitting down. Try it lying down. Film it to see what happy accidents emerge. This might throw up something that looks much more complex. Choreograph it again to capture these accidents.

Just because you have invested so much time and energy into the unison does not mean that you are stuck with it. We often rehearse in unison before breaking it up. It helps attain a unity of quality and helps build the communicative powers of the performers. It is an extremely useful tool to create work but it is a dangerous quality to attempt to perform.

MOVEMENT FOR NON-DANCERS/CHOREOGRAPHY THAT DOESN'T FEEL LIKE DANCE

Listed here are several task-based exercises that result in the creation of choreographed movement sequences without the group having to understand any of the basic tenets of choreography. Instead they take the form of tasks. By following a step-by-step approach, the cumulative effect is unapologetically choreographic without the participants having to think choreographically.

Chair Duets

This devising process keeps a large group busy with a fairly simple task. It is similar to and inspired by Hymns Hands (covered later and moving a little bit further into advanced territory) but is a group scene and captures a frenetic energy that, under your manipulation, can be comic and ultimately quite sad.

Chair Duets presents a very physical scene of touches, embraces, flirtations, rejections all played at a quite mesmerising speed. We have presented it as a sofa in a house that has seen the changing partners of all the people who have lived there. For it to work best we have found that it pays to withhold this information, this context, as it gets in the way of the participants achieving the speed this scene requires. If the task for them is just to achieve the choreography as fast and cleanly as they can, they will not get bogged down in acting the context. And they will need to know the moves extremely well to be able to take on the context later.

This works best with even numbers. Split your participants into groups of two and ask them to take chairs and find a space in the room where both chairs can sit side by side.

Try demonstrating the basic principle behind this. Two people sit on ordinary plastic or wooden chairs. They both face the front and remain seated. One of the partners is instructed to place a hand on the other. They can place this anywhere but the action must be firm and deliberate. (It is best to start simply so encourage them to use their partner's thighs and shoulders.) They should create approximately three moves, placing their own hands or moving the hands of their partner. They may choose to place these hands on themselves, their thighs, shoulders, knees, around their neck, or they may choose to place their partner's hands somewhere on the partner's own body. This might also include pushing their partner's torso forward or pulling them back into the chair. Once they have done this they remain in their final position and the other partner takes over. The same rules apply and then the original partner carries it on from the last position.

It is important to keep this simple and to make tiny, bite-sized chunks because they need to remember them and link them all together. It is also crucial to be on the look-out for a story being acted out. By that we mean look out for any attitude in the moves. Are they frustrated or flirtatious? Are they angry or petulant? Participants will generally try to give you more than you have asked for and more than you need. Remind them about the clarity of the task and the need to avoid *any* story.

Limit the couples to between 12 and 20 moves. (They can do more but it will impact on the overall running time of the final piece.) They should aim to achieve a smoothness in the transition of the hands and the transition between the partner that was leading and the partner that is taking over.

Now get the participants to keep practising this but avert their eyes from each other. Make them look out ahead and keep looking ahead. They need to remember these moves physically rather than visually.

Once they have grasped this and their moves are clean, fluid and fast, it is time to share the simple context. Tell them that what they are both looking out at is a television and they are both sitting on a sofa. They never take their eyes off the television and are oblivious to the touch and touching of their partners.

You can use a sofa but we stipulated chairs as we thought you were more likely to have them and it meant that everyone could rehearse at the same time. If you have a sofa, you could move the final piece to it once you have rehearsed on chairs. The advantage of making the work on chairs and not talking about the context is that you now have a very edgy and precise choreography to play with. This will contrast effectively with the lazy context. If you had placed your performers on the sofa and explained the couch potato context, then you might have had a job creating anything other than lazy choreography. Their physicality would have been the same as the context and would have effectively been saying the same thing twice.

You can run each pair's work to see how effectively they are managing to keep up the sharp physicality of the hands while still maintaining the couch potato physicality of the rest of the body and the focus on the television. It may take some rehearsing to achieve the mesmerising speed that is required.

To turn this into a group scene there are two ways to proceed.

First, number each pair and place everybody in a line so that the person in the left chair of couple 1 is next to the person in the right chair of couple 2. The person in the left chair of couple 2 is next to the person in the right chair of couple 3. Basically they are all in one line with no spaces between them. You are now going to work on the links that will turn this group of individual scenes into one piece of group choreography.

The person in the left chair of group 1 takes the person in the right chair of group 2 and makes a small version with them using the same techniques and focus as before. (It does not matter that they now know the context as they have been trained and know and have achieved the quality we are looking for.) Now that everyone has a new partner, pair up the remaining couple. This will be the person in the first chair at one end and the person in the last chair at the other. It is their new section that will allow the completed scene to loop if you want it to. If not, you can finish it with this new couple.

Once this stage is complete clear the room of all but one pair of chairs. These are the only chairs used in the scene. Everyone, apart from the first couple, is split into two groups – one in each wing. (For clarity, let's call the first couple group 1 and those in the wings groups 2 and 3.) Place group 1 in the chairs and get them to run their routine. Once complete the first person from group 2 runs on from the wings and needs to get rid of the person sat on the right-hand side of group 1 so that they can take their place and run their mini routine with their new partner from group 1. This expulsion of the redundant partner can be a brutal shove or swing off stage into the wings immediately followed by the new person sitting down and starting their mini routine. The same happens when the other half of the pair (from group 3) comes on and throws, pushes off the person from group 1 and starts their routine with their group 2 partner. The timing of the entrances should feel like an interruption and the couple in the chairs should not feel like they are waiting for someone to come along. This will take some mastering. It might help to go through the routine in front of the group and agree on what move the person running on is going to take as their signal. This helps emphasise how important clarity and consistency are as the moves have now become cues for people in the wings to run on stage. If they are not clear and consistent, then the person waiting in the wings will not get their cue.

Continue until the final couple get interrupted by the first person of group 1. (The whole thing can either loop or finish with the mini routine between the last person and the first from group 1.)

These transitions need to be swift but they can be creative and choreographed. You can either set time aside for this or just rely on the creativity of the whole group in the moment to offer suggestions or come up with new ideas.

Now that everything is in place it is time to reinforce the context. Remind everyone about the television and how their focus must never wander from it. Remind them how crisp the choreography must be to succeed.

Try the complete routine with a strong and upbeat music track. We have often used 'Lucky Star' by Basement Jaxx featuring Dizzee Rascal. The energy will lift the physicality and the urgency of the performers. We unashamedly time the run and then set a target of knocking another ten seconds off in the next run. Participants usually embrace this urgency and are desperate to know if they have succeeded in getting their time down (without compromising the quality of the work, of course).

The humour of the couples constantly changing, of old partners being dumped for new ones, starts to emerge. An evening or a lifetime of their possible cuddles and caresses flit by in a flash and then they are gone but nothing changes. The television and their fixation on it remains.

You still have the choice of whether you want to finish this scene with the last couple or with an individual alone. If you decide on someone alone, what do they do? Switch the television off? Then what? There is still the possibility of emotional impact in this scene despite its comedy and physicality. The end result can be quite moving. You can also play with the pace and physical dynamics to explore this. Try a slow run and ask the performers to maintain their gaze at the 'television'. How does this change the story or the tenderness between the couple?

We find this a very successful way of engaging a large group in a physical task that does not require previous physical experience and training. It is fun and is a really good way to focus the participants and get them committed to the success of the scene.

Ways into basic lifting techniques

There is something absurd about trying to tackle this within a book, but it seemed even more wrong to ignore it. So here it goes ...

Getting people lifting is a careful process. There are all kinds of preconceptions, hang-ups, fears and concerns to overcome. Make sure everyone is warmed up as they are all going to be working their backs, arms and legs. It would be good to start by playing a game of Clear the Space (see page 115) as the 'Person' command gets people gripping, holding and embracing each other without a thought for decorum or protocol. Such abandon or ease with physical proximity is crucial before you start working on lifts as people will have to be able to relax into their partner and not recoil away.

Then there are the preconceptions. Many people may consider a lift between two people to be an act of strength – one person imposing their strength upon another more passive person. The kind of lifting we would recommend does not necessarily require strength. It is mostly about simple technique.

Even though it is impossible for us to demonstrate physically from within these pages there are certainly some rules that will stand you in good stead. This list is probably not exhaustive.

1   Get your core lower than that of the person you are lifting. Basic principles of martial arts like Judo are all about using and controlling your partner's or adversary's weight from this position.
2   If you are being lifted, do not deny your partner your weight. Give it to them freely. Do not push away. Pull in. If anything, push down on or into them. And think about going up, about the lift succeeding, not all the ways it could fail.
3   Don't look down at your feet. They won't go anywhere with you looking at them.
4   If you are using strength, then you are not using technique. Lifting can be more about positioning and balance than brute force.
5   Be safe. Do not over-rehearse. Do not be over-ambitious.
6   Don't forget to breathe. Holding your breath freezes the back muscles you need to be active. Exhale slowly with control if you are catching.
7   Think 'rucksack'! Let us explain …

Everyone can imagine a cradle lift: Picture lifting a baby, or the way a muscle-bound hero might emerge from a burning building in a Hollywood film carrying the beautiful heroine. That is the preconception we need to fight. If possible, get a couple to replicate this image. It will be hard work for the lifter so make sure the people demonstrating are safe and capable.

Now encourage the person being lifted to be active: Get them to pull their weight into their partner, putting their arms around the shoulders of the lifter. Ask them to bring their knees up to their chest, engaging their stomach muscles in doing so. They should put their head on the lifter's shoulder and make themselves as small and all tightly packaged as possible to get as close to their partner as they can.

Now talk to the lifter. Can they take their arms away? Can they literally wear their partner around their shoulder? Can they walk and turn as if they are just wearing some enormous human scarf? If so, then the 'lift' has become the work of the lifted and they are being worn just like a rucksack. They are no longer passive or like a fainting heroine in *Gone with the Wind*. They are now active and working with the lifter.

This is an extreme but effective example of how much work is involved in being lifted. It is also an example of how easy lifting can be if the lifted partner is active and the weight is placed in the right place.

Working with lifts is a practical exercise and cannot be dictated by books, but what we hope to have offered are some simple rules that can open up and simplify a way of working that can seem far too ambitious and frightening.

If you take participants through Push Hands and Round/By/Through they can then find the opportunities to use these lifts. The right moments just present themselves. This is so much more beneficial than have two people stare at each other working out how they are going to use their new lifting skills!

Flight Paths

This was an exercise born on a British Airways flight. The magazine features a double page spread that shows all the destinations that the airline have operating out of London and around the world. Each flight path is represented on the world map by a single red line. As well as being an impressive indicator of the extensive corners of the planet serviced by this behemoth, it also serves as a creative tool for the bored artistic director. A prolonged episode of staring at the patterns of this map gave rise to the following physical exercise.

It uses the principle of creating duets that would only ever come to look the way they do because of the challenge of the task. Because of this, it is an exercise we like to use with participants of all levels as, in every instance, it promotes the capacity of the performer to make work outside of their own particular physicality. It forces people into physical response and by following a very simple principle, assures the creation of a sequence that would not be the primary physical instinct or response of the two duettists.

To begin with, two performers stand face to face and assume an A and B status. For the first part of the exercise, A is active and B is neither assisting nor resistant. Using the idea of B's body as that of the map of the world, A traces a flight with thumb and forefinger that takes off from one singular and specific body part and lands somewhere new. For example, this flight might depart from rear left shoulder blade and land at right Achilles tendon. A then repeats this action several times more. Three would be the minimum number of flight paths and five would be the maximum if this were the first attempt at this exercise. At this early stage, it is important that each flight path is treated as a separate flight rather than a continuous flight that happens to stop off in a number of locations. Departing flights might be made using the fingers of alternating hands. All flights have a smooth orbit around the surface of B's body and A should be encouraged not to make the flight path occur too far off the surface of B's body. B then repeats this process.

For the next stage, A and B return to facing each other. From here, both participants are to execute their flight paths at the same time. Of course, the task becomes very different. A and B should run their separate (but now entwined) sequences very slowly in order to accommodate the new information regarding the surface of their partner. In some instances, after setting off from the point of departure, the point of destination might actually be travelling towards your fingers, in which case, there should be a moment of suspension as the destination pulls closer. In other instances, and more frequently in this exercise, the point of destination moves considerably. This is by no means a problem within the exercise. It is actually the essence of it.

In trying to stay true to the two points of departure and destination, each person is required to twist, turn and wrap themselves around the ever changing body of their partner. This makes for intriguing shapes from the outside but also for some very complex-looking relations between the two participants. If we include the idea that both A and B have flights that depart and arrive at the exact same moment, we create an exercise that relies on the partnership to develop a sense of rhythm and of the other body in space. It can create moments of smooth entropic or explosive movement followed by the stillness of the 'landings'. It also sets up the idea of your own physical actions having a very immediate consequence on that of your partner. This is a skill set that is absolutely key to even the most basic forms of physical duet or group work.

In taking this exercise further, A and B might be encouraged to maintain as much eye contact as possible during this new duet. Original versions of this exercise almost always render both performers unable to look away from the ever-changing surface of their partner's body and this is no bad thing, just something to play with as an advancement of the task. Another development might involve the partners attempting to identify the direction of their combined flight paths and attempting to move across the floor following the impulse or the direction of their combined flight path. This element sounds very simple but is the introduction of the physical body operating on two levels so will need to be given time and care in order to be introduced effectively. We have seen the carnage that resulted from this last element being introduced too quickly but we have also witnessed some beautiful results when we took a bit more care at this stage.

This is a simple task that can lead to endless complexity. It can serve the non-dancer and the highly experienced movement specialist. Even in its early incarnations it reminds A and B to read the movement of their partner while remaining essentially true to their own material. It is about communication and being open to the possibilities it presents. This is a useful lesson for any performer.

Taken further, it can incorporate lifts and huge shifts through the space. This simple principle can be the launch pad for incredibly dynamic choreography.

The important thing to keep an eye on is that A and B remain true to the process and continue to think about that constant exchange of information between the two of them. It is very easy to get carried away as the movement becomes bigger and bigger to leave the process behind and find ourselves just throwing the shapes we always do. The exercise was about finding new shapes. It was about communication and adapting to a partner. It was about reading the movement of a partner and using that energy and dynamic. Returning to the basic principle should help the participants from falling into the trap.

Flight Paths works very well as a skills building exercise. It demands that its participants never become isolated in their own thoughts and movements. It is a very useful building block for any contact work, not just as a choreographic devising process in itself.

Fluff

This is another very simple starting point that can lead to more complex choreography. It can work for any level of experience and can help you create a bit of harmless comedy or something much more complex and heart breaking. It is just as valid for dancers as it is for actors or young students. The process can veer into either world further down the line. What it requires from all participants is precision and, especially important for those wanting to get on and throw shapes, restraint.

The beauty of this exercise is that a theatrical context and subtext can emerge almost instantly, allowing you to explore character and potential development. Conversely, both context and subtext can be ignored (or delayed) and it can develop as a much more technically complex process with layers being added, each asking more of the performers physically.

This exercise was a very important part of the creation of *Lovesong*. Nearly all of the choreography within *Lovesong* sprang from this simple exercise.

It started as a simple fascination with the way that people who are comfortable with each other can betray that and so much more through a simple, absentminded touch, for example, the removal of fluff from someone's shirt, a rogue eyelash from someone's cheek, the slight adjustment of clothing. This is an act of intimacy where one person is allowed access to the body space of another and essentially grooms them. They alter the image of the other ever so slightly, moving them closer to their own preferred version.

The reason why this simple exchange became so fascinating to us is because it is actually a bit more complex than that and all of that complexity is betrayed instantly and silently. We, as observers, note that someone feels they have the right to remove that fluff from another. We also note that they were given access to the fluff. There are many telling reactions a person can

Sam Cox and Sian Phillips in *Lovesong* (2011). Image by Scott Graham

have to having fluff removed from their person. What does it say if that person watches the hand come towards them and sees the fluff get removed? What does it say if they do not even notice the act at all? What if they stop the hand before it makes contact? What if they stop the hand that has picked the fluff off and make that hand return the fluff to where it was? What if the look alone was enough to stop the hand that wants to remove the fluff? The moment can be intimate, provocative, invasive, clumsy, tender, comic, tragic, heroic, stoic, etc. That is not a bad start for simply picking a bit of fluff from someone's shirt.

All of this very quickly reveals character, context, subtext and history. The process is a useful tool to explore almost any intimate relationship on stage. It is not always about finding out what a character would do. It is just as valid to find out that the character would not, or could not, do something.

The process can go much further.

Sit a couple opposite each other close enough to have their knees touching. Get them to find, for example, five moves where they might be removing fluff or adjusting hair or glasses on their partner. They should take turns at finding this string of five moves. When they have their string get them to perform them and have a look at them. At this stage keep it very simple. Let Person A do their five and then Person B do their five.

Then you can get them to start to play with the sequence. Try getting them to do it alternately so Person A does their first move and then Person B does their first move. Person A then does their second move, and so on.

Something new might already start to emerge here. It might start to look a little antagonistic or tactically provocative.

Change the rules again.

They can now decide how they want to divide the sequence. That might mean something like this:

Person A – 1st move
Person A – 2nd move
Person B – 1st move
Person A – 3rd move
Person B – 2nd move
Person B – 3rd move
Person B – 4th move
Person A – 4th move
Person A – 5th move
Person B – 5th move

They should look to avoid a predictable rhythm. This is a simple and easily remembered sequence of ten events. Look out for stories starting to emerge.

This is when the performers start to imbue the moves with an attitude of, for example, anger or frustration. This emerging context or subtext is not helpful if you want to take this process further but it can be useful or entertaining in itself. Note that this process follows that familiar pattern of many of our tasks and starts simply before building up to new complexities. Each building block is a perfectly good stopping off point however.

Already they will have something more choreographically complex. Take this a step further by asking them to change the pattern slightly. Now they should look to do one of their moves at the same time as their partner is doing a move.

This changes the dynamic of the movement. No longer are they remaining passive while the other moves. You can play with this passivity. Does it disappear if you get both of them to fixate on their partner's fluff and just let their choreography move fluidly. They are now unaware of their partner's fixation on their own fluff but they still have the difficult task of staying true to the rhythm of their choreography. This might present two people picking at each other like fascinated gorillas grooming each other.

This can be fun but it completely ignores the tension we had highlighted above. How do we feel about the touch? Is it ok? Is it intrusive? Does this always happen? Is this the first time? Is this the last time? Do your feelings change throughout? Are your actions pointed acts of revenge?

Play with these directives. Fascinating little relationships of surprising depth can emerge.

Slow it down. What if one of them looks at the hands moving and sees the fluff leave the clothes while the other just looks into the eyes of their partner?

What if they both keep their eyes closed?

What if you change the touch from picking fluff into a softer touch? With the eyes still closed does it become a desperate need for reassurance? 'Are you still there?' What if the hand lingers longer?

What if the eyes remain closed but the fingers never make contact with the body? Does this still express the desire to make contact halted by fear or restraint?

Already we are running away with ideas but you can see the potential behind this simple exercise. It reminds us that a touch can say a lot. It gives us so much information about the two characters.

Think about the touch. If it is the first touch then nothing will ever be the same again. You have disturbed the universe slightly but unalterably. It might mean the touch was not so easy to do. After all, we do not touch random strangers on the street. If we do, it usually comes with some kind of repercussions.

We must not throw this touch between people away, like it was taken for granted. There is the universe before the touch, there is the universe during the touch and then there is the universe after the touch. They should all be different.

OK, what about how the movers might use this? Let's think about this sequence of touches choreographically. Get the couples standing up and get rid of the chairs. Go through the sequence standing up. Already it will feel very different.

Change the touch. Make it grab the clothes and pull. Let that tiny dynamic of pulling the fluff from the clothes become an extended action that pulls your partner forward. This will alter the physical relationship. The partner will now have to work hard to reach the point of the body that contains the fluff for the next move. They stretch to make contact. As they pull they might spin their partner around or drag them across the stage towards them.

Return to the set sequence as set out above.

They can use the whole space and should explore long pulls and tiny pulls (more in keeping with the original fluff exercise). What if you get them to change a pull for a push? And what happens on that moment you asked them to move at the same time?

As before, once you have the sequence you can explore the quality. Pulls can become grabs; can become sticky hands that move their partner across the room.

Again, go through the exploratory section that investigated touch. Don't take the touch as a given. There could be a complex series of thoughts from both sides of the touch. What if the partner being touched feels the magnetism before the contact and is compelled into the hands of the other?

What about taking the hands out of it altogether? You have rehearsed it often enough. They should know the impact and twists demanded by the partner. Can they replicate this without touch but just showing two bodies that want to be touched? Each twists and aches for the contact the other might provide.

This is potentially complex stuff, both choreographically and emotionally but importantly you have created this complexity without asking anyone to think about aching for someone's touch, etc. This is another example of getting to a place of emotional sophistication without making your participants uncomfortable (see Headsmacks – The Off Switch).

This simple process, beginning with a single touch, can be pushed to create highly physical choreography. Pulls can propel someone into your arms; can throw them across the room. Pulls can also become lifts. It is all about how far you want to take it. Just remember the building blocks, though, as there are many valuable discoveries to be made along the way. Keep pushing for restraint and don't aim for the hugely dynamic straight away.

NEW PHYSICAL VOCABULARY/RESTRICTIONS AND FREEDOM

The following exercises are designed to bring surprising choreographic qualities out of your performers. The aim is to develop a kind of physicality that might be impossible to achieve were it not for the specific demands of these exercises. They can be used by the inexperienced to create movement but also help the experienced break free of their regular stock physicality.

Phone numbers

We had been trying to think of a way of making the learning of complex choreography seem less daunting. We have often seen what happens to people when they are swamped with information. They stop taking in new information or begin to leak stored information. Worse still they begin to beat themselves up about it and become stressed and angry. We have been in that position many times. The rage and self-loathing totally incapacitates you and you become useless. It is an absolute waste of energy.

There is complex choreography within our daily routines. The tying of shoelaces is a beautifully dexterous dance for the fingers. Picture someone tying a tie. Now take the tie out of the picture and what you have is a hand dance Lea Anderson would be proud of.

These all come from repetition but the learning of these routines is embarked upon with the understanding that mastering it IS possible. The repetition takes the effort out of it as the action becomes linked to physical memory. This shows that we are all capable of learning this complex physicality.

We wanted to find a way to create choreography that accessed our ability to retain information physically in a way that was not daunting or intimidating. We were interested in finding a way of using a process that we have already shown an aptitude for. We noticed that there were times that someone might want to tell you a phone number but could not do it without having the keypad in front of them. That meant that the number sequence had been retained physically rather than numerically. This is often the case with our debit card PIN. When people try to remember it they often imagine the keypad and do a little finger dance to help them recall!

We wanted to devise a process that drew on this quite literally. We tried this out at one of our regular practitioner skill sharing events where we share new devising techniques with our workshop practitioners. We got each practitioner to stand roughly six feet away from and facing the wall. We asked the performers to imagine a huge numerical keypad in front of them, exactly as they have on their phone, stretching from floor to ceiling. We then asked them to tap out their phone number. We suggested that it did not have to be their own number, or they could alter it if they wanted to. The reason we chose phone numbers is that it is a sequence that we have little problem learning quickly when broken down into code and number. To point to number one would require them stretching to top left, to point to number three would mean stretching to top right.

1	2	3
4	5	6
7	8	9
	0	

We asked them to only use their right hand and, keeping their arms outstretched, point out their phone numbers as if pressing the numbers on a huge keypad. Including the code, this should be around 11 moves. Once they have remembered these moves they then paired up and taught each other their moves. They put them into a sequence of 22 moves.

This was all achieved very quickly. Already it was clear that if we had asked them to create a hand sequence of 22 moves without the keypad and the known number they would have struggled. The keypad helped them translate numbers into physical memory.

We tested this choreography. What if it was smaller? What if it was the head that was looking towards the numbers rather than the arm pointing? What if it was the whole body swaying? What if we move the keypad to the floor? What if their eyes were closed or they seemed preoccupied with something else as their hands moved in unison?

All of these created interesting unison. It was a very useful experiment but we had the chance to use this devising technique on the Damon Albarn opera *Dr Dee*.

The show was about the brilliant mind of scholar, mathematician, astrologist and alchemist, John Dee. We wanted to somehow capture, choreographically, the mechanics of his brain, how his mathematical mind must have worked in many dimensions, the sheer effort and pressure of his calculations. We thought, with a few tweaks, the phone numbers exercise might work.

We realised that we could not suggest to Damon or Rufus that we base our choreography for a scene on people's phone numbers! They both were knee deep in research of Dee's life and Damon had assembled a band of musicians playing old English instruments to capture an authentic sound. Actors were researching ancient astrological charts to get an understanding of Dee's calculations. We needed to dress up the process in something that made it look more considered and bespoke but still served the same purpose and offered the same support in creating and remembering lots of choreographic moves.

Inspired by John Dee's fascination and study of Astrology (much more a science then than it appears now), we decided to replace phone numbers with birthday dates. For example, 15.20 on 23 September 1984 becomes 152023091984.

Damon's music for this scene was meticulous and in keeping with the mathematical theme and the magical significance of certain numbers it was nine bars of nine beats. Having 12 number meant we needed to trim down our dates to match. We dropped the 19 of the year as everyone had that in their birthday. That meant we had ten numbers.

1520230984

We dropped the first (the hour) number, as it would only be a 0, 1 or 2 so that gave us nine figures.

The performers learnt their own using the giant keypad (we did not tell Damon about the giant keypad!) and then taught the others. Then it was someone else's turn to teach their numbers, always referring to the (secret) giant keypad. This process was achieved in chunks, as so many numbers is a real brain melter!

We also had only eight performers in the scene and used their figures to fill the first eight bars. To fill the last bar and add to the credibility of the scene in the eyes of our collaborators we chose the birth dates of Queen Elizabeth I and trimmed them accordingly. Dee would have used these figures as he searched for the optimum date for her coronation.

It is important to think of devising processes as malleable. We have stated this many times but the meaning does not come from the process. It comes from the context in which you place the work created by the process. The fact that this process comes from our physical dexterity with and propensity to remember phone numbers does not rule it out from being used on a show about a sixteenth-century mathematician.

Just don't tell Damon.

Passives

Many of our devising tasks are designed to find a way of getting beyond what a performer may think they have to offer, that bag of tricks they may pull a move from when asked to create a string of choreography. That bag exists in the subconscious and is linked to many aspects of the performer's personality. It is full of the moves that they feel comfortable doing; the moves they think are impressive; the moves that they think work; the moves that they think are right for the task; the moves they think are right for the show; the move they think the director is looking for. Sometimes you need to find a way to get beyond this.

This task takes away all of that need to please and moves far from the safety zone of what the body has done before and feels safe to return to. Before it starts to sound too grand, the task simply presents an environment where the performer should find themselves moving in a way that is genuinely new to them. The performer is cut free from habit and pattern and from the unconscious limitations we impose upon ourselves when we feel we are making choreography for a particular moment in a play. In this exercise the performer is just making shapes.

If any of the performers start to think 'I know where we are going with this', the later instructions should keep the movement that is created fresh and unfamiliar.

This is a very simple process and could be adapted and applied in many different ways.

1

Put the performers in groups of three or four. One of each group is the 'passive'. The rest of the group take and lift the legs and arms of the 'passive' as they lie relaxed on the floor. This can start as a gentle massage, stretching and calming the 'passive'. They should be able to wiggle the head and all limbs should move independently. You need complete relaxation from the performer on the floor. A good choice of calming music might help here. No need to go all dolphins and crystals. Just something that makes the performers focus and relax. This exercise will not work if there is laughter, awkwardness or if the environment is not conducive.

This in itself is a really good relaxation exercise. Aside from the extraordinary sensation for the 'passive' of having no responsibility for the movement of their limbs you also have a room full of people becoming more comfortable making contact and handling each other. You have the 'passives' having to concentrate and really think about letting go of their limbs, dislocating their movement from the rest of their body and from their own control. It is surprising how hard it is for some people to completely relax like this. For the 'passives' it is also a trust exercise. As they relinquish physical control they also potentially hand over their dignity, as they will end up in all kinds of strange and potentially unflattering positions! It is worthwhile asking them to think about relinquishing the control of their joints as well as their limbs here too. This might add a little more time onto this stage but is well worth it. You should start to see this latter effect on the quality of movement in the limbs almost immediately.

Allow time for the performers to become comfortable in their duties. They need to be comfortable touching and being touched. They need to feel that they are giving the weight of their limbs to their partners. They should not see the limbs as chunks of meat. They should explore all possible articulation. This should extend to the hands and fingers. This should help the group explore a full range of movement from the sweepingly dynamic to the minute and intricate. Once they seem to be achieving this range of movement in a fluid, focused and relaxed way you can move on to stage 2.

2

It is now the job of the performers manipulating the 'passive's' limbs to set a string of 20 moves and shapes upon the 'passive' on the floor. The 'passive' remains passive throughout. The movement vocabulary should come from all of the moves they have just explored – moments where hands are adjusted minutely, legs are twisted, torsos are raised and dropped, bodies are turned over. The performers should, without causing any discomfort, seek to explore physical positions and angles that are far from everyday positions and movement. Just manipulating the head at the top of the neck and vertebrae is itself a whole wealth of positions and angles that are rarely adopted by the passive individual. They must resist telling a story with these moves. They do not have to find anything spectacular. Just keep it as simple as it was but make sure it is now completely precise.

After a while they should be able to perform the string of material where they manipulate the 'passive' who remains on the floor yet gets twisted, shunted, moved about. Allow enough time for all participants to attain a level of precision about all of their moves. This string of 20 moves should contain the full range of movement explored and can last as long as two minutes to perform.

3

Now the focus shifts to the 'passive'. They now repeat the moves of the string without the touch of the manipulators. They are still working as a group. The manipulators can teach and return to a move to help the 'passive' remember it. Some of it will be impossible but the 'passive' must try to capture the essence of the move.

Everything is in the detail. The manipulators must try to help the 'passive' capture the exact movement set but can only instruct from the outside. Every twist, shunt, lift, turn, stretch. All of these moves were created from the outside and initially felt completely alien to the 'passive'. This section is now about taking ownership of the moves. In doing so the 'passive' is using a set physical vocabulary that they would not have been able to achieve on their own.

You might find that the two-minute string of material naturally condensed to roughly one minute once the 'passive' is able to capture the moves and perform them on their own. Try pushing them to getting the string of moves down to about 30 seconds, not by editing but by putting a bit more energy behind it. They must still aim for the exact dynamic of the initial string. This might not lead to a fast string but repetition might just take most of the pauses caused by trying to remember.

This process can create a contorted and disturbing choreography. It is always useful to play with its theatrical potential even at this stage. Place the 'passive' in the middle of the room and get the rest of the group to observe from a distance. Try lighting the 'passive' if possible. Try different music tracks. Give the 'passive' different instructions regarding tempo, urgency, eye contact or closed, vocalisation, etc. The results can be very interesting.

This simple exercise will not necessarily lead to a choreographed scene but it will take a performer beyond their usual bag of physical tricks as the moves have come from somewhere impossible for a performer to find on their own.

There are various things you can try now to test the potential of the physicality you have created.

If you have arranged the room with several groups of 'passives' and 'manipulators' then you can now place two 'passives' next to each other on the floor and get them to close their eyes. Instantly they are a couple in a bed. Get them to run both of their independent sequences at the same time but warn them that they might bump into each other and not to be shocked by this. They should let a touch become a caress if it feels natural. It might be advisable to get them to do this very slowly at first.

As you run the exercise with the rest of the group observing, look for happy accidents, moments of what looks like deliberate and potentially complex choreography and moments where a story might start to emerge. Sometimes the most startling moments are events where one might appear to reach for the other as the other rolls away, or when they both move towards each other. Sometimes it is just physically interesting moments that appear to canon, echo or reflect each other. This presents moments where they appear as a united couple and then in an instant they are distant individuals sharing different dreams, all in a flicker of a movement.

These are beautifully complex moments and can serve early character exploration just as well as choreographic scenes. To the observer the 'passives' are displaying subconscious desires and intentions towards and away from their partner. Moments of synchronicity can suggest a history between the two. A missed embrace can open a telling window on this relationship. Depending on the complexity of the moment that missed embrace could be comical or utterly tragic. The notion of sleep gives the 'passives' an innocence and an honesty. These are moments where their needs are being expressed without them knowing and may give the scene a delicate voyeurism.

154

It might also present a couple of performers with their eyes closed, smacking each other in the faces with flailing arms. That is the risk. The trick is to not give up. Adjust the tempo. Try different tempos for each of the couples. Have one remain still. What does this say? Start one of the 'passives' slightly later so that all of the interaction will be different. Feel free to play, remembering that this does not have to lead to a polished choreographic scene. The exercise could continue to present new thoughts and situations each time you run it with a little variation applied. You might want to get the 'passives' to bring some of the character they are playing into the exercise. What does this do? Does it present something more complex or is it all a bit obvious now?

Keep playing! Look for illuminating moments. Get the observing group to comment. What do they see?

It does not have to stop there.

4

Get the 'passives' on their feet and see if they can replicate the movement while standing up. This will be hard but it takes us back to the original intention of the exercise, namely accessing a new movement vocabulary for the performer. It gives the performer a movement palette that could not have been imagined if they had set out to devise them while on their feet.

Try putting a pair together where the 'passive' works through their sequence and at the same time, the standing person tries to be the exact reflective image of the person on the floor. This is both an example of 'cross-pollinating' and also taking the standing person way out of their regular physical pattern.

This exercise was a crucial part of the creation of the Lovesong Bed sequence (see Lovesong Bed). It was used to break down the usual movement vocabulary of the actors and give them a whole new and strange palette to draw on. It would have been so easy for their preconceptions or habitual movement patterns to influence and ultimately limit the potential of the scene. This is not unique to them. It is true of the genesis of any scene.

Headsmacks – the Off Switch

When creating *Beautiful Burnout* it was clear that there was a wealth of physicality to explore in the highly energetic, ballistic and controversial world of boxing. We looked at the training, the boxing, the skipping, the way cornermen touched and patched up the boxers, the peculiar way the referee moves around the ring, balancing observation with intervention and the need to be invisible to the crowd.

We worked hard to replicate this physicality but we felt that copying it would not really reveal its strange grace and potential in a new light. We had to find a new way of looking at it. (This approach is most clear in Refs.)

So much of the movement of a boxer happens at such speed you have to carefully dissect every split second to appreciate the lightning shifts of balance, the feints and strategies employed. We watched fights on DVD and trawled the internet for these complex, chess-like moments that, without the benefit of slow motion, are lost on the casual observer.

One of the more obvious observations but no more easy to replicate is the boxing stance. While working with our actors it would always become instantly apparent when the correct stance or form had been lost. Parts of the body would become exposed to attack. We would bark reminders to bring the elbows in to protect the ribs and the stomach but the most common reminder was to protect the chin, to drop it behind the guard. Within boxing the chin often gets referred to as the Off Switch, as a well aimed punch causes the body to crumble. This was fascinating to us.

We decided to look at what happens when a boxer gets caught on the off switch.

We looked through footage of knockout punches and observed the way the off switch impacts on other parts of the body. We found that the punched boxers did not react in the way you might imagine or may see in a fistfight on a film or TV. The head does not fly back and they are seldom propelled across the canvas. The first things to respond to the off switch are the knees. They buckle as the legs turn to jelly. They flail for balance. They fail the top half which might still want to fight on!

Watching this in slow motion presented an extraordinary physicality. Only then did we get a sense of how the information travels through the body, how the body fights to stay upright, how it twists and ripples as it tries to resist the inevitable demise.

We looked at the shape of the boxer's body when it receives impact, how the neck might twist, the head might recoil, how the legs might buckle. We set our performers off exploring this. They would return to the DVD or internet footage trying to capture the same quality of movement and dislocation.

This, however, only creates a facsimile. It does not necessarily offer something new or interesting. It just presented people who were pretending to be boxers and were being hit. The key was to stop pretending they were boxers.

We asked them to take their arms out of the equation; keeping them by their sides or letting them flail naturally if the movement of the body dictated. The explicit context of the previous attempts was stopping us seeing the action for what it really was. This simple adjustment allowed us to focus on the peculiar, almost Egon Sheile-esque contortions of the body.

Inspiration can be taken from observing infinite facets of life. When we look at them closely they may become startlingly new to us but by merely replicating them we run the risk of presenting something less interesting than the original inspiration. You have to look for that little twist of perspective that makes the movement come alive again.

This process and the resulting choreography was used sporadically within Kittens in *Beautiful Burnout* but that twisting of perspective was a vitally important part of all how we represented the boxing world on stage. It was not enough to present something instantly recognisable, no matter how well observed it might be. An audience would only see what they already know and in doing so they would not see the fascinating detail you discovered in the process. The much more interesting and ambitious intention is surely to present something in a slightly skewed yet still truthful way that results in an audience having some kind of epiphany about the movement of the boxer.

This process is very useful in workshops. A quick demonstration of the relationship between the Off Switch and the body can replace viewing DVDs.

Make sure that everyone has a good warm-up focusing on the necks. When they get to rehearse their full string they will be throwing their heads around quite a lot.

We tend to put participants into small groups, usually between three or four, and have them individually, create a very short string of, say, four impact moments. They should not tell a story. They should not use their arms in a boxer's stance (remember, making the context explicit actually stops us from seeing the movement with fresh eyes). Each impact does not have to logically relate to the next. They do not have to play tired or hurt. They don't have to play punch drunk. It is purely about applying the logic of what we have discovered about the relation between a blow to the Off Switch and the response of the body.

When they have a short string they teach it to the others in their group. The group then has a string of between 12 and 16 moves. They need to rehearse this to capture the dynamic and ballistic quality that inspired it. We use a strong and fast track to get adrenalin levels up and push the performers along.

When performed at speed the body is full of impossible contortions as the body responds to one impact yet powers into another. When performed in unison you can have a very powerful dance of impossible twists and contortions.

When taking inspiration from such a literal source you run the risk of presenting movement that can seem to only mean one thing. We run a useful exercise after Off Switch that reminds the performer of the fluidity and flexibility of meaning when applied to movement.

We ask a participant to take an iPod and earphones, put them in, close their eyes and go through the moves on their own, slowly and fluidly, taking their body to the same extremes as when they did it fast. This is not easy. As this is a demonstration, choose your participant wisely!

We change the music and take the rest of the participants to the other side of the room to be an audience.

The music is usually a beautifully haunting track called 'Nude' by Radiohead. It is an immediately surprising choice and changes the atmosphere dramatically.

While the performer is slowly contorting we might ask them to smile or to talk to themselves imperceptibly. Try throwing in simple commands.

When the song finishes we then ask the audience what they saw. The usual responses talk about the ecstatic, the erotic, the private, the brave, and the sensual.

These are a million miles away from the origins in boxing but these comments are essentially a response to the same choreography. All that was changed was the music, a prop and a little directorial spin. It is surely proof that the movement itself meant nothing as we have shown it was capable of telling a vastly different story. It was the context that had changed, which suggests the same devising process could have been applied to make incredibly sensitive choreography. The erotic, the sensuous, came from boxing!

There is an important point behind this trick. If what you want is sensuous and erotic it is often the hardest thing to ask from a performer. They will feel exposed, as if they are being asked to bare their bedroom technique! This is even more of an issue with the younger, non-professional performer. What this exercise shows is that there are ways to getting that quality of performance you are looking for without crashing into the insecurities of the performer. It creates a safe environment to create choreography that is not limited by the expectations or insecurities of any party. Also, by taking this route the choreography itself should not be clichéd or derivative because it was never made with the end product in mind.

This is a fundamental element of how we approach the creation of choreography. Allow the performer the freedom to create within clearly stated confines. Take that choreography to new places so that it has the potential to surprise and present that subject in a new and informative way.

There are other areas to explore now that you have this choreography. We have placed two people face to face and asked them to hold on to each other's shoulders. They then attempt their string of material slowly.

What can emerge is an incredibly powerful scene where they are desperately imploring each other, or are trying to get away from each other, or are wanting to embrace but cannot. Try experimenting with eye contact. What happens if they are looking into each other's eyes throughout?

What happens if they never look at each other but face away from each other? What if only one of them places a hand on the shoulder or elbow of another? Try that touch in different places. Try different grips. Try different music.

What happens if...? Well, we don't know. And neither should you. That is the whole point of trying it!

Villette Floor

This was an exercise developed during rehearsals for *Villette* in 2005 with director Laurie Sansom. That seems quite a long time ago now but the process, while specifically developed for *Villette*, still has relevance and serves as a useful way of developing choreography with both actors and dancers. Depending on where you take it can provide vastly different outcomes.

The Brontë novel posed various challenges for us as movement directors. One was the accurate portrayal of the protagonist's complex internal life, often unreliable and quixotic. Another was the demand of depicting specific events that take place in the novel such as a storm in a dormitory, an extended nightmare sequence and a fire in a theatre. It was this last challenge that informed the following exercise. For us, the end result was to portray the public panic of bodies in space.

As an exercise, Villette Floor is a layered, sequential progression that might be adapted to suit a number of theatrical requirements or scenes. It encourages participants to orchestrate spatial dynamics, creating fast patterns of energy and physical movement that switches between control and abandonment. Although the exercise promotes unison work, this notion of unison is more about a unified sense of energy and intention rather than physical detailed precision. Each stage is (as ever) incremental and requires each new detail to be fulfilled before moving on to the next stage. The ultimate effect is reached only when the group are extremely confident of the space in which they are moving.

The room itself should be fairly large for this to work effectively. Split the group into four groups of equal size and place one in each corner of the room. They should establish this point as being 'home'. From here, each group creates a pedestrian floor pattern. From 'home', they set off as a group walking into the space at a speed slightly slower than pedestrian speed. After a certain amount of time the group should come to a still point. This is their point 'A'. From here they set off and walking in the space come to settle at another point, their 'B'. They repeat this twice more, establishing points 'C' and 'D' before returning 'home'. The route of this should not be something known but discovered by the group with no one particular person leading. The

Georgina Lamb as Lucy Snowe in *Villette* (2005). Image by Scott Graham

shape of the group should not be regimented like a line but should be an easy, shifting 'blob' with all members of the group staying in close proximity to each other. Once at 'home', each group should repeat their floor pattern a couple of times but now at a slightly-faster-than-pedestrian speed. (If the room is small you might ask the groups to work two at a time in order to allow them to make good use of the space.)

Watching the groups executing this very simple task you will probably note that most of the members of the group are looking at the floor in order to establish their route around the room. Point this out and then ask the groups to walk their floor route and this time to use the perimeters of the room and its details as their 'markers' for when to come to a stop at each point. For each person these markers should be different. For example, someone might use the light switch to their left and its proximity as their reference for when to stop at point 'A', a fire alarm switch on the wall straight ahead as their reference to point 'B' and so on. Ask each person to become aware of how the walls of the space are moving both away and towards them as they move around the room. They should very soon be comfortable too with using a relaxed combination of prime focus and peripheral vision in order to map out their location within the room at any one time. This part of the exercise is a basic step in spatial awareness but should not be passed over. It is surprising how this exercise can fall apart without this. Not least of all, it promotes a confidence in the space where faces are confidently scanning the walls rather than a group of people all moving around the room with their heads down (though this might eventually be a desired aesthetic of course! It sounds quite interesting!).

For the next stage, the group should consider the points at which they turn from point 'A' and head towards point 'B'. At the moment this change in direction is totally without cause. From point 'A', ask the group to choose a specific body point, e.g. the front of the left shoulder. This is their 'impact point'. In imagining taking an impact in this specific spot, each person plays with the capacity to isolate that body part, twisting it in the direction away from the point of impact and only moving the rest of the body in accordance with this event when they absolutely have to. In the instance of an impact to the front of the shoulder this would mean twisting through the shoulder to its full extent before bringing in any subsequent movement in the arm, ribs, hip, head and finally feet. For this reason, this part of the exercise should be undertaken slowly in order to discover the logic and precision of the impact and its effect on the rest of the body. The impact should also be such that its direction will send the group to their point 'B' in the room. Once at point 'B' the group chooses a second impact point and does likewise. This is repeated at points 'C' and 'D' too before the group return home.

This is the most detailed part of the exercise and time should be given over to this in order to fully discover the logical physical progression involved in such an event. In choosing body parts such as the centre of the chest, as points of impact, it is important to discover just how much mobility exists in the upper middle section of the vertebrae in order to truly communicate this information to us as observers. Any movement in the shoulders should be as full as possible before any engagement with the arms and then finally the hands. It is important to figure out in this instance whether the hips might start to move forward with the shoulders or whether there may be some delay between the two events. Points like the fronts of the knees and the backs of the elbows are impossible impact points to use (unless you are teaching a class of chickens) but any folds in the body (elbows, hips, knees, necks) are all useful places to start. There should be encouragement for more ambitious choices as long as they follow the logic of what it is to receive a physical impact at that point.

With all four impact points established, ask the groups to run the floor pattern with these impact points. From the outside you will notice now how the pedestrian speed is at odds with the impact points, which will look like sudden moments of slow motion. The next stage of the exercise is for each group to now increase the speed of these impact points to match the walking speed. There is also the chance that groups are coming to a standstill and pausing before the impact moment. This should also now be removed so that the literal moment of impact is something that happens within their stride pattern and not as they come to a standstill.

An advanced layer, which might be added, is to introduce a moment of propulsion. It is likely that all the impact points operate on a horizontal level. That is, the incoming object is travelling in a straight line horizontal to the floor and at a constant level from it. Each group now chooses one of their four impact points and imagines now that the object is travelling up out of the ground towards the point on the body. With this change in direction, the body point still reacts in the same way, except that the group now play with the idea that the impact of this object lifts them momentarily off their feet. Within any string of material, there will be body points that are more useful to use in this way. (In being knocked off their feet in this way, it is useful not to involve both feet landing at the same time but landing one at a time in order to allow easy movement towards the next point in the room.)

From here, with each round, the groups should increase the speed with which they move in the space. In keeping with the last stage of the exercise, this also means that the speed of the impact points should also increase. In becoming more and more violent, these sudden physical explosions should be moments of controlled abandonment, with the limbs full of weight, the propulsion moment (if used) meaning that the group leap higher and higher into the air. At faster speeds we finally see the impact points as being the only reason why the bodies change direction in the space as they are now finally, truly being knocked off course. Even at increased speed, the group should be encouraged to remain together and unify the moment at which they are all simultaneously impacted upon. It might be worth spending a minute or two on the general rules for unison (see Ways into Unison). That way the desire for unison will not slow the group down. The moves can remain fast and full.

Try getting groups to run their sequence two at a time. They will have to spend time finding the paths through each other's journeys. There is a welcome element of chaos here that gets harnessed at this stage. You will not know how the groups will meet each other and at what stage in their sequence they will be. Once you see it you can get them to look out for hitting certain pleasing moments and committing to safe and exciting routes through each other.

When the groups are in command of their moves you can play with the context. Remember our initial starting point was to capture the fear and chaos of people trying to flee a burning theatre in the production *Villette*. By the time it came to reminding our cast about the context they had almost forgotten the reason why we were making this work! This is no bad thing. It meant they were working without the end product in their mind. They were not self-editing options. They were just working within a group to a set of specified and very simple tasks.

The return to the context was exciting. Now we could explore the real reason for the moves. Every twist became escaping the lick of the flames. Every change of direction became about falling timbers and blocked exits. Every direction had a clear and crucial imperative. It made every decision important.

We then gave them permission to scream and shout, as you might within a burning theatre! This took the energy levels through the roof! It was as thrilling to watch, as it was to take part in. (There is more about the merits of this process in 'Dance Face and the Permission to Perform'). It meant that we had moved the audience's potential focus away from the mere spectacle of the physicality on stage and onto the fear and panic in the eyes of the performers. The performers might have been in a highly energetic and choreographed movement section but they remained real characters in very real peril and this was at the heart of the finished scene's success.

If you were using this process you could play with the order in which the groups run and find the most pleasing.

A variation would be running individuals from each group. That way you have more space for more complicated pathways and potential interactions. You could get the first person in each group to set off together. When they return, the second people could set off. You could play with mixing individual runner and groups. Just remember that you are playing with chaos. It is always important to have a slow and steady run or mark through of the routes, as, with all that adrenalin pumping, it would be easy to deviate from a route and potentially cause a painful collision. Start slow and build the speed.

There are other interesting choreographic spins you can employ. Take the routes that you have created but forget the 'fire in the theatre' context. Try decreasing the space within which the teams run. How does this change the way the performers negotiate each other? Do they now have to touch? What lengths do they have to go to NOT to touch?

Decrease it until it is barely a metre squared. Place your groups on the apexes of the square. All it takes now is one step into the square to set off a writhing mass of bodies all trying to work their way back to the home corner. Make sure people are being true to their original material.

Try it with twos, threes and fours. Try different tempos. What happens if a couple have to maintain eye contact? You might find that material that was created thinking all about their own body now looks like it is responding to, longing for, or repelled by another body. What if they are always looking for something on the other's body? What if they are looking for someone else in the room?

What if you take that duet and made the square so small that they have no choice but to be in contact throughout? You might find an extraordinary quality or vocabulary that your performers could not have created together if you had told them you wanted a writhing duet. Of course you can adapt the material at this point. Not everything will work. The point is that you are using an established source material with clearly designated routes and paths. This takes the awkwardness out of intimate duets. Performers can find themselves skirting around certain areas of their partners bodies, keen not to seem like they are being lecherous or insensitive. This shapes their choices and over-complicates the relationship between the performers. Taking this route towards intimate choreography might not give you the polished finished product but it will help you and your performers hurdle this awkward stage.

This is an example how of one process can be used to create a movement palette a million miles removed from its starting point. This can be a safe route for creating some challenging material. Remember the *Villette* cast almost forgot all about *Villette*. All casts can become nervous and inhibited by the prospect of approaching difficult moments in a production. These moments can loom over the rehearsal room and effect confidence and morale. Sometimes it can be very useful to be taking the long route when creating work for those scenes. This was certainly the case with the fight in *Stockholm* (see 'Stockholm Fight and the Crooked Path' on page 32).

WORKING WITH LARGE GROUPS

The Fives

Many of the devising techniques have focused on duets but that does not mean they are only for couples. Round/By/Through is harder with three but yields something much more complex and rewarding when engaged by a group of three.

We encourage you to mix things up a little bit. It should all be play.

We have developed a process for working with larger groups that allows you to build gradually, gives you time to observe the scene develop and ultimately create something complex out of something very simple.

Be warned! This can get count heavy, depending on how far you want to take it. It may be worthwhile spending some time on Quad to get the group used to counting. Also get them used to ordering bars of counts. For example, we have recently found that we were presuming that people knew what we were talking about when we were counting bars of 8 out loud like this,

1,2,3,4,5,6,7,8,
2,2,3,4,5,6,7,8,
3,2,3,4,5,6,7,8,
4,2,3,4,5,6,7,8,

It was not the case and we were actually just confusing the participants. It is easily resolved and understood, however. The bold number at the beginning of each line is the bar number so that we know we might be talking about the third count of the fourth bar.

We started with something that would feel familiar and manageable. We got the group to start on their right foot and walk forward for eight counts and then turn left on the eighth count. They continue walking for eight counts and then turn left again. We continue this until we are back at the beginning or until the group appear to be comfortable with the counts, rhythm and transitions. They are essentially marching in a square. There should be nothing challenging about this. It is merely the first building block.

The reason it is familiar is that we are always starting a direction on the same foot and that, as we listen to most of our popular music in bars of eight or four, we are using the rhythm.

The next stage is to test that. Try turning every five counts. (It can be any odd number but we used an odd number less than eight because that would allow us to be more complex in the room without taking up more space.) The strangeness of this number will present a challenge. We are not used to how five feels, unlike four and eight. We are also beginning each turn on different feet.

Amanda Drew as Judy in *The Curious Incident of the Dog in the Night Time* by Simon Stephens, 2013 Cast. Image by Scott Graham

Once this is more comfortable you can insert a bit of complexity. Try walking forward for five counts and then immediately set off on a circle of five count/ steps that finishes where it started. This should look like a loop that leaves the straight line but joins back from the departure point after five counts. Then continue forward for another five. Next you can turn to the left and walk for another five counts.

This is four bars of five counts. The circle is on the second bar. The left turn is on the fourth. Bars one and three are merely walking forward.

Bar five turns left again and you are now facing down the room. If you imagine the original marching square has now become a rectangle and you have worked your way up the right hand side and across the top of it. Bars five through to eight are a repeat of the actions of bars one to four and should ensure you return to your starting position at the bottom right of the rectangle.

Once this is secure you can start to play with bars, adding complexity. This is about choreographic complexity at this stage but once that is mastered it can be about character complexity. We shall come to that soon.

At the beginning of bar four, instead of turning to your left, try turning to your right and walking backwards across the top of the rectangle, as if suddenly in reverse gear. This should still begin on the left foot and means that the transition into bar five should still be on the right foot. Remember bar five onwards is, at this stage, identical to bar one, two and three (you have just changed bar four).

All of these bars are up for grabs. Once you have this you can be as complex as you like.

Halfway through the seventh bar of our version we had all the men reverse direction and run to the top left of the rectangle. They took the remaining of the seventh and the whole of the eighth bar to complete this. The women would have continued on the original pattern meaning that they are at opposite corners of the rectangle at the end of the eighth bar. On the beginning of the ninth bar we repeat the original sequence but now there are two teams working opposite each other.

This is an important moment because they will now be heading towards each other. On the tenth bar both groups will be circling and this should be embraced as a moment where they can pass through each other before they both straighten up on the eleventh bar and head away from each other. These moments present a strange order emerging out of chaos. Keep an eye on interesting moments of connection or near miss. You can return to this later when you are adding character quirks and personality.

If all this talk of counts and bars is feeling daunting, rest assured it is much simpler to do than it is to read or write it!

And now to think about context. We used this process to create a scene within *The Curious Incident of the Dog in the Night Time* where Christopher ventures to the train station for the first time and is mesmerised/overloaded by the barrage of information and is confused by all the people walking with purpose and drive through the concourse. Everything in *Curious* is seen through Christopher's eyes and to him they are a group unified by movement. We wanted them to possess a pattern and drive that frightened and alienated him. This is what a busy station concourse must look like for a bewildered Christopher.

Only once our group felt confident with the basic pattern did we introduce the context. It remained a choreographic task until then. Performers did not have to worry about character and nuance. Just getting those counts and steps into their muscle memory. When that happened we started to talk about context.

That allowed us to get performers to look in set directions, reading information screens and checking for departure times, all set on certain counts. We could choreograph quirks and intentions for different characters. We could also cut into the pattern and pull focus onto individuals. This could be people running late or looking for their date partner across the concourse. These isolated moments would not stand out if there were no unison. It would just be chaos. We also choreographed unison moments where the whole group would look for a certain screen or simultaneously check their watches. We could look to create more complexity because of the building blocks approach. We could feel confident in their ability to take on and retain new information. In the technical rehearsal we even started giving them props as we felt they did not look real enough! This meant that they were now doing all of the choreography with a brief case or while simulating a chat on the mobile.

If we had introduced these elements earlier there would have been a mass brain meltdown and possible walk out! The important lesson is to observe and gauge the group. Have they reached saturation point? Could they handle one more detail?

Also, choreographically, this process allows you to let chaos emerge from order and vice versa. You have taken inspiration from seeing things happen in front of you. This is an important luxury you must allow yourself. The more you create in a void the more others will feel it and look to you to fill that void. That can be an uncomfortable pressure. This approach gives your cast a manageable structure and you valuable time to think.

OBSERVATIONAL INSPIRATION

Physical dexterity and complicated choreography can feel like the most difficult things to master. Of course we are forgetting that we do this every day. Driving a car is a complicated dance of mind and body that a lot of us take for granted. We just need to look at it in a different way to see the dexterity our bodies possess in simultaneously steering, putting the clutch down and changing gear.

Realising this can help give us the confidence that we can master complex choreography. Of course, learning to drive a car takes lots of practice and time and not everyone gets there but there are other examples we can refer to that show our ability to absorb complicated movement into muscle memory and, in doing so, take their beautiful complexity for granted.

Ties

For example, in the rehearsals for *Lovesong* we gave two of the performers a tie each and asked them to tie it around their necks. They immediately did so without any hesitation. We got them to watch each other as they did it again and they realised that they did this in quite different ways. They had different 'dances'. We took the ties away and got them to replicate the moves with their hands only. This presented two fascinating little hand dances. To stop it looking like a mime we asked them to take their hands further from their bodies. This helped reinvent the movement as something strange, fluid and alien. We did not take it for granted anymore. It was not a mime. It was choreography.

Also, when you next tie your laces, look at the dexterity of your fingers as they dance and loop around each other. It is quite beautiful.

Both of these examples teach us two things. One, we are capable of meticulous and complex choreography when repetition converts the thought process to muscle memory and, two, the actions we take for granted, that exist in the background, are often beautifully mesmerising when presented in a new context.

Refs

This understanding was behind our intention to study the movement of the referees of a boxing match for the production *Beautiful Burnout*. When people picture boxing they are most likely to imagine the two boxers slugging it out. Few will consider the ever-present third that dances around and between them, who gestures instructions from within the cacophony, who signals to the crowd and indicates any foul play or penalty incurred.

We decided to look at hours of footage of boxing matches and focus only on the movement of the referee. It became instantly apparent that this character, which mostly pulls off the trick of being invisible, has a vast palette of absurd shapes, leaps, gestures and manoeuvres at his disposal. He is light on his feet, ready to pounce in a split second. He is looking around corners, through limbs and into the eyes of the boxers. He is both not there and totally

Ali Craig, Margaret Ann Bain and Matthew Trevannion perform Refs in *Beautiful Burnout* (2012). Image by Scott Graham

there, prepared to be decisive and definitive at any moment. It might be this dichotomy that lends him the unique physicality.

We asked three of our performers to study the footage and create a string of material each using the physical quirks of the referees. They remained separate while they did this, as we wanted to be able to draw on three very different strings. They were instructed not to worry about any story or logic, just to concentrate on the moves. It would not really help them to get caught up in imagining a couple of boxers. That would merely place the quirky movement back in the world that inspired it. It would make it normal. We wanted their string of material to be a quick succession of moves randomly put together.

What followed was the familiar process of teaching the other performer your string of material and learning theirs. We wanted to make a much longer scene where three referees moved in unison in this strange, alien way.

While rehearsing the finished unison one of our performers made a spectacular error that saw her setting off in completely the wrong direction from the other two referees. This was a thrilling moment, taking us totally by surprise. It was a brilliant reminder about the perils of unison and perfectly illustrated what we have written about unison elsewhere in this book. It is a brilliant way to create work. It is a hellish way to perform it!

We immediately set about cutting into the material, creating moments where one referee would freeze and then catch up with the string further down the line. We would reverse the direction of some sections too. That created a more complex routine of three referees in unison, suddenly bursting out on their own and then surprising us by re-joining the unison seamlessly.

This two-minute sequence was made entirely of moves pulled from footage of referees doing what referees do. It was the act of looking at them afresh that made their movement so rich and fascinating. And that was the point. We wanted to highlight what we take for granted.

The lesson is look for stimuli in the unusual places. Everyday actions can have fluidity or a dexterity that the best choreographers or dancers might melt trying to create from scratch, yet we are all capable of them and do them without thinking.

A colleague of ours, Dan O'Neill, made an award-winning short film about the actions of a linesman at a football match (*The Linesman*). He observed the behaviour the casual observer might look beyond and found an extraordinary palette with which to play. Dan had his linesman become a wannabe ballet dancer but the clever part was placing the root of this exaggerated behaviour in the linesman's natural physicality.

This is just one example of looking at behaviour with fresh eyes. You could look at almost any aspect of life and find the peculiar choreography at the heart of its day-to-day rituals. It is not particularly clever to just copy and mime these actions. It is much more interesting to make them new for the audience. The point is to NOT recognise the movements we take for granted. We need to be shown them from a new perspective to make them interesting and surprising to us. This is what makes them special. Remember that we already have a history of taking these moves for granted! Don't just remind us of the original context. Shine a new light on these sophisticated moves. That is why it was important for the three *Beautiful Burnout* performers to ignore any impulse to tell a consistent story with their referee moves. If they had done that they would have instructed the audience to see what is NOT there, i.e. the boxers. Then it becomes mime.

Dee Birds

This was an exercise we used during the creation of *Dr Dee*, an ambitious and rich rehearsal period for a new opera under the direction of Rufus Norris and Damon Albarn as composer. Taking the extraordinary life of the unsung British hero John Dee as the source of the piece it involved an ensemble of singers, dancers and actors.

The show was to begin with the arrival of several real ravens flying onto the set. A later scene would revolve around an epic game of chess between Dee and Lord Walsingham, a powerful figure within whom rests the possibility of high patronage. Walsingham's power and reach was represented by a number

Clemmie Sveass and Victoria Couper in *Dr Dee* (2011). Image by Scott Graham

of acolytes dressed entirely in black, who would surround and swarm him and the stage whenever he appeared. Essentially they were the ravens. We wanted them to have an otherworldly quality. Dressed in black masks with long snouts (modelled on Elizabethan plague masks) the acolytes were to watch and crowd Dee with an eerieness that only birds possess! This chess game marked their first appearance in human form but their physicality was to be a direct link to and reminder of the ravens that had shocked the audience as the lights went down. The idea was that these spies can be everywhere. (Scooby and Liza were the names of the ravens, in case you were wondering.)

There are many actors who have had the excruciating experience of being seen publicly as part of a group of drama school students who are lead around a zoo on a mission to discover and observe 'their' animal. An experience only made the more appalling by the inevitability of having to be their 'sloth' in front of classmates sometime later that week after ruminating on the observations made from standing in front of the aforementioned creature for what was seen as an expected amount of time. Time was not in short supply during the making of *Dr. Dee* but we still felt that a visit to London Zoo would bring back unwelcome memories from some of our company. A mixture of dancers and actors, we knew we wanted to start a creative exercise with some kind of inspiration – a source that the entire company could relate to in some way that would allow for a sense of something without necessarily drawing too many parameters around the possibilities of the exercise.

We are long-time devotees of the work of Chris Cunningham and it is probably true to say that we are always looking for any appropriate occasion to use his work as a reference point. Despite his own misgivings on the process and eventual result, Cunningham directed a stunning music video for Madonna on the release of her single 'Frozen'. It is a shady and shadowy work (if you don't believe that there is a distinction between these two terms, just watch this video for proof). In it, the singer appears on a desolate beach at twilight in an undulating black cape which is, for the most part, Cunningham's point of focus for the video. It forms a dark, sinister choreography, wrapping itself around the lone female figure, engulfing and revealing to extraordinary effect. Cunningham uses reversed footage at times to add to the sense of unease.

At one point during the video, Madonna stands up and immediately falls backwards. Upon impact with the cracked surface of sand, her cloaked body shatters into a flock of black birds that take to the sky. This moment is perhaps why we were initially drawn to this video. However, after several viewings, we realised that it was the story of the cloak that was more useful. Whereas the birds did just what you might expect from a flock of menacing birds, the cloak was another beast altogether. It had a rhythm that was singularly odd, flowing one minute and jerking and snapping into odd configurations the next.

The blackness of the cloak created shadows within shadows that suggested the depth of movement around the human body.

It is worth pointing out that it is always a risk when presenting a room with a Madonna video when that room is full of cultured, experienced and varied individuals. We held our nerve and set the cast off on the task. It was simple. Watch the movement of the cloak throughout the video noting its surprising twists, flows and jolts.

We watched the Cunningham film many times so that the company could really observe the qualities inherent in the cloak. We then looked at clips of crows, magpies, blackbirds and ravens. We asked the performers to look out for the more surprising elements of movement and behaviour. We did not spend long on this. In the case of the Madonna video, this was about informing their creative minds with something very specific. With the latter, it was about simply finding a moment or two.

After an hour or so, the room was alive with twitchy, swooping, elegant, awkward bodies and we were richly furnished with the physical language we wanted. The performers were asked to create a string of material that lasted a number of beats or counts (two bars of eight). We then put the performers into two 'flocks' with around five birds in each. We asked them to teach one another their own individual sequences, ultimately making for a long unison sequence from both flocks. This latter stage took a few sessions over a number of days. This is the period where you can see where the performers are inspired, where they are challenged (good) and where they are habitually happy (bad). Even at this stage, it is always worthwhile nudging, suggesting, urging, shaping a little – all the while beginning to figure out what it is you might want to do with this material in terms of its choreographic potential.

The birds had to enter with a genuine fascination in Dee and his work. They also had to have an air of threat. We talked about how as individuals they could probably be swatted away. As a flock they had a terrible strength. (Alfred Hitchcock had already demonstrated this beautifully, of course.) They should be inquisitive, apprehensive and full of an unpredictable potential to burst into movement. This is often what terrifies people about being trapped in a confined space with a bird.

We looked at the arc of their time on stage in this scene. It started with entrances, then introductory behaviour, then flock mentality. They entered. They observed. They mimicked. They tested surfaces. They engaged Dee in a challenge. They are defeated. They will not forget this. They will return stronger. By applying this very simple progressive development, we gave ourselves a dramatic arc and the audience an introduction to wordless characters who would suggest something sinister and (taking bird form) timeless – that establishments can always reach into the lives of its people and find a way to crush them. The scene was about Dee winning the battle but the suggestion must be that they would return and win the war. Presenting Dee's easy victory over the birds was to simultaneously suggest his intellectual ability and that this will ultimately make him powerful enemies. There always needed to be the sense that the birds would return. This is where engaging the imagination of the audience pays great rewards. All it would take was for the suggestion of a dark feather on stage to announce that the moment for revenge had come.

The actual chess match was taken from a classic game plan where checkmate is achieved in a very small number of moves. Again, this was sourced from YouTube. During the game the birds would highlight their bird-like qualities – sharp head adjustments, necks pulled in, claws skittering across the hard surface of the table. We had presented the court of Walsingham as jeering, sneaky, cowardly birds; cowardly as individuals but dark and threatening as a flock.

Not all the moments of bird-like movement were the most obvious if we were to look at a written list of bird-like physical traits. That is the pleasure of engaging talented eyes on a simple observational task. They see something that you have missed. One performer found a moment of bouncing across a table with knees locked but bent. He had somehow captured the essense of these birds. There was an instant 'Yes!' from everyone else in the room – one of those instances where we would not have believed it to be true if described to us. You had to see it to know it was true. It was a moment of magic.

chapter five

Devising and words

This chapter examines the practical starting points of both words and images as creative stimulants. Drawing on our experience of collaborating with many writers, this chapter also looks at the keys to a successful relationship with a writer in a collaborative environment.

Words as starting points – working physically with text

When working with text you may be setting out on a piece of collaborative new writing or working as choreographer on an existing text. You may even have the title 'movement director' and be asked to consider all physical aspects of the production. We will try to touch on all aspects of creating physicality from words.

For a long time we maintained that the words always came first in our devising process. That rule is not so hard and fast now that we feel more confident about working from images and through physicality. Our experiences on *Stockholm* and *Beautiful Burnout*, both with Bryony Lavery, and *Lovesong* with Abi Morgan have shown us that the physicality can be just as inspiring to the words as the words have proven for the physicality.

When looking for the physical potential within the words, we have to look at those words in several ways. Is there enough space in the text for physicality to flourish? Is there a rich subtext to explore under the words?

Do these characters really mean what they say? What do the stage directions offer?

Space

One of our main requirements when commissioning a writer is to consider space. By that we mean the unsaid. This could be rage or sadness or unrequited love. By remaining unsaid they offer rich pickings for choreographed physicality.

Not all of our writers have necessarily delivered this space. That presents us with problems and, shall we say, challenges and opportunities? With some writers the concept of space and the physicality that filled it was central to the writing process. Chris O'Connell's *Hymns*, Abi Morgan's *Tiny Dynamite*, Bryony Lavery's *Stockholm* are all examples of this. We have had to fight for this space on other productions, notably Brendan Cowell's *Rabbit* and Mark Ravenhill's *pool (no water)*. It is important to consider this 'space' when you set out to approach the text physically. Are you empowering the production by having your cast dance across the stage? Are the moves breaking up the rhythm of the show?

We have fallen foul of this on *Stockholm*. We created a physical scene in what we thought was a missing beat from the play. We called it Tea Towels and it charted the mellowing of a couple after an argument. We absolutely loved this tender and complex scene of gradual and grudging reconciliation. Its complexity and simplicity was a bit of an achievement. In isolation it worked well and promised to be a charming crowd pleaser. When we considered it in the production as a whole it was clear that it was destroying the rhythm of Bryony's play and it had to go. It was hard saying good bye to good material but cutting that scene was the most grown up thing either of us have done in our lives. (For those who know us, that will not be such a big surprise.)

For more about this scene, see 'Stockholm Fight and the Crooked Path', page 32.

Subtext

The subtext is crucial. It is very important to aim to express what is not said verbally. If you are reinforcing what has been said verbally, then you are just saying things twice.

The difficult thing to gauge is whether, by articulating the subtext, you are giving the audience something new and valuable or are you just doing their thinking for them? There is little more infuriating and patronising for an audience than to be presented with the latter.

In one of the early drafts of *Hymns*, writer Chris O'Connell was so desperate to give us opportunity for physicality that he set it in the basement of the home of a deceased street performer. The hope was that the numerous props would inspire physicality or, crudely, give us something to do! We had to convince him that his text was full of physical opportunities as it was. It was the characters and what they were saying and, more importantly, not saying to each other that was so rich (see 'Lullaby', page 50).

Hymns was about four men mourning the loss of their friend. It was inspired by the disproportionate number of suicides among young men and how this appeared to be brushed under the carpet. It was about how people do not talk about such things. As this was the case how could we then have our characters, four ordinary men struggling to come to terms with a tragic event, suddenly buck the trend and become eloquent on the matter?

Hymns required a brave writer as all that the words could truthfully express was the characters' inarticulacy and their small talk. It was the physicality and the subtext that had to possess the eloquence. The writer, now fully aware of this, left plenty of space and kept the words bordering on the banal while suggesting this torrent of emotion and questions existing underneath. It became a writer happily writing for the possibilities of a physical approach, allowing images, silence and movement to carry scenes and recognising that, as a writer, he was only part of the theatrical process. (In practice, especially with *Stockholm* and Bryony Lavery, we found that this actually extended the writer's vocabulary rather than limiting it.)

Stage directions

The most obvious area within a text for physicality to flourish is in the stage directions. They are, after all, the bits the writer admits they do not want to express through words. They are, however, a minefield.

On our first production (*Look Back in Anger*) we embraced the stage directions as autocratic demands from the omnipotent author. They were vocalised by the performers and served to highlight how unnatural and uncomfortable they were for characters we wanted to set free. On reflection we were probably just naive, reactionary and trying to make some point that escapes us now. Our adaptation, while aiming to find the original fire at the heart of the play, was less than respectful to the existing text. Stage directions felt like interference and led to a long-standing and unhealthy disregard for them.

It was while working on *Tiny Dynamite* that we developed a new interest in stage directions. Rather than interference, Abi Morgan's stage directions felt like windows through which we could grasp a greater understanding of the world she was creating. This might sound obvious, but what was wonderful about these stage directions was their impossibility. We were instructed to glow in the dark, to climb to the top of an electricity pylon, etc. They were all clips from the film of *Tiny Dynamite* that existed in Abi's head. With the wrong writer this can be a nightmare. Somehow, with Abi, this was a joy – probably because Abi treated the stage directions as windows and opportunities too, rather than demands for prescribed theatricality.

Tiny Dynamite was probably the easiest rehearsal process we have ever experienced. Everyone shared a knowledge and understanding of this film version and everything just fell into place. We knew the world we were aiming for. We knew what it smelled like, tasted like and so on.

Every bizarre stage direction appeared to be linked to an emotion, an effect on the beholder. It was not just about actually being able to climb up the pylon in the middle of an electrical storm. It was the feeling of watching your drunk friend climb up the pylon in the electrical storm. We never spoke about how we were going to literally achieve the pylon and when the scene was presented to Abi, she never questioned its omission because we had captured the essence of the situation – not the construction of metal and wires but the human predicament played out upon it.

Abi also presented us with some unavoidable challenges. She directed the characters to swim about in a lake! We were fearful of being asked to come up with some swimming physicality, but we found a way of solving the issue and, with designer Julian Crouch, decided on how to present the lake. We talked about only ever showing the beginning or end of the swim, the leaping in or scrambling out. The 'lake' became a hole in the decking that constituted the set, under which lay a small plastic paddling pool with an inch of cold (very cold) water in it. We would baste ourselves in the water before surfacing through the hole, dripping wet and exhausted from our 'swim'.

This was one stage direction we were very happy to pass on to someone else. It was also a sign of a true and healthy collaboration that the designer felt he could step in to solve something that could so easily have been someone else's problem.

While working on *Villette* as movement directors we were faced with a script that had physicalise written in bold every few pages in what appeared to be a fairly arbitrary fashion. As it turned out, writer Lisa Evans's instinct for what should be a physical scene was pretty sound. Our reticence or reluctance was just a mardy residue of our earlier suspicion of stage directions and their interference in our judgement.

There was a particular stage direction that struck the fear of God into us.

A fire breaks out in the theatre. There is panic.

In what appears now to be a sustained bout of stupidity we feared that what we were being asked to articulate physically was the fire, as it would have been difficult to present through design or lighting. We imagined we were being asked to create an expressive dance piece where people became flames, licking and crackling around the stage!

Once the fear and stupidity passed we realised that it was simply the human predicament that we must articulate. It was the panic and desperation of those trying to escape. It was the strange calm over the face of the one who had given up hope and was resigned to death. It was about strength and weakness. It was about terror and heroism. (See 'Villette Floor', page 159.)

There was nothing in the text to map out a story for us other than a fire starts, people try to escape, two central characters rescue a new and important character. This was perfect for us because it gave us everything to create in between the fire and the escape. Here was an example of a stage direction that had terrified us turning out to inspire us. Conversely, there is a stage direction in *Rabbit* by Brendan Cowell that we just could not wait to sink our teeth into: Alone in her parents' holiday home Madeleine wants to seduce her boyfriend, Spin, before her parents turn up. He wants to ingest a cocktail of drugs and then submit to the seduction. Convincing her of the merits of his suggestion she finally relents. Cue stage direction ...

Kids let loose.

Three perfect words that sum up the situation but also open up a world of debauched possibilities. It suggests Bacchanalian excess and frenzied indulgence. It also captured the social dynamic perfectly. This was a woman in her twenties with her slightly older boyfriend in the prized holiday home of her parents. All of the tension and desire added to the significance of the setting makes them 'kids' again.

Whether Brendan Cowell stumbled upon this phrase in his own rock-and-roll fashion or whether he took hours crafting it does not diminish its genius in our eyes. It was the perfect invitation to play and create. It is that invitation that makes the killer stage direction.

There was also a moment in *Hymns* where the characters flippantly embraced someone's words and turned them into a stage direction. The words 'We could just talk' inspired a camp and expressive torrent of small talk and gestural choreography all based on important subject matters like football, cars, women and DIY.

This scene (see 'Headwrecker', page 52) was more than a dramatic tension release. Set among four friends avoiding the main issues at the funeral of a friend, it also commented on how easy it is to talk. Talking was not the problem. Talking about their feelings and things that mattered appeared to be the problem. While *Hymns* explored this inability to open up, ultimately it was about our inability to listen when confronted with men speaking about those things that really mattered. The flippancy of Headwrecker set this up well.

Beware the misguided invitation, however! Some stage directions explicitly invite physical creativity, but the task is an empty one and does not move the narrative on. Sometimes they are quite prescriptive and much more like Beckett's stage directions. The author has had all the creativity and just wants you to act them out. We have received many scripts about rock climbing, horse riding, skateboarding, etc. because we are a physical company. This prescriptive physicality is not what we are interested in.

When working with a writer you have the opportunity to discuss such matters. The initial stage directions within *Hymns* were really just to give us opportunities to be busy. We convinced Chris O'Connell that we did not need them as his words were inspiring a physicality that could move the production on and liberate the writing from some of the storytelling.

It is important not to leap at any opportunity to be physical. Like any aspect of a production the physicality must earn its position. Does a physical scene really move things forward? Offering variety to the production is not a good enough reason to leave it in. Let the physicality breathe life into the production by saying something that needs to be said that cannot be said verbally.

How physical is physical?

It is important to remind yourself that you are serving the production as a whole and, in the case of movement direction on an existing play, you are serving that text. Therefore do not get hung up on the spectacular, dynamic or crowd pleasing.

One of our biggest decisions on *Rabbit* was to give the Mother character a tiny moment of stage time on her own. Every word she spoke, every opinion expressed was heinous, but we felt that there must be more to her than this. Here is a woman between a dying husband and a spiteful daughter. We did not want to forgive her obvious deficiencies. We just wanted to present her in three dimensions.

We choreographed a tiny moment when she knew she was alone and allowed the façade to drop for a second. Frightened and unloved by her family, she cradles the live rabbit they have procured for dinner. She holds it tightly. Too tightly. Even this rabbit is going to die and leave her. It was a moment of fear and uncertainty of the future. It made our audience reassess her slightly and by changing the theatrical focus right down to a close-up on her, the unexpected moment of human weakness was as spectacular as any firework.

The Residency Model

From the very beginning we have been making self-contained shows in residencies around the country and now around the world. The aim is to make a show from scratch and perform it with full technical support for a public audience, often within four days. These are often extremely intense periods of creativity and prove equally exhausting and inspiring for both the performing participants and us.

This process has become central to our Ignition programme. Ignition is designed to unearth male talent from all walks of life, to nurture and develop it and ultimately use it for Frantic Assembly shows. This came about through recognising a dearth of professional male physical performers despite us seeing that our workshops and processes were going down a storm with teenage boys in schools. They were clearly not making the leap towards this as a vocation. We aimed to redress this imbalance. As we came from non-theatre backgrounds we could testify for the value of the creative experience and for how our non-theatre skills were transferable. It meant that we went looking for these boys in street dance groups, sports clubs, parkour, martial arts clubs, etc. Basically, the places where we might have found ourselves if we had not been lucky enough to get switched on to theatre.

We would hold taster workshops for the boys to see if it was for them and then invite them to trials for the four-day intensive, based on the residency model. The trials were always in workshop form so that no one would feel exposed and would at least leave having had fun. We always sought to create an inclusive and non-alienating atmosphere.

Those successful would attend the five-day intensive. This essentially becomes very similar to the process of any residency. Possibly a little more intense, though!

Below we are going to use *The Fear* as an example of a residency. This was an Ignition show in October 2009. We hope it serves to outline the process of a typical residency, capturing the creative process, the levels of input from the participants, the division of labour and the intensity of the effort involved.

On the morning of Day 1 we meet our company for the first time. On Day 5 we present a performance normally lasting around 45 minutes long that is based on the experiences of the company, based around a theme or subject that we have decided upon prior to rehearsals. During those days, the performers are treated as professional performers and as if they are a proper company. Residencies are a very intense period and when held in schools we make sure we have full access to the students over four or five days. This means getting students off timetable, which is becoming increasingly difficult. In the case of *The Fear* and other Ignition shows, we are working with

Zuck Harris rehearses for *The Fear*, Ignition (2011). Image by Scott Graham

Lindokuhle Nkomo in *From Me To You*, Ignition (2013). Image by Helen Maybanks

performers from across the country that are mostly out of education but nonetheless we plan them for half terms to make sure that people have maximum availability, and to ensure we are given the hours needed to create such an ambitious piece.

Over the years, we have created many, many pieces in this way. They have sometimes been a very useful way for us to try out ideas and material for ourselves but more often, they work simply as a way of having a creative blast. This is a slightly guerilla mode of working where we have to think fast, make fast and present as fully and as beautifully as possible. Often these residencies have felt like a recharging of tired creative batteries, an antidote to the trials and tribulations of extensive touring and development of work. The performers are always brand new and completely unknown to us so we are truly starting from square one with them in terms of a working relationship.

In most instances, the process will begin with a single meeting between us, where we present possible ideas or themes that might work well for such a process. Themes that have been successful are ones where the participants, though unknown to us, will be able to contribute. This means that the subject matter must speak to them all in some way. Preferably in a way that allows some kind of emotional response. Subject matters need to have an element of soul searching, but they need to stay safe – the last thing we would want is for the initial stages to feel like compulsory therapy sessions among a roomful of people that have never met before.

The idea for *The Fear* came from a song by the band Unkle, called 'F.E.A.R.' We sat down and chatted with Neil Bettles, our Frantic associate who was also a co-director of the piece, and the following images emerged...

Hands suffocating a talking head
Lined up against a back wall
A cluster of microphones suspended in the air
A mass of clowns
How we fight fear
Chris Cunningham videos
Music tracks by John Metcalfe, Nine Inch Nails and Olafur Arnalds
An extensive list of actual phobias

In addition, we created the following questionnaire:

Describe a fear you once had but not now.
Describe a fear you have now.
Have you ever really frightened anyone?
Who is the most frightening person that you know. Why?
What is the phone call you fear making the most?

Who were/are you scared of at school?
What does fear feel like?
How do you physically overcome fear?
Is there anything about this project that you are nervous about?

So far so good, and all done within the space of an hour. In many ways, this is the key to a successful start. Enough of an idea of where we are heading but no expectations of what we might get back from the participants. This allows us to think within a defined parameter in terms of music, images and physicality so that the three of us can come together at the start of the week and have a few creative tools at our disposal.

Day 1 working list looked like this...

Day 1
Name Circle
Quad
Stretches
Lifts
Round/By/Through
Questionnaires

All the exercises above are described in detail in this book and are pretty formulaic 'ways in' for us. What this does allow us is a full day of being able to watch the company and see where their strengths lay in terms of physicality and skills. We are also able to see how quickly they can pick up instructions, how well they are able to generate physical material and how they operate within this new group dynamic.

The Name Circle is always a good starting point. It ensures that the group knows each other by name and the exercise creates a great, physical dynamic in the room where the performers are soon yelling each other's names as they charge at full speed towards one another. Quad plays the more jovial card and is a great signifier in showing whom in the group is familiar with using counts in music and who is not. This will play an important part when we begin to select certain performers for certain types of physical sequences later on. The stretches were done in pairs and they are there to test how confident and comfortable the performers are with close contact. We encourage and assist in this part of the morning by making the exercise feel very much 'task based' and in no way about any kind of emotional connection or performance. The task is about giving the partner a good, deep stretch in preparation for the day. The lifts section is one where they are taught four or five standard lifts, in order to get their heads around the concept of squeezing the lifted person into yourself and in this way, make the principle of lifting your partner that much easier – ensuring it becomes a technique that does not rely on pure strength. Again, this encourages reliance on one another and close contact work that is about copying what we are showing them. Round/By/ Through takes these contact elements and creates a creative task for the performers. At this stage, it is very likely that we will use the material they create here once we have found a way to attach it to the theme of the show. This is not declared to the room at this time – it is important that they do not become aware that they are now creating for us. In this way we keep them safe from any anxieties about 'making'. From our side, they have just made their first sequence for us.

The questionnaire is held at the end of the day and involves sweaty, tired bodies sitting around with a paper and pen answering each question as a group but sitting in their own space so that they can reflect on each one. We always play music tracks in the background (as has been the case all day) in order for it not to suddenly feel like an exam room. They are then sent home – usually early on this day – and told to take a bath and rest well...

The rest of this first day is probably the most crucial in the making of any residency. This is the session where we, as directors, look over the material in the questionnaire results and read aloud what we have. With *The Fear* we made, among others, the following discoveries:

- The boys were afraid of wasps, plugs, toys and being in a room with more girls than boys.
- Fear felt like sandpaper through veins. It gave you sticky hands.
- Dads were frightening if they were aggressive.
- The man on the train with the white contact lenses was scary.
- A short prayer would put you to sleep and save you from the Sleep Cops who come after you if you don't go to sleep.
- One frightening dream involved fingers falling off.

From this, we started to create a number of 'scenes' that were a response to the day and the ideas that sprung from watching the tasks play out. At the end of this session we had the following on our list of 'possibles'...

Physical sequences

- Response to bangs and loud noises.
- Approaching a fearful object.
- Scary clowns.
- Bodies falling apart.
- Comforting another body.
- Thrashing in a bed trying to get to sleep.

186 THE FRANTIC ASSEMBLY BOOK OF DEVISING THEATRE

Text

- A definition of fear.
- The biological effects on the human body.
- A roll call of phobias.
- How to defeat the Sleep Police.

So already, we had ten 'scenes' and the sudden need to find a bed we could use as a prop! From here until the actual performance, the rest of the week is about clever planning and time management. Working backwards, we knew we had to have everything made and completed within the next three days as the final day would be taken up with going into the theatre and setting everything up, running a tech session for the entire show and then a dress rehearsal of some kind.

As an initial approach, we look at the physical scenes and see which ones will be the most difficult. As this is an Ignition residency, we also work hard to ensure that every performer gets to play to their strengths and has significant stage time, but also performs in ways that are not their normal territory. A phenomenal street dancer will be chosen as part of a delicate, emotional duet for instance. At the heart of this is our desire to create an ensemble on stage in the truest meaning of the word. If achieved, it will always belie the fact that the company has been in existence for less than 45 hours.

On the morning of Day 2 we spoke to the company about their answers to the questionnaire. It is not always the case that the answer given by performer A will be said by performer A during the show. Sometimes it will be performer B. This might be because performer A might not be comfortable revealing certain things about themselves but has no problem if it comes from the mouth of performer B. Sometimes it is more interesting for the responses of the tiny, diminutive, bird-like performer C to have his answers played out in a speech spoken by the hulking brute that is performer D. In some cases, we will ask a performer to extend or expand on a short answer if we feel there might be more to discover or understand. Like in any rehearsal process, we will spend time with any performer that has text, directing them and getting them to a performance level – something that is still time-consuming, even if they are speaking about themselves in a wholly naturalistic way.

On the second day we had a list for the week that looked like this...

Day 2
Fear Approach sequence (inspired by the idea of a birthday gift that seemed frightening in its box).
Comfort Duets (sequence using the material we saw from the Round/By/ Through exercise on Day 1).

Bangs sequence (based on the idea of what the body does when it hears a loud bang).

Day 3

All texts and monologues so far (Lecture 1 – Definition of Fear; and Lecture 2 – The Effects of Fear on the Body).

Phobia List (one by one the performers come forward to the microphone and describe a phobia and react accordingly).

Clowns sequence and text (Johnny has a speech about his life being ruined by a fear of clowns as four horror clowns approach from behind before executing a menacing sequence on and around him).

Day 4

Pre-show torch sequence.

Breaking Bodies sequence/Jordan text (Jordan speech about fear of the body breaking down – opening out into six bodies doing just that as a physical sequence).

Callum Ending text.

Stagger through entire show.

Day 5

Get in and tech/company interviews and appraisal.

Dress rehearsal.

Evening – performance.

For each of the rehearsal days, we would create the new material in the morning session and then in the afternoon, return to existing material and run it again, adding, changing, shaping as required. In every instance, we would set the performers a task of creating a short amount of physical material based on the ideas listed above. Working with music tracks, we would then collate the physical results and start to put it together. This would often involve performers learning each other's material to create longer sections of movement.

We also pre-arranged a late night rehearsal session. In our experience, these are always a very useful session to have up your sleeve. They are different and often feel exciting. This late night work might not be the world they know! Everything feels and looks different. This is well beyond school hours and we are here because there is very important work to be done. Invariably this session feels special. We were working in a rehearsal room with huge windows on one side and as the darkness fell, the whole of Canary Wharf began to light up and we felt like we were somehow suspended up in the darkness. We told the company that we had a short session at our disposal as we needed them to be rested for the following final day, but that we also had to create a whole new physical sequence from scratch. We had finally sourced a bed that we liked and we wanted to make a ballistic, dynamic physical sequence that involved everybody. Up until now, most sequences had involved roughly half the group. This planning is based on the need to sometimes have two exercises running at the same time when we needed to optimise efficient time use and also playing to strengths of the performers as well as constantly shifting the visual and physical dynamic of the company on stage during the performance. At one point on the afternoon of Day 4 we actually had four different groups rehearsing four separate sections (Bangs, Breaking Bodies, Clowns and Biology). This was possible through clever planning in terms of which performers we used in which sequences and also the fact that there were three of us directing *The Fear*. Throughout the rehearsal sessions we would constantly be playing different music tracks and making decisions as we went along. Final edits of the music tracks would have to take place during the Friday morning technical session as, until this point, we would not know how long the music tracks would need to be.

Day 5 was an exercise of military precision. By this time, we had invoked in the company a sense of responsibility and camaraderie.

In the afternoon we collect the company on stage and give them a little surprise – we have one more scene to make. It's the end scene and involves the entire company retiring to bed and 'blowing out' stage lights as they do so. It's a huge ask of the company at this eleventh hour and it creates a fantastic focus and intensity (and yes, we did plan it all along). We create it in less than 20 minutes. So we finish the show and then run it from the start. It's rough. It's not ready. Perfect.

The final few hours before our audience arrive are spent creating a sense of energised calm – those times when the company are encouraged to be in the space, running lines with each other, going through physical moments with their partners that didn't quite land in the afternoon dress run, walking through the show scene by scene (there are large posters on each side of the stage in the wings with a scene list containing words like 'Fearwalk', 'Bangs' and 'Jared's Comfort'). The three of us divided the speeches between us and spent a last session with any of the performers that had text in the performance, giving them last minute notes and suggestions.

The final 45-minute performance played to a sell-out audience and was shockingly powerful and polished. This is often the case and we always have to wonder what would happen if we were forced to make all our work with a little more of the 'guerilla' tactic. At every stage, we tell the company that they can only ever move forwards, that every run or attempt at a scene or sequence must improve on the last. That all notes we give them must be absorbed as quickly as possible. These time constraints are very real and we have a finite amount of hours and a very real, expectant audience at the end.

For us, it is always a feeling of real achievement. The quality of the material is often incredibly high. In practice, this is a result of a week where we are open to anything in the room being interesting or worthy of exploration. A week of fast decision making. Of hearing a single word and that being enough to kick off a whole new section. It is also a week of locking things down and holding them in place so that results are achieved every day. It is about not really knowing the end point but ensuring that the company always, always feel they are being nurtured, nourished and supported every step of the way. Ultimately, these residencies are about unlocking potential in the performer, and making it clear that intense, honest work is often closer to their own personal experience. That the crafting of an entire production can be made to look smooth and considered after only a few days. That all this is only possible with devotional amounts of mutual trust and respect.

The questionnaire and devising from a theme

As stated above, we run many residencies at schools and colleges throughout the world where we take a group, work with them as close to full time as we can get and make an original show with them. These are usually a week long and culminate in a performance at the end of the week. They are very intense periods of creative activity when our devising skills are stretched and tested to the full.

Each residency is different, but one of the consistencies is our use of a specially created questionnaire. We go into each residency with little more than a theme and a few trusted processes to fall back on because we want the show to be about the participants' lives and experiences.

The questionnaire

The questionnaire has been a big part of our creative process. It can be used to inspire both words and physicality. It is a way of opening up worlds unknown and tapping into the experiences of your collaborators. Below is an account of how it came to be used and how we have gone on to use it.

In 1998 Frantic Assembly collaborated with writer Michael Wynne on *Sell Out*. Due to the peculiarities of working with a small-scale touring theatre company, Michael was invited to be part of a project that already had a name, a tour and a poster design before a word had been written. He even had a brief that went along the lines of 'An argument among friends spirals out of control and things can never be the same again'. This was pretty much what we had offered venues to entice them to book the show.

This was the first time we had worked with a recognised writer other than Spencer Hazel and it was a new process for Michael too. Previously we had devised and written together (*Zero*) or worked closely with core collaborator Spencer (*Look Back in Anger, Klub, Flesh*), drawing on our own experiences, ideas and projections. The fear was that Michael could come in and strip that control away from us, although that was also the challenge, and cause for excitement and the reason for engaging this writer in the first place.

Michael's first act was to engage the cast in a series of workshops. One aspect of these workshops was the questionnaire outlined below. The genius of this move was that it invited the cast to offer stories, opinions, details without burdening them with the job of turning that information into a scene. It felt purely a fun exercise with, as you will see, a balance of absurd and probing personal questions. It was also confidential and to this day only he has seen all of our answers.

The brilliance of this approach is that it gathers acres of material, all of which has been collected through what looks like a chaotic questionnaire but is actually a carefully crafted and gently disarming document. It creates a buzz of excitement as the information gets handed back to the writer. It instantly sets up a level of trust between writer and performer and gives the performer an immediate input into the creative writing process.

But this is not play writing by committee. Such a process could have been disastrous and would have been a huge risk considering there was already a tour, a poster, and copy promising certain things to our potential audience. This was still clearly a writer in control. This was his research into the dark possibilities of destructive relationships. The reason for this process was for him to encounter something that would surprise him, to take him into realms he had not considered. It also allowed all the other creatives to have their say in a structured manner and still feel that they were part of that creative process. It asserted order where there could have been chaos.

We have used this process often when devising with young people in residencies. Often these residencies have a broad starting point or theme, e.g. people's experience of their birthdays, or their understanding of loss and death. We all have vastly different experiences and this process allows us all to share or offer our ideas in a safe and confidential way. The revelations from the returned questionnaires are often staggering. We live such varied lives and this gives us an insight into things beyond our imagination. Furthermore, all information is taken as true by the director. It has to be respected. It gives the director an understanding of the life experiences of the people he is working with and, often, making the work for. Invariably the questionnaire responses inspire scenes and text.

When this happens with your questionnaire, the next stage is to talk privately with the person whose questionnaire inspired it. You are about to make the private public and this must be done without dissolving the trust you have recently developed (and need to rely on). You must ask permission to use the information given. It may also be a good idea to encourage the person to lead this scene as it gives them ownership over the idea. Equally you must judge whether it is better, once given permission, to explore the idea maintaining confidentiality.

The questionnaire is a crucial part of disarming and engaging the participants of the many creative residencies we lead at schools and colleges around the world. It is important to construct your questionnaire so that it is full of open questions (i.e. questions that require more than a yes or no answer). You must also find the balance of engaging the participants in a fun and open experience while still creating information that is of use to you. We often start with the questionnaire before telling the participants what the show will be about. This, importantly, keeps their minds open and they don't feel the need to respond in a certain way. The following is Michael's questionnaire for *Sell Out*. It is worth remembering that *Sell Out* was a show that debunked the 'friends are the new family' notion so popular at the time. It was a show full of back-stabbing and sexual shenanigans but, as you can see, the questionnaire seeks to disarm, engage and inspire the participants just as much as it is designed to dig and delve into the scandal of their lives. It should also be remembered that *Sell Out* was made in 1994 and some of the questions have, well, dated somewhat!

The Sell Out Questionnaire

What is your favourite smell? ....

Describe a discovery about a friend that shocked you, including your response and that of your pals. ....

What position do you sleep in? ....

List your drunk and drugged regrets. ....

What is the worst thing you have stolen? ....

How do you like your eggs? ....

Describe something you discovered about a friend that didn't bother you. ....

Describe your best friend's gestures or expressions. ....

Have you ever been drunk on your own – why? ....

Describe a situation where you were misunderstood. ....

Describe being dumped. ....

How many Maltesers can you fit in your mouth? ....

Have you ever been dumped not face to face?...

Mobile phones – discuss. ....

What have you done that was illegal?...

What were you really into when you were young that you now really hate?...

Is there anything you wanted to do when you were young but not now – what changed? ....

Describe an argument that made you storm off. ....

Faxes – discuss. ....

Ever been caught slagging someone off? ....

What have you bought that you really didn't need? ....

If depressed, what cheers you up? ....

Internet/E-mail – discuss. ....

Have you ever insulted or offended someone and regretted it? ....

What do you want most in the world? ....

What are our generation's specific problems? ....

What makes you get out of bed? ....

Did video kill the radio star?...

Devising through Research and Development

People are often intrigued by what we take into the first days of rehearsal and what we get from a research and development session. The process is different for each show, but we thought it might be interesting to focus on the development of *Stockholm* (written by Bryony Lavery), specifically the notes from the first and last days of the session.

As is clear, the discussions were broad and at times fairly random. We didn't set any particular end point or agenda on the day. Instead, it serves as a record of the free association we like to encourage in the room and how such diverse thoughts and references have an uncanny way of constructing a kind of intellectual parameter, an outer limit that inversely begins to define the space in which the eventual show might begin to form itself. Where a book title is referenced, it might have been that someone simply asked whether anyone had read it. On some occasions this might have been followed by a discussion of the central issues it covered, but this was not always the case. One of the most controversial joys of the modern intellectual age is the capacity to 'believe' something to be the case without having actually experienced it. Dangerous but in some instances quite handy. We know for a fact that some people in the room talked about the Brian Keenan book as if they had read it from cover to cover when we now know this was not actually true. Not that this got in the way of some healthy discourse you understand. In the case of quotations, we rarely make a note of who said what. This might be to protect the person or might be an act of abject laziness. It's most probably a bit of both.

Brian Keenan book *An Evil Cradling*.

Patty Hearst.

A Carol Churchill text presenting a list of atrocities as 'a love story'.

John Fowles book *The Collector*.

Manipulative uses of language.

Question – does power shift as soon as one person commits a physically violent act?

'I was there to be smacked for something that had happened years before.'

Lolita and the idea that the man is not to blame at the critical moment.

'To whack someone is really a strategy to have your needs met.'

Could loving [physical] material lead to fighting?

Could fighting [physical] material lead to loving?

The Cornelia Parker effect – how a lunch box, a laundry basket and a coat hanger, once inanimate objects, become deadly weapons.

Film – *What's Love Got to Do with It* – scene in the car where Ike and Tina fight then are forced to step out of a limousine into a high-profile event with blood on their clothing.

'Close the fucking door' – is it more aggressive when loud or quiet?

Audience – to give them a sense of observation, of involved responsibility, of being questioned.

Control = a little girl with dolls.

Cushioning – making things seem quieter, more stable.

'If you fall in love when you are young, you can always remember them as something else. This else-ness is very important in understanding why they are together.'

Film – *Code Unknown.*

Film – *The Piano Teacher.*

The idea of physical proficiency as a signifier for shared history together – they move beautifully together – sex, the washing up, shopping away.

Songs and singing – why do you sing? What do you sing? Singing to yourself or to them?

Music – why do you put it on? To appease, annoy, dupe, unsettle, cover up?

The sound of meat slapping on a table.

Music – the characters are hearing it and are in control.

Appetite – knives and forks dance. Eating each other.

Film – *9 Songs*

Music – album plays constantly. Music as apt commentary. Incongruous music.

Periods of prolonged silence.

Taking loved music off so it's not tainted by a bad experience.

Asking about the best sex ever had, not just between them.

Dali painting – Autumnal Cannibalism.

Beautiful South record cover for We Are Each Other.

Not being able to commit to the argument because the football scores are on so even the argument is rubbish.

Question – when does 'I' become 'you' when telling of an event?

Arguments – where and how do they happen? Hanging a painting, map reading, moving furniture, wrapping presents (being reduced to the function of a finger pressed for sticky tape).

Physical Exercise (A practical exercise):
Pull partner in to yourself so there is no space between you. Give full support. Take the weight. Little lifts. Take them to the floor.

One pair on the floor, one pair on the table.

The list above shows the range of discussion on just day one. Over the next few days we explored all aspects of a loving but destructive relationship and the associated themes of Stockholm syndrome.

Over the rest of the week we explored many contexts and situations, physically. We set tasks incorporating functional kitchen duties and wild romantic dances across work surfaces. We played with the simplicity and complexity of touch between lovers. We explored just how lonely a shared bed can be. All week our characters hardly uttered a word. Everything was physical and choreographic. Throughout, we, the observers, felt more and more in love and angry with our protagonists. We were invited into their lives and made part of the problem.

On the last day of the development we devised what we called a recipe. We felt that these were all the ingredients that had come out of the development and should go into the further development of the text, of the story. We had unearthed a vast amount of information and ideas in the preceding days. We tried to distil them into the simplest form to provide a framework, a skeletal structure we could then flesh out. The recipe is also set out as a dramatic arc:

A couple
Us
A day
Some events
A plea. Some demands. (An ultimatum – the deadline is reached and passed)
A recipe/A confession
A meal is cooked
The last dance
(The end of the world)

It might be really useful to think about your development work progressing in this way. Of course, you should not necessarily be reductive, but devised theatre and the nature of devising theatre can often mean that we take our focus off things like the dramatic arc.

The final production proved remarkably faithful to the recipe above. The recipe served to consolidate all of the input from a sprawling development session and then take us forward in a structured fashion.

(It should be pointed out that the development session was sprawling only in the amount of good work that needed to be processed, not in the amount of time we had to indulge. We are very careful about this. We even stopped the *Stockholm* sessions two days early because we felt that we had created enough. We believe you have to look out for the point where research and development or even rehearsal stops being productive and stop it there. (Otherwise you taint the whole thing.)

Actions speak louder than words?

Sometimes they do. It is also good to remember that sometimes actions fall completely flat, can seem obscure, strange, pretentious, needless, pointless, clichéd, simplistic, indulgent … (the list goes on).

Movement has to earn its place in any production. Even for a 'physical theatre' company we have to be sure that the decision to create a movement scene is based on it being the best way of telling the story. No writer worth their salt wants a production to merely dance all over their words. Movement has to fight for its existence at every turn.

When thinking about movement versus words we often consider distillation. How can the crux of the matter be distilled and presented most effectively?

If that choice is to present something physically, then we have to ask ourselves whether we have created a three-minute movement scene to put across what it would have taken three seconds to say verbally. If so, then you may be saying the same thing for three minutes if the meaning is obvious in the movement, or it may be that the movement is so obscure that it takes a full three minutes for the audience to get something they could have got in three seconds. Either way does not make for a happy audience or good theatre.

We would encourage you to think about this distillation. An example of this kind of thought is the Happy Hour scene from *Dirty Wonderland*.

The basic premise was that the central character, Alex, lost his girlfriend in the sprawling hotel as soon as they checked in for their dirty weekend. He is told that she is down in the bar. It is happy hour. He sets off to find her but only encounters a couple trying to relive their honeymoon but failing miserably. There is a suggestion that he might be seeing a future version of him and his girlfriend. What is clear is that the fire in this other relationship has gone out no matter how hard they try to go through the moves.

We wanted the audience to know that the couple really are making an effort and that there was a time when they really would have set the room alight with their love. Now that this has faded they are left with little more than routine and mutual contempt.

We believed in this rich scenario – even more so when one of the cast found out that his parents actually did have their honeymoon in the hotel we were performing in and even returned years later to find that it had lost its magic! This seemed to validate the scenario. (The resulting scene cast no aspersions over the strength of the performer's parents' marriage!)

We talked about how we could get the history of these people across to our audience and how this history comes crashing to the ground in the present moment. It became a complex thing to solve through text. There seemed to be an unavoidable need for dull exposition. There appeared to be more merit in their sudden physicality expressing the exposition. Instantly this was about love and passion. Just as instantly we could see it fade and be replaced by bitterness.

The scene played out as follows:

The couple sit side by side as a singer appears to croon forlornly. They, apart from Alex, are the only people in the bar. The man gets up and gestures, ordering a couple of drinks. The two of them sit together again. Suddenly they burst into a passionate and provocative dance. It is full of daring and danger. Just as suddenly their dance ends. They are sat again. Their drinks arrive. The waiter places a gin and tonic in front of the lady and a pint of lager in front of the man. When the waiter leaves, the man reaches for the gin and the woman reaches for the pint.

Just when you think this is the joke, they both casually spit into the drinks they hold and place them back in front of their partner. Then, seemingly oblivious or knowing but past caring, they both drink from the drinks in front of them. This moment is a shocking acceptance of the contempt from their partner. It may even be an acceptance of guilt for letting the spark die.

This became so much more complex (and pleasing) than we could have hoped for if we had opted for words. The moment and the physicality had been distilled into a single action (the spit). The exposition was the passionate precursor to this act.

(Think about the ending of Brokeback Mountain. *The beautiful economy of the shirt inside the shirt, reversing the way they were kept before, and the simple, enigmatic 'Jack, I swear …' Perfect distillation of words and action. God bless Ang Lee! See 'Working with writers', below.)*

If it is not about distillation then, alternatively, aim for progression through your choice of physicality. Demand that it moves the story on! Consider what words cannot do or can only do in an obvious or laboured way. In *Hymns* we chose movement and clichéd jokes to suggest frustration and verbal inarticulacy. The characters' discomfort grew and exploded as they skirted verbally around the real issues that concerned them. It would have been wrong in the context of *Hymns* to have the four men eloquently express their pain and fear of words through text. That pushed us towards movement as, in this context, actions would definitely speak louder than words.

Simply, we would like to think we don't just throw shapes because we can. There are many tools at your disposal as a theatre maker. It is crucial to use the right one at the right time.

Working with writers

Your practical relationship with writers is as idiosyncratic as the writers them-selves and the project you are working on. We have not committed to any one process because every time we think we might have found one something comes along to blow that out of the water. Any single and constant process would surely be reductive or claustrophobic anyway?

This is the most important relationship to have clear and understood from the start. You both must know what you expect of each other. Sometimes you can only find this by getting together and trying things rather than talking about it, as from the outside we can all have a slightly different understanding of ourselves and how we actually are under pressure. Any research and devel-opment session you can find the time and money for could be crucial to this understanding. You need to know where your creative references are. You need to know whether the writer is expected/willing/able to write in the rehearsal room. You need to know if your writer is going to take inspiration from the devising processes or whether they need the privacy to follow their own clear line of creativity and then pass that on to you/the devising company.

This is not something we have always got right. It is from bitter and exhausting experience that we stress the importance of this relationship.

Acknowledging the range of possibilities here, we will not try to advocate a single process. Instead, what follows is taken from a workshop we held for writers looking to gain an understanding of how to incorporate physicality into their work. Or how to bring the inherent physicality out. The rest of this section sees a slight change in focus as we address the writers themselves.

This workshop dealt with the writer's desire to bring physicality to their work. It hopefully showed how to write with this in mind while always leaving space for the input of other collaborators. Areas we wanted the writer partic-ipants to consider were:

1 Inspiration for words.
2 Harnessing physicality.
3 Helping others to harness physicality.
4 Space and economy.
5 Other worlds and ingredients (music, songs, lighting, etc.).

The writers were shown four images and asked for their first responses. This basically explores the cliché/truth that an image speaks a thousand words. The images were promotional images of Frantic Assembly, but they could be any reportage photography, or even the work of photographers like Gregory Crewdson. In their responses, the writers talked in depth about the stories behind the images. There was not necessarily agreement but there was always emotional depth.

The writers were then shown an edited promotional film of *pool (no water)*. None of the participants had seen the show yet. This film has roughly chronological images but no sound. Instead there is the track 'The Moment I Said It' from the album *Speak For Yourself* by Imogen Heap laid on top.

Again they were asked to give their reactions. It was remarkable how much of the story they had got just from the edited images. More intriguingly they had a very strong sense of all the emotional relationships that existed in the real show. It was then pointed out to the writers that they had been manipulated by the ingredients of the film – the selection of music, the editing, the choice of focus, the colours, as well as the performances.

The exercise served to show the economy with which you can manipulate emotion and tell a story. And all without a single word. This was not to make the writer redundant. This was to inspire the writer to think about writing in a different way.

Bedworld

We used a couple of volunteers to be the couple in an exercise called Stockholm Bed (see website). We ran the exercise and then noted the complex and fragile stories that emerged. The writers were then asked to state the instructions for the task as succinctly as possible while capturing something of the essence of the world the performers create.

It was agreed that these short descriptive sentences could effectively be the stage directions for the Bedworld task. (It was pointed out that this was how the stage directions in *Stockholm* emerged.) If those words could sum up the instructions, could the same words then work in reverse and inspire the delicacy and sensitivity of the Stockholm Bed task? This example showed the writers how stage directions could be incredibly simple and inspiring if they have an idea of the world they wish to explore. Imagining that world should draw upon their freedom of imagination. It should not be bogged down by thinking about the technicality of the resulting choreography. Leave that to the particular skills of the performers/choreographer/director. That is why they are in the room.

We talked about stage directions at length, using our chequered history of being on the receiving end of them to illustrate examples of good and bad practice.

Writers can be just as guilty as performers and directors of giving their audience too much. To illustrate this we followed Stockholm Bed with the Leg of Lamb exercise (see page 211) showing that a whole new story can emerge through the most minute change in dynamic within text. (The change of tense again prompted the story of a woman confessing to having killed and cooked her husband!) This led to us discussing economy within writing.

Economy

We considered things that were greater than the sum of their parts. We played a few songs including 'Wichita Lineman', written by Jimmy Webb and performed by Glen Campbell. This song is a masterclass in suggesting depth and troubled human emotions. It presents a telecommunications worker fixing lines beside the road. He is tired and missing a loved one but is compelled by a sense of duty and concern for the job in hand to keep working rather than take a holiday. If you were to look at the words, this is all they convey.

But this song has the power to bring tears to a glass eye! Surely there is more to it than this? We then considered the ingredients:

- *The words*: There is a tension in the scenario between the duty to the job and the implications for many people if the job is not done properly versus the tiredness and love and longing for another person.
- *The delivery of the words*: Glen Campbell imbues the words with a considerable weight. This is not a fleeting thought during a lunch break.
- *The music*: The bass is heavy and mournful. The strings are highly emotive. The general tone is sad. We are not music experts. These were the comments and observations from the listeners.

All of this appeared to overwhelmingly suggest that we were listening to some epic story of distant love and misguided duty. All in three minutes and seven seconds, the last 37 seconds of which was just slowly fading music; and in just 15 lines of text, three of which are a repeat.

It has an incredible economy. We looked at the writing specifically and noted that we had all projected a greater meaning onto what appeared to be there. How had this happened? And what had we projected onto the song? What had we brought to the experience of listening to the song?

The text presents a very succinct tension.

The sound of the loved one is crashing into the Lineman's mundane work. He is not taking time out to think about this love. It is forcing its way into his head. He is trying to focus on the work despite this voice calling him back. Remember, the Wichita Lineman is *still* on the line.

The tension within these lines gets carried through the rest of the song so that lines about needing a holiday but being worried about his workload begin to express a tragic human frailty, the dangers of a life unlived, economic pressures on the working man, time passing by, and the utterly heroic act of a man putting the effectiveness of a phone network above his own heart and body!

By the time we had got to the killer lines about needing more than wanting and wanting for all time we were all virtually in tears!

This song is epic. It is minute. At times our projection of backstory can seem absurd, but this is what we bring to things with this kind of economy and power to suggest and engage. We, as listeners, have done most of the work in telling this story.

Is this accidental? Jimmy Webb has said that 'Wichita Lineman' was written as a response to a challenge where he said he could write a song about anything and then saw a lineman at work. It could not be simpler. There is nothing accidental about the tone of the music or the delivery of the lyrics. They are surely working to engage us in seeing the Lineman's life in a certain way without being explicit about it.

It was clear that the complete song is successful because of the way the ingredients had been considered and played off one another and with each other to suggest so much more than they explicitly say. This is why it is so successful and affecting for the listener.

There are many lessons to be learnt here, not just from the economy of song writing but also through this use of ingredients. All composers and lyricists write songs to be sung. Writers need to remember that they are writing plays to be performed and should give full consideration to the potential ingredients involved.

Writing Silence

Writing Silence was another task designed to get the writers to think about writing in a different way.

We played the end of *The Ice Storm*, the film directed by Ang Lee (making sure that those who did not want to know the score looked away). The scene (again, look away if you do not want to know the final score) involves Tobey Maguire's character returning home on a train after it has become trapped by an ice storm. He is obviously pleased and surprised to see his family pick him up from the station. He does not comment on the fact that his younger brother is not with them (he has been killed in a freak accident the night before; Tobey Maguire does not know this). When the family get in the car, the atmosphere changes and it falls to father Kevin Kline to break the news to his son. He turns to look at him in the backseat and his son smiles back obliviously. This is too much for the father and he breaks down crying. The mother caresses her husband's back and tears well in the eyes of the young sister. Slowly there is a terrible dawning across the face of Tobey Maguire. The film ends without anything else being said.

Again this is a brilliantly brave example of craftsmanship and economy from Ang Lee and his creative team and performers. It is a very brave scene as it never gives us what we think we are waiting for – namely, an answer to the question 'how is he going to break the news?' Instead it gives us something much more human, complex, engaging and ultimately more rewarding.

The first impression was that this near-silent scene had been shown as an example of what writers cannot write. It was actually meant to display the opposite. This being film, every aspect of this scene would have been written to allow for the correct positioning of cameras and lighting. There would have been a very clear script for people to follow.

We were not suggesting that writers dictate the angle of a performer's face or the lighting design. We were suggesting they take inspiration from the complexity and precision of scenes that were written to be silent. We wanted to stress that a writer can write their ideas in images when it is apt to do so.

The events

When asked about the physical scenes that are integrated into our productions we have often talked about the need for space in a text. This space allows the possibility of physicality or visual image telling the story. At times the quest for the absolute integration of words and movement, both existing simultaneously, has seemed like the search for the Holy Grail but ultimately found to be a red herring. We have tried and have found ourselves layering languages on top of each other and creating a convoluted mess. When it works it can be fantastic but there are times when a much more simple approach is necessary.

Every Frantic Assembly show goes through research and development sessions, testing the kernel of an idea and trying to flesh it out. We try to involve as many of the creative team as possible at this early stage. There is nothing revolutionary about this but what might be different is the way each participant is asked to think about his or her own input. In many cases the challenge is to think about what you don't have to do to make a story work rather than what you do have to do.

This stems from a conversation with Bryony Lavery where she spoke of the ambition to take a moment to the point where she writes silence. This is the moment where words are redundant. The image, the light, the sound will do all of the work.

This economy and efficiency is encouraged in all departments. Each will think about whether another department might best serve a moment. This means each department is speaking in the single language of the production and is not suggesting their work for the sake of it. This is how we find our scenes without words, our physical scenes and heightened physical moments.

Sam Cox, rehearsals for *Lovesong* (2011). Image by Scott Graham

Sometimes, despite all the research and development sessions and the various drafts a script might go through, there will be events in a production that you will not find in the published script. Sometimes this is because inspiration comes late but at other times this can be by design.

We had always said to Abi Morgan as we were developing *Lovesong* that there should be space for a visual language to complement the written word and that she should feel free to write without the limitations of thinking about how things would happen practically on stage. The only major physical scene we all agreed should be in the script was the highly energetic bad scene where all couples morphed in and out in a frenzied blur of memory and reality. (See 'Lovesong Bed', page 72.) This was because this scene captured our whole ambition and aesthetic for *Lovesong*. This physical scene was not an afterthought. To legitimately reach this point was the ambition of the production.

Giving Abi this freedom led to a beautiful script that at times captured moments of physicality that we had explored in development and at others presented something quite impossible (characters disappearing and appearing elsewhere). This was not a fault. This was the opportunity we had asked for.

We needed to create what we called Events to help the production flow and to avoid dull blackouts. (We have a long standing aversion to functional blackouts.) Abi's script, by design, had focused on all the crisis moments that litter a long-term relationship. The Events could go some way to redressing the potentially gloomy take on a marriage by capturing some of the lighter, more flirtatious and provocative moments.

The Events were little moments that happened between the scenes that opened a window upon a character's feelings or situation. They allowed a much more liberal physicality as they were often about the words unsaid. They were mostly private moments of crisis or contemplation, moments of levity and, although partly necessitated by the need for flow and other practicalities, they became crucial parts of the story.

For example, in *Lovesong* there is a moment where Bill is left alone in the kitchen dealing with the terminal illness of his wife. He turns towards the fridge. We have seen through the earlier scenes of their younger selves that his drinking had become an issue for them. We have also seen that he now drinks soda water while she drinks gin. He looks at the fridge and then strides towards it purposefully. As he opens it (presumably to take the gin out and pour himself a drink) the younger form of his wife emerges from the fridge and drapes herself around him. She is held aloft and ends wrapped around his shoulders before slipping away from him. The memory of her has stopped him drinking. In this moment we see that he still retains the youthful look and feel of her. It is palpable, tangible and vital. This is crucial to our depiction of love, ageing and death. The past had to simultaneously exist in the now. The memories had to burn with vibrancy if we were to give them the weight they deserved.

Remember this scene only came about through two 'problems', both of which were created on purpose. One was that Abi did not write that scene. It is a valid moment of very important storytelling but she did not feel the need to put it to words as she recognised the power of movement to do the work for her. Secondly we needed a way to allow the older Maggie to leave the preceding scene and enter the next written scene in a new costume on a new day. These were the structural problems we asked for. They were the 'problems' Abi was brave enough and trusting enough to allow.

chapter six

Textual analysis

In this chapter we present some simple exercises to encourage practitioners to see text from a basic physical viewpoint and from there attach the discoveries back to the text.

The Lecture

We make no apologies for the simplicity of this exercise. Sometimes it is important to address the basics.

Working with actors on Shakespearean text showed us how easy it is, when we don't really understand something, to retreat behind an adopted tone of voice, a faux classical RP and crash on with a jaunty rhythm in the hope that the audience know what we are talking about. 'As long as we are making the right noises then nobody will ask any questions.' (See 'Dance Face and the permission to perform', page 39.)

To combat this…

1 Give the performer some time with the text.
2 Ask them to consider and identify the subjects that are addressed within the text.
3 They can now use objects to represent those subjects. They can place them around the room or have them on their person.

4   Now present the text as a lecture. Don't act it. Keep emotion to a minimum. If it helps, use a pointy stick and a blackboard! Think of it as a PowerPoint presentation to the uninitiated.

We feel this process helps the actor to really get to grips with the task of communicating the meaning of text. It might seem simplistic, but we would be ignoring one of our primary tasks as directors if they were not communicating the words clearly.

The lecture has to be clear because its primary objective is to make people understand and not necessarily convey emotion. Despite all of the writhing and torment an emotional reading may produce, it might only tell us one thing – the character is upset. Presenting the text as a lecture gives the performer an opportunity to think about and express the many facets of the text. It is from this point of understanding that they can start to add emotion.

If we inspire people to embrace movement then great, but we don't want to be accused of encouraging people to neglect the basic techniques behind clarity of thought and presentation. Devised theatre should not lack the skill and depth of literary theatre. Otherwise it will be forever sidelined.

PHYSICAL CHARACTERS AND RELATIONSHIPS

These are exercises that look for the physical truth of a situation through a variety of means. Each one demonstrates a different practical device in attempting to locate this truth.

Time Passing

Think of a simple setting for two characters: on a sofa in front of a TV; in a café; a date in a restaurant. Ask your performers (or characters who inhabit the setting) to picture their moves over an extended period of time – all the changes of position and the different poses that one might get into quite naturalistically over the space of a couple of hours. If it helps to visualise it, think of a CCTV camera spying on the event and capturing the moves.

Get the two performers to set their individual moves, taking care to include moments of stillness and rest. If you then run the two individuals together in the space, a physical story emerges. There may be moments that you want to hold on to, to set. Others you might want to change.

Give your performers a section of fairly sparse dialogue from a script of your choice. Let the performers run the moves under the dialogue while the rest of the creative team look for moments where the moves and the words really work. (Look for moments that possess a pleasing dynamic relationship rather than an obvious literal relationship.)

Now encourage the performers to give plenty of space to the words, to take plenty of time. As the moves have a life of their own it might appear like this simple conversation has taken all night to run its course. Or it might suggest that the characters are very uneasy and are desperate to escape from this situation. The very least you should find is that the characters are possibly saying things that they might not believe. Their physicality is undermining their sincerity, although there might equally be moments where the movements actually enforce the sincerity. Either way what you have discovered is the important relationship between context (the café, the dialogue) and the subtext (the discomfort, the need to escape). It is a great example of how, from simple physicality, a complex subtext can emerge.

This exercise is about finding a subtext where we may have not considered one. Of course when we know our play inside out we are well aware of the subtext that runs through each scene. We can still use Time Passing to help the performers experience that subtext, even if the physical quality achieved never becomes part of the performance. It serves as a physical memory of the richness and depth beneath the text and will enhance a naturalistic performance.

Variations

Get your performers to set their moves. Now place one of the performers in 'the café'. Without saying a word they can start their moves and loop them so that we can see the repetition. What does this do? Do the moves look comfortable? Is the character practising for something?

Introduce the other character somewhere else in the café. When they are settled they can start and loop their moves. Try setting them off at a slower pace to see if anything emerges here. Do the two people, oblivious to each other, comment on one another or some mutual situation? Physically they are not now 'together' so what has this done to the emerging story or context?

Start again with the first character. Introduce the second character and place them together. What happens if only one of them speaks their side of the dialogue? What happens if they say nothing but just look into each other's eyes as their bodies act out a whole evening of naturalistic adjustments?

Can these naturalistic gestures be taken to an extreme? Is there greater movement potential in these gestures?

This is another starting point for the creation of choreography. To do this you must let your performers break free of the original framework. The moves are not naturalism now. They do not have to say more loudly what they said before. They are a new palette with which to create choreography rooted in the frustrations, desires, anxieties found in the earlier exercise. Remember that although you are now moving away from text, you have, very importantly, come from text.

Stockholm Post-Its

This task came up in the rehearsals for *Stockholm* and works well for exploring the intimate details of modern relationships. It is useful background work, but the process was so successful and enthralling to watch that we even tried to incorporate a similar scene into the show itself. (It did not survive a final cut!)

For our version we used the *Stockholm* set as it was a domestic kitchen, but it does not have to take place on set and in character. It can be an informative process in itself.

1   Split the group into pairs. Ask your performers to write ten Post-it notes to their partner or lover within the play. These could range from the mundane to the earth-shatteringly important but, more importantly, have to be the kind of thing you would commit to a Post-it note and leave for your partner to find.
2   Get the performers to take on these considerations. At what stage in their relationship were these notes written? What would have prompted them? What would they have written?
3   In turn, get one performer from each pair to leave their notes around the set for the other to find. They then leave and the other performer enters the empty set. When this performer finds the notes they must respond appropriately for the next ten seconds. This is not a great big theatrical response. Just a moment of thought.
4   When they have found all the notes they then leave their written notes for the other performer to find and we repeat the process.

This is all about the effect the other has on them when they are not even there. It is about memory and intimate personal history. It is very much inspired by the effect of the editing and direction in the sex and post-sex scene in *Don't Look Now* by Nicolas Roeg. It is a useful character exercise in getting performers to think about the other characters they share the stage with and how they really feel about them and how they affect each other.

Here is another task from *Stockholm* that could work for other productions.

The two characters in the central relationship had to compile a track list of a CD they would create for their partner. These are the songs each individual thinks they might share and hold dear. They should both think about songs that meant something to them at different times in their relationship. This allows the

210

performer to imagine a rich and varied backstory existing alongside popular culture. The choice of music cannot fail to suggest aspects of their characters.

They both create two separate lists and swap them. The results can be shocking and illuminating. You might want to discuss them and encourage the performers to defend their inclusions. The CDs might be the choices of the individual character or they might be the soundtrack to their love. Either way they should cast a light on what one performer thinks about the couple or their relationship. You may find that both performers have vastly differing views. This is not a problem. It just opens up discussion, as it did in *Stockholm*. Some of the choices made our blood curdle, but they were no less valid than the choices we loved. It is a character exercise for the performers and an excellent opportunity to throw up some surprises. It is also a simple and effective way of separating performer from character as the performer is not asked to list their own personal favourite tracks. They are asked to list the right tracks as their character. It would then be up to you whether they should work their way to a definitive couple CD or leave the exercise there.

In addition you could ask the performers to be more detailed. They could write out individual lists for their relationship after three months, after two years, after five years.

Playing with words: Leg of Lamb

This task is an example taken from *Stockholm* rehearsals where words are taken on in a creatively lateral way to examine their potential.

We have stated many times the importance of playing with the physical material you create. We have encouraged you to test its validity and flexibility to throw up new meaning and create new stories.

This section takes a similar approach towards text. The following is an account of an exercise from the *Stockholm* research and development. We were looking at how words might *suggest* a story rather than explicitly tell it. It was principally for us to find a way to hint at a horror lurking under a domestic bliss.

We knew that we wanted our characters to prepare a meal during the show. We also wanted to explore the suggestion of death and destruction (the characters' names were Todd and Kali ('Tod' being German for 'death', and 'Kali' the Hindu goddess of destruction).

We cobbled together a mock recipe and had a play.

1   Bone the leg of lamb. Do not strip the tough meat from the knuckle end. Cut the meat you have removed from the bone into large, rough chunks. Remember that most casseroles and stews require larger cuts. Trim fat and gristle off the meat.

2   Roast the bone and the knuckle at 225 degrees for 15 minutes, put carrots, onion, celery in a pan. Add a bay leaf and half a bottle of good red wine, drinking the rest yourself! Once you have brought it to the boil, allow it to simmer very gently for 1–2 hours. Strain the stock through a fine sieve.

3   Rinse the prunes.

4   Heat your oil in a large frying pan. Soften the garlic, onion and carrots. Add all the spices, and fry for a few more minutes. Transfer to another pot. Heat some more oil in a frying pan. Brown the meat and add to the softened vegetables.

5   Bring to the boil, then reduce immediately to a very slow simmer. Simmer for two hours. Add the prunes and cook for another hour. Test after this time. The meat should be extremely tender.

6   Serve with mashed potato.

Read at face value it was an instructive guide through preparing and cooking a leg of lamb with prunes. We asked one of our performers to sit at a table facing us. Another performer sat in front of her with his back to us. She read the recipe to him. Then she tried to learn it. Then she read it to him again.

Already, this makes the recipe strange but there is not necessarily another story emerging. There are more questions than answers. Who is she? Why is she relaying this recipe? Who is the man sitting in front of her? And does he want to know about this recipe? Is he bored? Has he asked her to do this?

Next time she spoke the recipe she had to change every present or future tense into the past tense.

'I boned out the leg. I didn't strip the tough meat from the knuckle end. Most casseroles and stews require larger cuts. I trimmed any fat or gristle off the meat.'

'I browned the meat and added it to the softened vegetables.'

'By this time the meat was extremely tender.'

'I served it with mashed potato.'

What emerged was quite startling. The performer was struggling with the task, which gave a methodical and deliberate tone to the words but more importantly a whole new context had emerged. This time it was a confession. To all of the startled observers it was clear that she had disposed of a body. The detail of what she had done to the meat was blood chilling. The man was taking her statement. Impassive. Professional. There was no escape for her. This was a confession and acceptance of a horrific deed.

This find was exactly what we were looking for. Not the murder story in particular but the potential to engage the audience in the telling of a complex story without explicitly using those words. We wanted to know if the couple within *Stockholm* could betray another story under the surface or scream for help as they talk about their wallpaper or the food they are going to cook.

We are in no way promoting an absurd approach. This is not about a disregard for the words. It is an exercise in how those words, just like the physicality, can tell a completely different story with just the slightest directorial adjustment.

chapter seven

Some things to think about

Some DOs and DON'Ts

DON'T make somebody become a table or chair that then gets sat on – this is not physical theatre, it is demeaning.

DON'T hold your breath when attempting particularly difficult physical movement – you need it. Breathe out during exertion.

DON'T, when working with jumps, create all that energy running through the space only to jump off both feet together in order to launch into the air – you just wasted a perfectly good run-up.

DON'T stand stock still facing the audience unless that really is what you mean to do.

DON'T stand back to back, link arms and lift one another by tilting forward – it doesn't mean anything. Honest.

DON'T treat movement any differently to text – they should operate under the same rules. A spoken sentence gets us from one point to another, is progressive, repeats only when necessary and has consequences. There is no reason why movement should not do this also.

DON'T allow language to become strange when combined with movement. If you close your eyes and listen to a scene where you have combined language and physicality and the language has strange rhythms and inflections you have just committed a grave sin. Start again.

DON'T look out above the audience as soon as you begin to move. They're still there.

DON'T always aim for the end point when creating physical work. When directing, don't be afraid of withholding information to support this practice. A love duet might have started out as a fight duet that got slower and slower and vice versa. This is how interesting material gets made.

DON'T be afraid of breaking every one of these rules if it is absolutely right for the show you want to make! We have!

DON'T make your show in 'a Frantic style'. This won't work for either of us.

DON'T make excuses for your cultural inspirations. Be it Cocteau or Kylie, if it speaks to you, you're all good…

You will notice a lack of **DO**s. Sorry. That is just the way it is. It is much easier for us to say what you should not be doing. That is how we have learned what we liked, just as reacting to what we are *not* has defined what we *are*.
Instead we suggest some things you might like to think about:

- *The positive opportunities in making choreography with non-dancers.*

- *Making choreography using clearly defined limitations.*

- *Responding to stage directions, good and bad.*

- *Making choreography and then testing it. Workshop the story.*

- *Music and audience manipulation.*

- *Movement and storytelling.*

- *Building blocks – we will keep banging on about the importance of these in our devising.*

- *Articulating the unsaid – when physicality can suggest a repressed subtext.*

- *Text vs. movement (and what comes first?).*

- *What inspires the movement?*

- *Is movement the best way to tell this story?*

- *Movement and time passing.*

- *Making theatre from non-theatrical inspiration.*

- *Who is your audience likely to be? And is this any different to the audience you would like to have? If the answer is yes, does this matter to you?*

- *Consider the relation between your work and your prospective audience – thematically, formally, spatially, and economically.*

- *Have you looked at your work from anywhere other than the prime audience location? Watch it from behind! From above, from the side! Do it now before it is too late!*

- *Could this piece of work be made by anybody or is there some quality within that is unique to you?*

- *How many of your old tricks did you use to make this work? Happy with that?*

- *What have you learnt? What were the mistakes you nearly made? Do not forget them! They can be incredibly helpful in the future.*

- *Remember chaos makes unison more surprising and more powerful. They both refresh the other. Try to find the balance that complements both.*

- *Get your headphones on. Turn your track up and just watch the world choreograph itself in front of you. It will be surprising, complex and dynamic. It might well be inspirational.*

Bibliography of inspiration

We have always championed accessibility to our creative process. This is not done to show how smart we are. If anything, it is the opposite. We were desperate to demystify the artistic creative process and show where ideas really come from and how they are shaped by the things around us.

Within our education packs we have written about process and development but at the back of each existed a simple list we called the 'Bibliography of inspiration'. In this list we laid bare the ingredients that were crucial in the genesis of the production. They were shamelessly personal and could reference the banal as easily as the highbrow.

Below is an example from *Lovesong*. We have our reasons why the things on these lists are pivotal. Without going into those reasons they just look trivial. But then that is the point we are making – inspiration comes from the oddest of places and is utterly subjective.

There are more examples of these to be found on the companion website (www.routledge.com/cw/graham). We hope these lists can inspire you to look a little closer to home for your own creative inspiration. If you are thrown by the lack of academic index, we would advise you to use an internet search engine. It might throw up some unexpected and inspirational results. Go on. Live a little!

The Love Song of J Alfred Prufrock and *The Wasteland* by T.S. Eliot

John Donne's love poetry

Essays In Love by Alain de Botton

A Lover's Discourse by Roland Barthes

The Time Traveller's Wife by Audrey Niffenegger

The Dead by James Joyce

Tiny Dynamite by Abi Morgan

Abi Morgan's brilliant but unplaced Tennessee Williams reference about knickers in a pocket

'Starlings' by Elbow

www.justsomelyrics.com/2013552/Elbow-Starlings-Lyrics

'Friend Of Ours' by Elbow

www.songmeanings.net/songs/view/3530822107858708247

'The Birds' by Elbow

www.elyrics.net/read/e/elbow-lyrics/the-birds-lyrics.html

Video for 'Paradise Circus' by Massive Attack (sexually explicit content)

The music of A Winged Victory For the Sullen

Pretty much everything on Erased Tapes record label

The petal effect on Yeah Yeah Yeah's performance of 'Maps' – MTV awards www.youtube.com/watch?v=xOj6hm09rOo

The music of Rene Aubry

UP, dir. Pete Docter

The Gruffalo *animated film*

Numero 2, dir. Jean Luc Godard

Carry On Up The Khyber, dir. Gerald Thomas

Magnolia, dir. PT Anderson

Legend, dir. Ridley Scott

Freaky Friday (1976) dir. Gary Nelson

The touchingly serious moments in *One Foot In The Grave*, BBC

Terry Pratchett: Choosing to Die

TV ad for Gucci dir. Chris Cunningham

The work of artist Claire Morgan www.claire-morgan.co.uk/

'Beneath The Roses' series by artist Gregory Crewdson

A Couple Drinking Tea On Plymouth Hoe. A photograph by Joni Carter

Is a Dignified Death Too Much to Ask? www.guardian.co.uk/lifeandstyle/2011/jul/09/nell-dunn-partner-home-death

Film making of Chris Cunningham